W9-BMK-521

The Bretons against France

The Bretons against France

ETHNIC MINORITY NATIONALISM
IN TWENTIETH-CENTURY BRITTANY

by Jack E. Reece

The University of
North Carolina Press
Chapel Hill

Copyright © 1977 by
The University of North Carolina Press
All rights reserved
Manufactured in the United States of America
ISBN 0-8078-1304-4
Library of Congress Catalog Card Number 76-49657

Library of Congress Cataloging in Publication

Reece, Jack E
  The Bretons against France.

  Bibliography: p.
  Includes index.
  1. Brittany—History—Autonomy and independence movements.
I. Title.
DC611.B917R43   320.9′44′1   76-49657
ISBN 0-8078-1304-4

12-20-78

For R. H. C.

Contents

ઙ૰ Preface

Foreign visitors and Frenchmen alike have long regarded the mist-laden Breton peninsula as an idyllic land of mysterious forests, beautiful seascapes, and rustic peasant scenes. But these many beguiling aspects of Breton life so often extolled by Parisian tourist agencies actually conceal a far less pleasing social reality. Depressed standards of living, poverty, disease, alcoholism, unemployment, and massive emigration scar the lives of a large majority of Brittany's prolific and industrious population of nearly 3.5 million persons. It has been in part to protest these unfavorable conditions that during the past decade ethnically conscious Breton patriots have brought a campaign of terrorist violence against the central government in Paris, whose long-standing neglect of Brittany's vital needs and interests they consider the root cause of misery on the peninsula. The persistent refusal of Paris authorities to promote the social and economic development of the region has in fact since the turn of the century provoked local demands in Brittany for some form of home rule. This study of ethnic minority nationalism in twentieth-century Brittany is intended to contribute to an understanding of the conditions under which an ethnic minority comes to advance political demands for self-government. Moreover, since the focus of this study is a region of France, hitherto one of the most centralized and by all accounts fully integrated national societies in the world, both the pervasiveness and the significance of ethnic minority nationalism in contemporary Europe will emerge with maximum clarity.

Many persons have given me much assistance and encouragement in the course of writing this book. Several of my colleagues in the history department at the University of Pennsylvania—notably Lee Benson, Michael Zuckerman, and

James C. Davis—have read parts of it in manuscript and have offered valuable suggestions for revision and refinement. Marc V. Levine, a graduate student in our department, provided much-appreciated bibliographical assistance. But my greatest debt of gratitude is owed to Professor Gordon Wright of Stanford University, under whose supervision this study began as a doctoral dissertation nearly a decade ago. Even more than his prodigious knowledge of modern European history and his distinguished scholarship, his perfect decency, civility, and integrity have been a constant inspiration for me and an entire generation of young historians trained at Stanford.

Finally, I want in this space to express the inexpressible —my heartfelt thanks to my parents, brothers, and sister, who have steadfastly supported me in my educational efforts since I left the farm eighteen years ago and went off to college in Ann Arbor.

๑Introduction

Historians as well as most other analysts of modern industrial society have long taken it for granted that modernization and national political integration are directly related. They accordingly assume that as a state undergoes large-scale industrialization and other related modernizing processes of economic development the ethnically, culturally, and socially diverse populations that had originally been brought under its sovereign authority will be increasingly welded into a single national society. Indeed, given the powerful instrumentalities of mass persuasion, political management, and social manipulation at the disposal of modern centralized states—especially control of national information networks and educational systems—any outcome to the modernizing enterprise other than the formation of an ethnically and culturally homogeneous population with a single national identity could hardly be imagined. Since, moreover, these processes of change and opportunities for uniform nationality development have obtained for the longest time in the established states of western Europe, historians have generally assumed that in these societies the goal of complete national political integration has been most nearly realized.

The rapid development of national consciousness among ethnic minorities in many of the advanced industrial societies of Europe in recent years gives the lie to this standard view concerning the relationship of modernization and national political integration. Equally misplaced is the implied corollary assumption that long-term industrialization and modern economic development must inevitably lead to the lessening of ethnic tensions and the creation of a state of social and cultural harmony between minority peoples and their majority rulers. Such an optimistic view can hardly be maintained in a world where, as has happened in Europe during the past decade, Basque nationalists assassinate Spanish prime ministers, Corsican separatists murder French policemen, German-speaking Tyrolese sabotage Italian trains and kill Italian nationals, Fleming dissidents firebomb the French-language University of Louvain in Belgium, Breton autonomists blow up French communications installations, and, finally, Irish terrorists make death and violence facts of everyday life in the United Kingdom. So serious is the challenge posed by various ethnic minority nationalist movements to the governments under whose sovereignty they live that many observers now fear, or at least predict, the eventual dissolution of several of Europe's long-established nation-states.

Wherever it is found in contemporary Europe, ethnic minority nationalism typically involves the formulation of political demands and the organization of protest movements by ethnic minorities against the centralizing efforts and assimilationist tendencies of the majority cultures in which they find themselves. Yet until very recently the phenomenon of ethnic minority nationalism has failed to draw the professional interest of most scholars. Mainstream liberal historians, particularly those who specialize in the study of nationalism, have instead focused their attention almost exclusively on those nationalities that have succeeded in establishing independent nation-states of their own. Thus one searches in vain through the works of C. J. H. Hayes and Hans Kohn for even passing references to national feeling among ethnic minorities in Wales, Scotland, Catalonia, and the Basque country. Occasionally, it is true, a representative of this historiographical tradition will fleetingly acknowledge the existence of nationalist movements among such minority peoples. But even in these cases nationalist phenomena are dismissed almost casually as vestiges of the relatively unimportant, if vexing, problems for central governments to handle as best they can. At most they are considered problems that will surely be liquidated by the passage of time and the onrush of modernization.[1] Liberal historians in any event regard ethnic minority nationalist movements as so pathological that they are more than happy to leave these phenomena to social psychologists and sociologists for discussion and analysis, devoting their own time to the presumably far more important question of political development within the majority culture.

Marxist scholars have hardly shown any more interest in ethnic minority nationalism, although certain among them, particularly those not noted for their orthodoxy, have at least glimpsed its significance. Herbert Marcuse, for example, apparently includes members of ethnic minority nationalist movements among "the substratum of the outcasts and outsiders, the exploited and persecuted of other races and other colors, the unemployed and the unemployable" who alone remain capable of mounting revolutionary opposition to the "one-dimensional society" that he despises so much.[2] E. J. Hobsbawm likewise views the recent growth of ethnic minority nationalism as the opening wedge of a far larger and more generalized popular revolt against governmental intervention and unresponsive bureaucratic rule. Expanding on Hobsbawm's notion, Suzanne Berger speculates that such attitudes develop first in regions with distinct ethnic characteristics because there the symbols of protest against the center —resistance to long-standing patterns of linguistic and cultural persecution, for example—are already available through shared historical experience.[3] Similar themes run through a 1973 symposium published in *Les Temps Modernes* in which French Marxists belatedly sought to incorporate into the political and ideological program of the extreme left the increasingly insistent demands of France's ethnic minorities.[4] These examples notwithstanding, however, Marxist scholars have not generally distinguished ethnic minority national feeling from more traditional forms of nationalism. Instead they regard such minority feeling as only a variant of the characteristic legitimating ideology with which national middle classes arm themselves in their efforts "to wrest power from feudal aristocrats and each other, to capture the market, and thus to obtain economic profit."[5]

This nearly universal neglect of ethnic minority nationalism on the part of professional scholars has as a consequence that almost nothing is known about the origins and subsequent historical experience of even the most important of the minority movements in contemporary Europe.[6] Two general reasons go far to explain this perennial lack of interest in ethnic minority nationalism. First of all, the common tendency of historians and other social scientists to focus on social theories and historical processes that posit the incorporation of ever-expanding areas of human activity and organizational existence into some central nexus like an empire, kingdom, state, or bureaucracy has become possibly too ingrained for these scholars to have glimpsed the enduring reality of ethnic minority feeling. Secondly, and perhaps more important, students of European nationalism have been almost completely preoccupied with the development of majority national feeling on its seemingly irreversible march toward full realization in France, Germany, and the other nation-states of Europe. Some observers, it is true, predicted that the triumph of majority nationalism was not, in fact, permanent. They assumed that it would disappear when its institutional basis in the nation-state gave way under the impact of overwhelming economic, social, and political forces to the formation of a larger continental organization. Thus it was widely expected in the immediate post-1945 period that the surviving war-shattered states of Europe would soon coalesce into a single political unit, a dream of European unity that quickly faded amid the divisive realities of the cold war.

Whatever its ultimate fate, most scholars took it as axiomatic that majority national feeling grew at the expense of local ethnic sentiments, and few lamented the disappearance of the latter into Trotsky's famous "dustbin of history." Any other result would have seemed a denial of progress and thereby in contradiction with the rooted belief of most western scholars in the inexorable forward march of the historical process. Indeed, in an important recent study of ethnic conflict and political development Cynthia H. Enloe insists that historians and other social scientists have consistently missed the significance of ethnic minority nationalism because most automatically assume that, as modernization proceeds, ethnic groups will fade away of their own accord.[7] For such scholars ethnic particularism therefore represents no more than the unfinished business of modernizing majority national elites. And if this job is done well (that is, if civic involvement is promoted while the broad distribution of the advantages of modern industrial development is facilitated), ethnicity should soon disappear as a salient factor in national political life even though it may remain an enduring basis for group association. The policy recommendation of all this is clear enough: authorities of the central state must genuinely encourage democratic and individualistic participation of the citizenry in public life and plan rationally for economic growth if they wish to eliminate disruptive ethnic conflicts from public affairs. Given this prevailing view it is hardly surprising that so many scholars assume when they make comparisons between social and political systems that the declining importance of ethnicity in a state's political life is a reliable index of modernity.

Unfortunately for the bulk of mainstream scholarship on ethnicity, however, the confident forecast that modernization must inevitably spell doom for ethnic minority nationalist movements appears to have come a cropper. Advanced democratic polities like the United States, Canada, Switzerland, France, and the United Kingdom as well as heavily planned economies like those in the Soviet Union and Yugoslavia are all experiencing ethnic minority tensions even as they try to cope with such postmodern problems as leisure, pollution, and suburbanization.[8] Undeterred by such inconvenient facts, most contemporary social scientists still maintain that modernization and ethnic minority feeling remain inversely related. Exceptions to this rule they explain (away) simply by acknowledging that scholars have perhaps overestimated the extent of modernization that may be attributed to advanced societies like the United States, the Soviet Union, France, and Great Britain. Or they may insist that even those societies that on the whole seem highly developed nonetheless include isolated pockets of traditional particularism in ethnically distinct regions that scholars, bewitched by nation-level analysis, have failed to perceive.

Even scholars who recognize the limitations of the nation-state as their primary unit of political analysis have missed the significance of awakening national feeling on the part of many of Europe's ethnic minorities. An important reason for this oversight has been their preoccupation with the postwar trend toward the development of supranational organizations. It is easy to understand how this could have happened since bodies like the Common Market and multinational corporations possess at least the appearance of power and economic significance, while at the same time seeming to promise a means by which long-standing national antagonisms between, for example, France and Germany may be accommodated. By contrast ethnic minority nationalist movements on the face of it appear to be historically lost causes of the weak and powerless or, worse still, they seem more likely to increase rather than to diminish the sum of violence that afflicts modern society. But it is precisely the potential of ethnic minority nationalism for generating social violence as well as the possibility that its spokesmen may be pointing the way toward new forms of political organization that make it imperative for contemporary social science to come to terms with this phenomenon.

Such a sense of urgency pervades Enloe's pioneering work on ethnic conflict and political development. No less pervasive is her refusal to be bound by the entrenched scholarly shibboleths that mark the theoretical literature on modernization. In particular she contests the notion that modernizing development and ethnicity are inversely related, indeed even that they are related at all. Instead Enloe suggests that ethnicity may be qualitatively much different—less rigid and tradition-bound, more resilient and adaptive to modern industrial conditions—than most scholars have long assumed. She goes on to argue that ethnic feeling may in fact respond to deep-seated human needs for community identity, thus forming "a basis for social relationships more enduring and less instrumental than occupation, status, and legal right." At the very least, Enloe intriguingly concludes, "ethnicity has become a major lever for forcing doubts about modernity into the open. Ethnic spokesmen are challenging the close connection of modernization and development. If modernity leads to alienation of the individual and to centralized injustice in the name of rational planning, then perhaps modernization is antithetical to genuine development." From such a perspective, then, the emergence of ethnic minority nationalism and its mobilization into political protest movements "may reflect the traumas of casting off tradition, but it also may portend innovative political forms for the future, beyond modernity."[9]

An increasing number of her fellow social scientists—Martin O. Heisler, Suzanne Berger, Michael Hechter, and Walter B. Simon, to name four—share Enloe's ideas concerning the growing significance of ethnic minority nationalism. They agree with her that even in the most industrially advanced and apparently fully integrated societies ethnicity is an enduring reality. They argue, moreover, that in such societies ethnic cleavages have long coexisted with socioeconomic class-based cleavages and speculate that in the long run the former may prove historically more important than the latter. Simon even contends that a frequently unremarked consequence of modernization is that ethnic and class cleavages actually coincide in many advanced societies.[10] This is so, he explains, because particular industries tend to recruit workers for similar jobs from specific cultural groups, a phenomenon of selective recruitment that has historically been found wherever people are brought together to live in cities. So it happens that the processes of "industrialization and urbanization tend to create groups whose members share language and religion as well as social class so that boundary lines created by diverse distinct characteristics often coincide."[11] Thus to the extent to which ethnic cleavages coincide with those that separate conflicting socioeconomic groups the resulting tensions will be exacerbated.

According to Michael Hechter, the most important of these tensions arise when members of ethnic minorities find themselves socially and economically disadvantaged as a consequence of systematic majority discrimination in the areas of employment, wage rates, standards of living, and educational opportunities.[12] Only then, he continues, may the long-standing ethnic resentments generated by official persecution of minority languages and cultural usages on the part of dominant majorities, as well as informal majority treatment of minority persons as objects of scorn, hatred, and violence, be mobilized into an ethnic minority nationalist movement of meaningful political proportions. Elsewhere Hechter suggests that once such a movement acquires a mass basis it may already be too late for central authorities to appease minority leaders with concessions on either cultural or economic questions.[13] Indeed, at so late a date the end of majority discrimination and the opening up of opportunities for social and economic advance to members of aggrieved ethnic minorities may from the point of view of the center only serve to make matters worse. On this point Hugh Seton-Watson aptly observes that when there were almost no French-Canadians in the Canadian business world members of this group didn't seem to mind very much. But once a third of the good business jobs in Montreal had fallen into French-Canadian hands Québeçois nationalist leaders found it intolerable that two-thirds were still held by the city's English-speaking population.[14] From this perspective the increasing frequency with which leaders of ethnic minority nationalist movements in contemporary Europe charge that their peoples are the chronic victims of deliberate patterns of structural discrimination in matters of social and economic life bodes ill for the continued political stability of many existing continental states.

Martin Heisler and Suzanne Berger also recognize that ethnic and socioeconomic class-based cleavages have long coexisted in many advanced industrial societies.[15] But while Hechter (and Simon would surely not disagree) accounts for the emergence of ethnic minority nationalism in terms of the merging of perceived patterns of majority discrimination against minority populations in both cultural and socioeconomic areas, Heisler and Berger propose a different explanation. They argue that until at least the end of World War II ethnic cleavages lay dormant or were obscured by class-based cleavages that dominated the internal political affairs of most European societies. But with the postwar creation of welfare states throughout western Europe most of the redistribution demands arising out of socioeconomic class-based cleavages were in the main satisfied. This change produced a general erosion in the traditional class bases of partisan politics, a development that, according to Heisler and Berger, in turn allowed ethnic cleavages to move to the forefront of political life.[16] Berger is thus led to conclude that in many cases ethnic minority nationalist movements seem "to be replacing organizations based on class, and, not as before simply inserting themselves into the interstices of a political system whose structures remain fixed by the old categories"[17]—the fate of most ethnic minority nationalist movements in Europe before 1945.

Berger also discusses another way in which the development of modern welfare-state systems has encouraged the growth of ethnic minority nationalism. She contends that in these new systems formerly politically sensitive socio-economic issues are transformed into essentially technical questions to be resolved within the context of the broadly agreed-upon welfare-state goal of assuring a constantly increasing amount of prosperity to all social classes.[18] This historic change has meant a gradual but decisive shift in the locus of political decision making in postwar welfare states from parliamentary arenas of power into technocratic locales. The effect is virtually to exclude from vital decision-making processes representatives from backward peripheral areas—areas where ethnic minority populations are typically found—since recruitment into the highly technical services that administer modern European welfare-state systems is through the great universities and training schools of the center. This exclusion generates among ethnically distinct populations in such regions increased feelings of isolation and neglect that—passing through the prism of resentment provoked by cultural and linguistic discrimination—are manifested in the form of ethnic minority nationalism.

No doubt all of the above arguments capture a part of the truth and contribute in important ways to the understanding of ethnic minority nationalism. Yet even Berger admits that until now scholarly literature on Europe's ethnic minorities has generally failed "to account for the circumstances under which a group with distinctive linguistic, cultural, and social traditions comes to formulate political demands for self-government."[19] In the absence of empirical verification, therefore, all of the explanations outlined above must in most respects be considered highly tentative, if not frankly speculative. In any case it is certain that these arguments do not in any meaningful sense constitute a coherent theoretical framework in which the genesis and subsequent development of nationalistic sentiments on the part of Europe's numerous ethnic minorities can be adequately explained. The formulation of such a body of theory awaits the accumulation of a substantial monographic literature on contemporary ethnic minority nationalist movements that historians and other social scientists have so far failed to provide. The following chapters are intended to make a modest contribution to that important scholarly endeavor insofar as ethnic minority nationalism in twentieth-century Brittany is concerned.

List of Abbreviations

ABES	Ar Brezoneg er Skol (Le Breton à l'école)
CCB	Comité Consultatif de Bretagne
CDIB	Comité de Défense des Intérêts Bretons
CELIB	Comité d'Etudes et de Liaison des Intérêts Bretons
CNB	Conseil National Breton
CNBL	Comité National pour une Bretagne Libre
CODER	Commissions de Développement Economique Régional
FLB	Front de Libération de la Bretagne
FRB	Féderation Régionaliste de Bretagne
GRB	Groupe Régionaliste Breton
MOB	Mouvement pour l'Organisation de la Bretagne
PAB	Parti Autonomiste Breton
PCB	Parti Communiste Breton
PNB	Parti National Breton (1919–44)
PNB	Parti Nationaliste Breton (1911–14)
PNIB	Parti Nationaliste Intégral Breton
POB	Projet pour l'Organisation de la Bretagne
PSU	Parti Socialiste Unifié
SADED	Strollad Deskadurezh an Eil Derez (Institut de l'Enseignement du Sécond Degré)
SAGA	Strollad ar Gelted Adsavet (Réunion des Celtes relevés
SAV	Strollad ar Vro (Parti Patriotique)
UDB	Union Démocratique Bretonne

UNR   Union pour la Nouvelle République
URB   Union Régionaliste Bretonne
UYV   Unvaniez Yaouankiz Vreiz (Union de Jeunesse
       Bretonne)

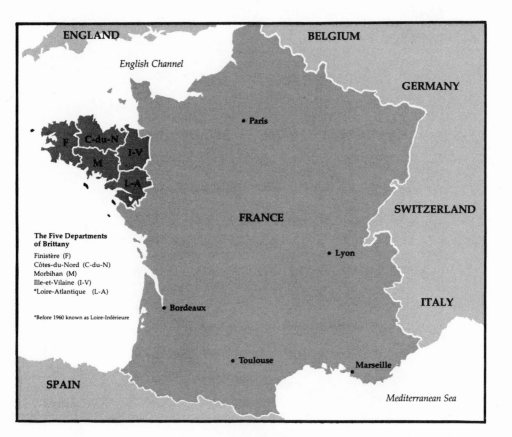

ENGLAND

English Channel

BELGIUM

GERMANY

• Paris

F

C-du-N

I-V

M

L-A

FRANCE

SWITZERLAND

Lyon

The Five Departments
of Brittany

Finistère (F)
Côtes-du-Nord (C-du-N)
Morbihan (M)
Ille-et-Vilaine (I-V)
*Loire-Atlantique (L-A)

*Before 1960 known as Loire-Inférieure

ITALY

• Bordeaux

• Toulouse

• Marseille

SPAIN

Mediterranean Sea

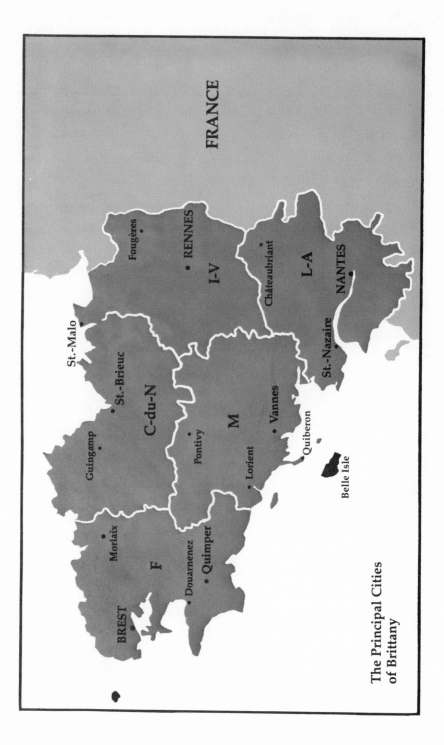

FRANCE

Fougères

RENNES

I-V

Châteaubriant

L-A

NANTES

St.-Malo

St.-Brieuc

C-du-N

St.-Nazaire

Guingamp

Pontivy

M

Vannes

Lorient

Quiberon

Belle Isle

Morlaix

F

Douarnenez

Quimper

BREST

The Principal Cities
of Brittany

The Bretons against France

CHAPTER 1

ᔕ The Historical Background

Most modern European states are products of the fortuitous convergence of dynastic ambitions, historical circumstances, and political and administrative skills wielded by a succession of able rulers. Once these states became firmly established, Ernest Barker persuasively argued a half century ago, they served "as the principal agents in the accumulation of that tradition which ultimately constitutes a nation."[1] Nationalists seldom accept so reasonable an explanation of the origin of nations. They maintain that the actual historical evolution is in the opposite direction. Behind the development of a given people toward full national self-awareness they glimpse the presence of an eternally existent nation acting as the primordial driving force of the entire process. Nationalists thus view ancient figures who thought they strove to accomplish the will of God, to make what they saw as the truth prevail, to advance the interests of a particular dynasty, or simply to defend themselves against an aggressor as persons who *really* acted so that the genius of a particular nationality could manifest itself and be fostered in the fullness of time. Incorporated into an officially sanctioned national historiography and propagated in a system of state-run schools, these largely fanciful notions have long been the moral lens through which individual Europeans perceive their national group identity.

Ernest Renan once remarked of the above phenomenon that "to forget, and I will venture to say, to get one's history wrong are essential factors in the making of nations."[2] Few people have been more susceptible to such historical forgetfulness and error than Renan's own countrymen. The centuries-long continuity and enduring territorial stability of the French state almost naturally incline Frenchmen to interpret its history in terms of the progressive unfolding of French national will. For both professional historians and their readers, the central meaning of this process is the unceasing advance of the timeless French nation toward its eventual realization as a sovereign state. In countless volumes of the history of France, therefore, learned discussions of the development of the French state under Philip the Fair, Henri IV, and Louis XIV slip easily into discussions of the development of the French nation under these monarchs. It is little wonder that primary-school children in France typically develop a mental image of their country already constituted as a nation when Clovis received baptism from St. Remy in 496.

The meaning of national historiography depends, however, on the point of view of the observer. Breton patriots look at the process of the formation of the French nation-state and see not the triumph of the French people, but the tragic history of the decline of Brittany and the dissolution of Breton national identity. They repudiate the notion that the French state is the inevitable product of an unfailing French national will. Instead they regard it as the violent creation of imperialist monarchs and their servants who built it out of the shattered fragments of nations that they had crushed by military force. Breton patriots equally consider the French nation itself an entirely mortal creation fashioned out of ethnic communities progressively denationalized by official policies of cultural uniformity and assimilation.

Breton patriots insist that the particular record of French aggression and hostility toward Brittany is not known because French historians have deliberately concealed it from their readers. Local historians of Brittany have thus sought to reinterpret the history of their homeland for modern Bretons so that the Breton people might know the crimes allegedly committed against their nationality by Frenchmen. From this labor emerged the image of an eternally existent Breton nation remarkably similar to, if no less fanciful than, the one that marches through the pages of French national historiography. It is perhaps a measure of how far gallicization has proceeded even among ardent Breton patriotic intellectuals that the conceptualizations they bring to historical inquiry have been so much influenced by French models. At the very least, the patriot version of the history of Brittany manifestly supports Renan's shrewd remark about the making of nations.

The historiographical point of departure of the patriotic revision of Breton history has from the outset been the work of two nineteenth-century historians of Brittany, Pitré-Chevalier and Arthur de La Borderie.[3] Relying mostly on selective quotation, later Breton militants have even tried to present both men as nationalists before the fact, the spiritual fathers of twentieth-century Breton nationalism. And there is no doubt that both Pitré-Chevalier and La Borderie were devoted sons of Brittany.[4] It is equally clear that for each the anchor of his national consciousness was France, not Brittany. Although he did admit that France had not always been just toward Brittany, "the most ancient and noble part of herself," Pitré-Chevalier nonetheless insisted that Bretons were wrong to seek redress on their own but must loyally await it from Paris.[5] As for La Borderie, it is true that he attributed a national past to Brittany, but he confined it solely to the pre-1491 ducal period of the peninsula's history. After that time he contended that Breton history formed but a part of the provincial history of France. In fact, he went further and declared that its history came entirely to an end with the administrative division of the peninsula into five departments in 1790. La Borderie considered the history of Brittany thereafter indistinguishable from "the immense and splendid mainstream" of French national experience.[6]

For many Breton patriots the histories of Brittany published by Pitré-Chevalier and La Borderie were both clearly inadequate. Early in the twentieth century, therefore, patriotic scholars on the peninsula resolved to interpret the history of their homeland from a systematically Breton point of view. The initial results of this effort were not very impressive, for the most part consisting of brief essays on selected topics in Breton history scattered through the prewar patriotic press. Far from providing a comprehensive view of Brittany's past, these little historical pieces generally focused on such figures out of the Breton past as King Nominoë and the Duchess Anne, who would in time emerge as the foremost heroes of nationalist historiography. Not until after World War I did a full-length history of Brittany written from an explicitly Breton point of view finally appear. This was the beautifully illustrated *Histoire de Notre Bretagne* published in 1922 by C. Danio, the pseudonym of Jeanne du Guerny, a young woman associated with the most militant branch of the interwar nationalist movement.[7] Her little volume may well be the single most influential publication ever to come from the pen of a Breton patriotic writer. It shaped the nationalist views of an entire generation of Breton militants, many of whom even reported that it was their chance reading of Danio's book that brought them to the nationalist movement in the first place. For these reasons this work provides much of the framework for the following discussion of the patriotic version of Breton history.

The point of departure of Danio's history is the Celtic origin of the Breton people and their distinct ethnic identity apart from the French. The Celtic ancestors of the Bretons, she explained, were a Germanic people who had preserved their ethnic purity in successive migrations from northern Europe to the British Isles and then to the Armorican peninsula of modern-day France. On the other hand, she argued that the French, although they could in the distant past point to the same Germanic heritage, had through contact with eastern Latin civilization become a polyglot people of uncertain ethnic composition. Danio stressed other factors, particularly those relating to physical appearance, moral values, and political attitudes, that she claimed ethnically separated Celts from Latins. Contrasting images of tall, blond, freedom-loving Celtic democrats and short, dark, authoritarian Latin centralizers were the result. The implied message is clear: peoples so different were bound to be bitter antagonists. Indeed, ancient conflict between Celtic and Latin civilizations —the one robust, pure, and original; the other debilitated, corrupt, and derivative—is the leitmotif of Danio's whole historical outlook. The developing twentieth-century confrontation between Breton nationalists and their French adversaries hence becomes the most recent manifestation of an ages-long struggle between inherently antagonistic peoples and cultures. In the process the Breton nationalist movement seems to acquire the legitimating sanction of historical tradition that it otherwise appeared to lack.

Danio passed lightly over the early history of the Breton population following its fifth-century arrival on the Armorican peninsula. She simply interpreted this confused period of never-ending tribal quarrels and endemic political violence as one in which Bretons successfully resisted Frankish attempts to subdue their new homeland and exact tribute from them. Local warrior chiefs with odd-sounding names like Gwerec'h, Maclaw, and Warok thus emerge from obscurity as the first bearers of "the eternal flame of resistance" that Bretons are said to have opposed ever since to their "long-toothed" Frankish neighbors to the east.[8] So spirited was the patriotic resistance of the local Breton population, according to Danio, that for three centuries the Franks were unable to occupy the peninsula. In her view it apparently counted for little in this standoff that the weak and divided Franks gave only sporadic attention to the task of conquering the Bretons.

This situation changed drastically in the eighth century with the emergence of a vigorous line of Frankish kings determined to establish their authority on the Armorican peninsula. In 753 Pepin the Short captured Vannes and combined it with the previously subdued territories around Nantes and Rennes to form the so-called Marche de Bretagne. Ruled for four decades by a collaterally related family of Frankish counts, the Marche was brought under the direct authority of the Frankish monarchy by Pepin's son and successor, Charlemagne, in 790. Almost immediately he launched a campaign to master the still-unconquered western portion of the peninsula. Although, according to Danio, the Bretons put up a fierce patriotic resistance that lasted for nine years, they finally yielded before the superior power of Charlemagne's soldiers. Relative peace obtained throughout Brittany until the death of the great Carolingian monarch in 814. For the next dozen years his successor, Louis the Pious, faced continuous rebellion in Brittany and twice personally led expeditions against insurgent Breton chiefs. Louis at last concluded, Danio recounts, that his subjects on the peninsula would be less troublesome if they were ruled in his name by a native-born Breton deputy. In 826 he therefore chose for this task Nominoë, a member of the local aristocracy near Vannes.

Nominoë loyally served Louis until the latter's death in

840. But, as Breton patriotic historiography would have it, he secretly planned to unite Brittany under his rule and at the first favorable opportunity separate it from the Carolingian state. During the confused period after 840 when Carolingian authority receded from Brittany as Louis's three sons Lothair, Charles the Bald, and Pepin struggled for supremacy, Nominoë supposedly found his chance. Nominally allied with Lothair to whom he had sworn an oath of loyalty on Louis's deathbed, he gradually established his personal sway throughout the western peninsula. Meanwhile Charles the Bald, awarded the western dominions of the Carolingian empire according to the 843 Partition of Verdun, prepared to make good his nominal suzerainty in Brittany. In response, Nominoë gathered all the leading Breton knights under his banner and on 22 November 848—the greatest day in Breton patriotic history—decisively defeated Charles on the field of battle at Ballon near Redon. Formally recognized by Charles the following year as Duke of the Bretons, Nominoë soon extended his authority over the eastern part of the Armorican peninsula as well. Thus for the first time, according to Breton historical tradition, all Brittany was united under the rule of an independent and native-born Breton chief. This achievement was officially recognized, Danio took care to explain, since in 848 Nominoë was consecrated king of the Bretons by an envoy of the pope in the cathedral at Dol. A short time later he is also supposed to have received from the holy Roman emperor the title of sovereign lord of Brittany. It turned out to be a brief three-year reign, for Nominoë died suddenly in 851 in the midst of a military campaign he was bringing against the count of Chartres.

Despite the brevity of his rule, Nominoë invariably figures in Breton patriotic historiography as the deliverer of Brittany from its Frankish yoke, the founder of Breton independence, and therefore the father of his country.[9] There is virtually nothing to support these claims except the hopes and dreams of twentieth-century Breton patriots. Otherwise, Nominoë looks remarkably like any other ambitious medieval princeling who, profiting from the breakdown of the Merovingian order, was able to find an advantageous position in the new Carolingian system that replaced it. He had, after all, entered into the framework of the Carolingian monarchy and faithfully served Louis the Pious as governor of Brittany for many years. Moreover, he and his successors organized their court and government along Carolingian lines. If his career merits any particular notice, then, it is only because Nominoë was one of the more intelligent and successful of a throng of contemporary dukes and counts who, seeking to extend their territorial authority as far as possible and without reference to the nationality of those who happened to get in the way of their ambition, finally dismembered the Frankish monarchy. But legends, especially those created by patriotic historians, do not die easily among Breton militants. Thus many Bretons still trek every year to see the ludicrously small statue erected several decades ago at Ballon to the memory of Nominoë, one Breton leader at least who defeated a French army.

Whatever the enduring historical significance of Nominoë's achievement, the kingdom that he fashioned lasted barely more than half a century. Badly governed by a succession of weak rulers, it steadily disintegrated under the pressure of marauding Norman bands that had been making forays into the peninsula since the time of Nominoë. With the death of 907 of Alain le Grand, the ablest of Nominoë's successors, Brittany was completely overrun and for the next thirty years lay at the mercy of Norman invaders. According to patriotic historiography, this experience deeply influenced the course of Breton historical development. Terrorized by pillaging, massacres, and other forms of Norman brutality, the Breton landed nobility as a body went into exile in neighboring Anjou. There, Breton patriots lament, this group underwent the initial phases of what proved to be an irreversible process of gallicization. Breton ecclesiastics similarly abandoned their ruined churches and monasteries and sought refuge even further to the east than Anjou. The wholesale departure of the top echelons of Breton society provoked virtual disaggregation at the bottom. Denied the protection traditionally offered by church and château, much of the rural peasant population fled into the mountainous, forested interior of the peninsula for sanctuary. The cities in turn experienced depopulation as fleeing urban dwellers sought refuge in the abandoned countryside.

With Danio in the lead, patriotic historians claim that Brittany was divested of its Norman despoilers through the conscious efforts of the Breton people themselves. In 936 the head of the Breton abbey at Landevennec is supposed to have called on Alain Barbetorte, a grandson of Alain le Grand then living in exile at the English court, to deliver his homeland from its enemies.[10] Alain accordingly returned to Brittany and raised an army of liberation. By 937 he had expelled the Normans from Dol, St.-Brieuc, and Nantes. With the victory of Trans two years later he drove the last of the northern invaders from Brittany and reestablished its frontiers as they had existed in Nominoë's time. Lacking the personal authority of Nominoë, however, he stopped short of assuming the kingly title. Powerful counts, viscounts, and other lesser nobles who ruled the territories adjacent to their châteaux with little regard for Alain Barbetorte's nominal supremacy over them would have risen in rebellion against such a pretension. He and his successors had to be satisfied with the title of duke of Brittany. The next six centuries of Breton history therefore constitute in Breton patriotic historiography the story of ducal Brittany.

During the first two hundred years of this period the dukes of Brittany swore homage to the Capetian monarchs who succeeded the Carolingians in 987. Except for the act of homage, however, Breton dukes tended to ignore the new kings of France, who for their part showed little interest in the day-to-day affairs of the peninsula.[11] Danio emphasizes Brittany's relative state of isolation during these centuries by recounting its history solely in terms of bitter and complicated struggles among the leading Breton noble families for primacy on the peninsula. Her implication is clear. Only so rich a prize as the national destiny of Brittany, always at stake in these struggles in Danio's view, could generate such emotion and effort. The actual situation was totally different. Since there was no Salic Law to regulate the succession, the death of a Breton duke typically precipitated a political crisis. These crises were usually resolved by force of arms and, though Breton patriotic historians glide over the fact, the ability of one of the rival claimants to win the liege support of the current Capetian monarch. Indeed, the only real advantage the ducal title conferred on its holder was preferment on the feudal pecking order presided over at the top by the Capetians. Otherwise the powers of the Breton dukes were virtually nonexistent, since Brittany at the time, in the words of one scholar, was "only an assemblage of counties dependent on various noble houses all of whom were ill-disposed to accept the authority of whoever held the ducal crown."[12]

Patriotic Breton historians argue that the weakness of ducal authority had, from their point of view, a baneful effect on the development of Brittany's landed aristocracy. Since the counts of Rennes and Nantes were the leading contestants for the ducal title, each sought to master the other by forging alliances with the ambitious heads of noble houses in western Brittany. Many of these nobles, calculating that such alliances would improve their family fortunes, established permanent residences near one or the other of the contending ducal candidates. The Breton landed aristocracy thus became concentrated in the Francophone east and, split into antagonistic factions based on Rennes and Nantes, soon became overwhelmingly French in language, culture, and mental outlook. At the same time the Breton-speaking western half of the peninsula fell under the domination of absentee landlords who took scant interest in the affairs and welfare of the local population. The outcome was, according to patriotic historiography, that Brittany's natural leaders in the landed aristocracy, instead of acting as the foremost protectors of Breton nationality, served for hundreds of years as the single most powerful social force on the peninsula for the denationalization of the Breton people.[13]

The two centuries of relative isolation during which Danio and other patriotic historians claim the Breton landed aristocracy underwent the changes discussed above ended abruptly in 1154. In that year Henry II Plantagenet, king of England, duke of Acquitaine and Guyenne, and count of Anjou and Touraine, also became duke of Normandy. Within a dozen years he had extended his rule to the Breton peninsula as well. He made his son Geffroi II duke of Brittany in 1181, who in turn was succeeded by his own son Arthur six years later. At the end of the century Arthur became embroiled with his relative "Landless" John who, after following his brother Richard the Lion-Hearted as duke of Normandy in 1199, resolved to have the Breton dukedom for himself. Arthur was able to resist this design through an alliance with the Capetian monarch Philip-Augustus. "It was like summoning the fox against the wolf," a Breton patriot recently observed, for the price of the alliance was the ducal succession itself.[14] After Arthur's death in 1203, therefore, the ducal crown for the next 138 years was worn by successive members of the house of Dreux, whose founder, Pierre Mauclerc, was a minor Capetian prince.

Patriotic historians explain the shape of Breton history during the two and one-half centuries that followed Arthur's death in terms of the accelerating struggle between the English and French monarchies for influence in Brittany. Flanked by powerful Plantagenets on the one hand and equally powerful Capetians on the other, the dukes of Brittany supposedly leaned now one way, now the other in order to preserve Breton independence. By so doing, one of Danio's successors has written, "they not only served their own personal interests but incarnated as well the national sentiment of an entire people."[15] This interpretation vastly overstates Brittany's role in the Anglo-French struggle, just as it exaggerates the amount of leverage enjoyed by Breton dukes during most of this period. The peninsula's involvement in the Hundred Years' War showed how little maneuvering space Brittany's dukes actually possessed and how slight was the role of Breton national sentiment in determining their political behavior.

The last of the Dreux line of Breton dukes died in 1341, touching off a war of succession that dragged on for a quarter of a century. Patriotic historians view this war as a strictly internal Breton affair that saw two families, the Montfort and the Penthièvre, struggle for the ducal crown. Coinciding with the first decades of the Hundred Years' War, it was actually a theater of that larger conflict, with the English backing the Montforts and the French the Penthièvres. For a long time the former had the better of the game and French influences that had grown rapidly in Brittany under the Dreux were halted for nearly a century. However, this situation hardly permitted local Breton culture and national sentiment to flourish unhampered by external influences, as patriotic historiography would have it. Instead, the ducal crown on a Montfort head meant only that English influences replaced French ones on the Breton peninsula.

The simple fact of the matter was that Brittany, centrally located in the struggle between the Plantagenets and the Capetians for domination of western continental Europe, would have its eventual fate determined by the outcome of that contest itself. Its dukes were more shuttlecocks than makeweights in this epic conflict, and their policies signified little more than whichever of the two contending forces was at any given time in the ascendant. Patriotic historians try to gloss over this unpleasant reality for the half-century after 1380 by extolling the "neutrality" of Jean IV Montfort and the wisdom of his successor, Jean V, who is said to have presided over a well-governed and prosperous dukedom. Both were in fact Breton puppets who danced on an English string. The latter's successor, François I, actually saw his dukedom become a possession of the English crown for a time during the first part of the fifteenth century.

The French Capetians finally prevailed, however, and drove the English from Brittany. Patriotic historians have had to account for the embarrassing fact that three Breton-born constables of France were among the most devoted servants of the Capetian monarchy in this effort. Two of these, Bertrand du Guesclin and Olivier de Clisson, are simply dismissed as traitors to Brittany. The third, Arthur de Richemont, is another matter. A son of Jean IV, a brother of Jean V, and duke of Brittany himself for a year in 1457–58, he "never forgot he was a Breton and remained faithful to his Duke and country."[16] Yet it was Richemont who was largely responsible for the recovery of Capetian fortunes after 1430, organizing for Charles VII the ultimately successful expulsion of English armies from the continent. Conscious Breton and at the same time loyal servant of France—this is a difficult combination for a patriotic Breton historian to explain away. Danio's feeble attempt to do so by arguing that Richemont above all else was driven by his hatred for the English at least leaves some room for the existence of Breton national feeling in the calculation of his political action. The more plausible explanation that he, like du Guesclin and Clisson, was a typical figure in the game of European dynastic politics as played in the late medieval period probably does not.

In any case, by 1453 the English held only Calais on the continent. Three successive Breton dukes recognized the new state of affairs by joining the French king in military alliance against the English. It soon became clear that the triumphant Capetians intended to absorb semi-independent fiefs like Brittany directly into the French monarchy. During a brilliant reign of twenty-two years Louis XI accomplished this for Burgundy, Anjou, Maine, and Provence. At his death in 1483 only the dukedom of Brittany remained outside the French crown. Five years later Louis XI's successor, Charles VIII, determined to resolve the issue by force. Therefore, at St.-Aubin-du-Cormier on 28 July 1488—the darkest day in the annals of Breton patriotic historiography—his army inflicted a decisive defeat on the last Breton duke, François II. Two weeks later François had to accept the treaty of Verger, which virtually stripped the Breton dukedom of its sovereign rights, even that of its ruler to arrange marriages for his daughters without the consent of the French king. François II died of sadness, according to Danio, a month after signing this harsh treaty.

The new wearer of the nearly worthless ducal crown was François II's eleven-year-old daughter, the Duchess Anne. Breton patriots implausibly portray her as the greatest heroine of their history, valiantly determined to avenge her father's humiliation and restore Breton independence. She was actually a bewildered child caught up in the antagonism between the Rennes and Nantes branches of the Breton aristocracy. Leaders of each faction, recognizing that Charles VIII would inevitably rule Brittany, outbid each other at Anne's expense in order to strike a bargain with the French king that would ensure their supremacy in the Breton social order. Grown impatient by three years of seemingly endless intrigue, Charles VIII simply occupied the dukedom and appointed a lieutenant-general to govern the peninsula in his name. Isolated at Rennes and abandoned to her fate by both branches of the Breton nobility, the Duchess Anne formally capitulated to the French monarchy on 15 November 1491. Eight days later she married Charles VIII and became queen of France.

On the subject of this marriage Dom Morice, a Benedictine historian of the mid-eighteenth century, argued that it was forced upon Anne and described her protest against it as the protest of the outraged Breton nation.[17] This theme patriotic historians have made their own, endlessly invoking it as their clinching argument in the legal and moral case they make against French rule in Brittany. Since Breton independence was violated by means of Anne's forced marriage, they claim, the French domination of Brittany is illegal and rests solely on naked power. The clear implication is that all conscious Bretons are thus duty-bound to resist that domination so that one day it might be overturned. In such resistance, moreover, all those means sanctioned by tradition and history —including appeals to the enemies of France for assistance— are legitimate. It was this sort of disjointed reasoning that inclined some Breton nationalists in 1940 to join their cause to that of Nazi occupation authorities in the hope of achieving the restoration of Breton independence.

The argument concerning Anne's forced marriage is in fact no more convincing than patriotic attempts to portray her as the courageous defender of Breton independence during the previous three years. Nor is there any evidence that her marriage was any less successful or more disappointing than such dynastic unions typically were. As was usually the case with such marriages, Anne's betrothal was regulated by a formal contract whose provisions were actually generous insofar as the Bretons were concerned. The contract stipulated that all taxes levied on Bretons had to be expended on the defense of the dukedom and that none could be collected until the formal approval of the Etats de Bretagne had been secured. It also conceded to Bretons the right to have their legal actions tried and resolved before Breton magistrates. In return Anne ceded to Charles VIII all her ducal rights in Brittany should she die before producing a child. If she were widowed first without children, then he yielded all his rights in Brittany, but only on condition that Anne marry the new French king if he desired such a union. The contract was surely unequal, but the two parties were hardly equals. St.-Aubin-du-Cormier had proven that inequality three years earlier; this nuptial instrument only confirmed the fact.

After 1491 Breton patriots portray Anne more as duchess of Brittany than queen of France. In their view she spent all her time struggling to regain as much as she could of what Brittany had lost since 1488. Upon the death of Charles VIII in 1498 his childless widow was even able to return to the peninsula where, according to Danio, she "resumed the entire government of the country." It seemed unlikely that the new French king, Louis XII, would exercise his nuptial rights over Anne, for he already had a wife. The real situation was quite different; before her departure Anne had signed a convention with Louis establishing that they would marry as soon as he could dissolve his existing union. An annulment was easily obtained from Pope Alexander VI and Anne of Brittany once more became queen of France. This time her marriage contract, which Breton historians claim she dictated, contained more favorable terms. The most significant of these was that the Breton dukedom would not pass to the eldest son of the royal couple but to a younger child, thus assuring that Brittany's dukes would not simultaneously be kings of France.

Although Anne produced several children for Louis XII, only two daughters survived infancy. Shortly after her mother's death in 1513 the elder of these, Claude, was married to the heir presumptive, who as François I became king of France in 1514. Claude showed no interest in the affairs of Brittany and turned its government over to her husband, the duke consort. To the consternation of later Breton patriots, in 1515 she simply gave her dukedom outright, in case she died without issue, to François I "in perpetuity and to do with as he saw fit."[18] In a will published a short time after her death in 1524, however, Claude left her dukedom to the dauphin. Breton historians like Danio consider this will a violation of Anne's marriage contract and "juridically null," since Claude "exceeded her rights by disposing of what did not belong to her." This fine legal point excites twentieth-century Breton patriots far more than it did the first magistrate of France in 1524. Instead, François I simply sought a means to transform the personal union of the crowns of Brittany and France into one based on law and the assent of the Etats de Bretagne.

François I achieved his goal eight years later with the pact of union of August 1532, which he negotiated with the

Etats. To this pact he attached a royal pledge to maintain ancient Breton rights in their entirety and a formal guarantee of Brittany's liberties and privileges, as spelled out a month later in the declaration of Plessix. Thus, "in his own name as well as that of his successors and in the name of France," he declared that the union of Brittany to France was regulated by the following provisions:

1. No tax levied at Paris could be collected in Brittany without the prior assent of the Etats;
2. Revenue from certain taxes levied in Brittany was to be reserved exclusively for use in Brittany;
3. The juridical sovereignty of the *parlement* of Brittany and the right of Bretons to have their cases tried in Breton courts would be maintained;
4. No Breton could be compelled to serve in royal armies outside the peninsula;
5. Ecclesiastical benefices in Brittany were to be held only by Bretons; and
6. No alteration in the legislation, the institutions, or the customs of Brittany could be made without the expressed consent of the Etats de Bretagne.[19]

As an earnest of his good intentions toward the peninsula, François I also had his son and heir crowned Duke François III of Brittany in a ceremony at Rennes on 14 August 1532. The young duke died four years later while still dauphin of France. He proved to be the last wearer of the ducal crown, for François I did not trouble to place it on the head of the new dauphin. After 1536 he and all his royal successors regarded Brittany simply as a province of the French kingdom.

The period between the pact of union of 1532 and the outbreak of the French Revolution in 1789 figures in patriotic historiography as the provincial phase of Breton history. Considered by successive French monarchs as a *pays d'état* and *province réputée Etrangère*, Brittany for more than 250 years kept intact the privileges proclaimed by François I at Plessix. The former dukedom thus maintained a separate administration within the French state and enjoyed a regime of relative political autonomy. Nonetheless, according to Breton patriotic historians, the kings of France throughout this period tried ceaselessly "to diminish our liberties." Thanks to the vigilant attention of the *parlement* and the Etats de Bretagne, however, Breton autonomy was preserved. Indeed, Breton patriots claim that after Plessix the history of these two aristocratic bodies, both the authentic representatives of the Breton people, is one of intransigent national resistance to the centralizing efforts of the French monarchy.[20] They insist as well that the spirit of revolt and resistance that forms the moral underpinnings of the modern Breton nationalist movement was born of this aristocratic determination to defend Brittany's liberties against the pretensions of French royal authority.

Patriotic historians find the first inchoate stirrings of the spirit of Breton national revolt and resistance during the French Revolution. All agree with Danio that Brittany's noble orders enthusiastically joined the countrywide aristocratic reaction against royal authority in 1788 and that Breton politicians took a leading role in the creation of a revolutionary situation in the spring of 1789. But few Bretons, they argue, truly wanted a radical revolution. Most aimed instead at the winning of governmental reforms designed either to improve the functioning of the state or to protect more fully particular Breton interests. No Breton, these patriotic interpreters emphatically insist, wished any alteration in the system of autonomy enjoyed by their province since the sixteenth century. Yet they admit that deputies from the peninsula acquiesced in —and a few helped arrange—the abolition of Brittany's autonomous status at the celebrated meeting of the National Assembly during the night of 4 August 1789.

This so-called betrayal of the Breton people by its own representatives still excites the scorn of Breton patriots almost two centuries later. They attribute the outcome of the 4 August meeting to the fluke circumstance that Brittany's delegation to Versailles was composed almost entirely of members of the peninsula's emerging middle classes. These were men, the patriots allege, who shortsightedly permitted their personal class interest to override their Breton national interest.[21] But what is more to the point here is that the abolition of autonomy and how it was accomplished have been used ever since by many Breton patriots as the legal basis for asserting Brittany's right to have that autonomy restored. They argue that since the pact of union was bilaterally negotiated in 1532, it could not be legally altered or abrogated by the unilateral action of one of the contracting parties. The National Assembly vote of 4 August was therefore illegal. Not even the presence in the abolitionist majority of the votes of the peninsula's middle-class deputies changed that fact. The forty-four representatives of the Breton third estate had been irregularly elected, patriotic historians contend, and they in any event possessed no mandate to alter the political structure of Brittany. Danio goes even further and claims that many of the Breton deputies who supported abolition made their affirmative votes conditional on the subsequent assenting action of the Etats de Bretagne. Since the Etats never again met after 1788, she concludes that the abolition of Breton autonomy and the incorporation of the former province into the new departmental administrative structure of the French state were rendered all the more illegal and arbitrary.

The above argument illustrates once more the extraordinarily fine, and perforce irrelevant, points of law on which Breton patriots so often construct their legal case against France. Since it rests on the highly dubious assumption that the real political issue in Brittany in 1788–89 centered on the conflict between provincial autonomy and accelerating French centralization, the argument in any case lacks persuasiveness. The real issue almost certainly lay, as Jean Egret has shown, in a double-edged assault on aristocratic privilege in Brittany by politically ambitious members of the third estate and a modernizing royal government.[22] Both logically focused on the leading symbols of aristocratic power in Brittany, the *parlement* and the Etats de Bretagne, bodies that served as the institutional basis of Breton provincial autonomy. The temporary convergence of these two attacks in the National Assembly majority that toppled the ancien régime in France during the night of 4 August necessarily engendered, therefore, the destruction of Breton autonomy.

Patriotic historians in any case attach great significance to the subsequent protests of prominent Bretons to the end of autonomy. The most frequently cited are those of the Vicomte de la Houssaye, an official of the Rennes *parlement*, in 1790 and of the Comte de Botherel a year later. Their protests, indeed the whole counterrevolution in Brittany after 1790, are interpreted as the authentic voice of an outraged people denouncing the violation of its ancient autonomy and right to nationhood. The conspiracy of the Marquis de La Rouërie and his Association Bretonne during the years 1791–92 have been presented in much the same fashion. None of this is very plausible and no real substantiating evidence has been brought forward. It is unlikely that such evidence will ever be produced, for these interpretations rest on a distorted view of the actual situation. The actions of Houssaye, Botherel, and La Rouërie were all incidents in the aristocratic counterrevolution in Brittany. They were thus part of the Breton nobility's attempt—in alliance with Bourbonism and aided by assorted vagabonds and adventurers from the French underworld—to regain the privileges lost during the night of 4 August. Class interest, not Breton national sentiment, formed the basis of their political action. It was surely no coincidence that the royalist Chouannerie began the very day that Botherel issued his protest against the abolition of Breton autonomy with an abortive march on Vannes of three thousand peasants demanding that their imprisoned nonjuring priests be set free.[23]

Despite its royalist character, the insurrectionary Chouannerie that smouldered on the peninsula until Napoleon finally suppressed it in the early 1800s is portrayed by Breton patriots as the movement of an angry Breton nation against French revolutionary tyranny. They do not seem troubled that the Chouannerie occurred in Normandy as well, thereby undercutting the Breton national basis they impute to it. The execution of the royalist partisan leader Georges Cadoudal in 1804 may in any case be taken as the end of the Chouannerie in Brittany. Thereafter, Breton patriots search in vain through the annals of the Napoleonic Empire for lingering traces of Breton national sentiment. They attribute its absence to local Bonapartist civil servants and military officials who labored mightily that a sense of French nationality would come to penetrate the whole of Brittany. So it happened, a Breton writer recently lamented, that "at the end of the Empire Brittany was not only a part of the French state but had entered into the French nation as well."[24]

According to patriotic historiography, Breton national feeling became so vulnerable to gallicizing pressures because of the wholesale corruption of the Breton elite during the revolutionary period. The peninsula's bourgeoisie had a lot to gain by abandoning its Breton national identity. Hungry for places in the bureaucratic apparatus of the new regime and bent on social promotion, the Breton middle class scrambled to embrace French nationality. Breton national feeling could no more find expression among Brittany's aristocratic classes. The upper nobility had long been gallicized, while the lower nobility had become increasingly so through prolonged contact with the French aristocracy during the emigration. The consequence was that after its repatriation the entire landed gentry on the peninsula, in the words of the Breton historian Joseph Chardronnet, "forgot its traditional role as defender of the rights of Brittany." As for the common people, the keepers of the "sacred flame" of Breton nationality, they simply lapsed into passivity, so tired were they of politics and bewildered by the many changes of regime since 1789.[25]

Patriotic historians nonetheless point to certain events during the nineteenth century to show that Breton national feeling, despite the powerful forces arrayed against it, still existed. The formation in 1829 of another so-called Association Bretonne is frequently cited in this regard. Promoted by a certain Beslay, the organization's aim was to organize liberals on the peninsula against violations of the restoration charter by the ministers of Charles X. Comparing Bourbon illegalities with those committed four decades earlier during the night of 4 August, Beslay called for the creation of an "all-Breton fund" to indemnify members of the association for any fines incurred as a consequence of their planned "refusal to pay illegally imposed taxes."[26] It would be extreme to say that no trace of Breton national feeling was involved in this incident. It really makes no difference, for the Association Bretonne was from the beginning an abortive affair. Moreover, its raison d'être, the restored Bourbon monarchy, soon collapsed and followed Beslay's obscure scheme into oblivion.

The fate of the Armée de Bretagne during the Franco-Prussian war is the nineteenth-century incident most seized upon by Breton patriots to demonstrate not only the immortality of the Breton spirit but also the implacable hostility of the French toward it. Part of the Volontaires de l'Ouest, this army of ninety-six thousand Breton recruits was formed to aid in the defense of the French homeland against invading Prussian forces. Breton writers allege that Gambetta and his ministerial colleagues at Tours distrusted this army and doubted its loyalty to France. One has written that they saw in it "the spectre of a well-equipped Breton army possessing all the facilities needed to profit from the disaster and national disarray in order to demand the concession of our ancient liberties and franchises."[27] Gambetta is accordingly supposed to have delayed the dispatch of food, clothing, and arms to Conlie where these Breton troops were quartered in winter camp. Thus the soldiers were exposed first to the ravages of cold, hunger, and disease and then to the murderous firepower of the Prussian army, which was allegedly permitted to massacre them in the battle of Le Mans during 10–12 January 1871.

These accusations against Gambetta actually stem from a report on conditions at the Conlie garrison prepared for the National Assembly by the deputy-historian Arthur de La Borderie.[28] He made no such drastic charges, although he did harshly criticize Gambetta and his government for incompetence, mismanagement, and confusion. It is almost certain that these factors, plus dissension within the officer corps, contributed most heavily to the tragedy of the Armée de Bretagne. If Gambetta did distrust this volunteer unit, it seems likely that he feared the royalist bias of its commanders far more than any specific Breton character that the troops may have possessed. He was aware, for example, that the commander-in-chief, the Breton landowner Keratry, was a notorious partisan of the Bourbon pretender. But even if their case is entirely conceded, pride that a Breton army could still inspire such fear in a French leader, not indignation at what would then seem understandable caution on Gambetta's part, might more reasonably be expected from Breton patriots.

The reconstitution of the Association Bretonne in 1873 (not to be confused with the like-named Beslay project) is the last nineteenth-century event invoked by patriotic historians to demonstrate the survival of Breton national feeling. This society had originally been founded as an agricultural study group in 1843 but was dissolved by imperial decree fifteen years later. Under the Third Republic the revived organization promoted the agricultural interests of the peninsula, encouraged the study of local history, and advocated a mild system of administrative decentralization for the five Breton departments. A politically conservative body that included thirty-seven Breton deputies of the monarchical right, the Association Bretonne was heavily dominated by Brittany's aristocratic and landowning classes. More than half of its membership at the end of the nineteenth century consisted of landowning nobles, while the remaining members were drawn largely from the aristocrat-ridden northern and northeastern zones of the peninsula. Since patriotic historians claim that the Breton aristocracy had become totally gallicized by 1815, it is difficult to see how the reappearance of the Association Bretonne could be taken as a sign of enduring Breton national feeling.

The Association Bretonne was generally isolated from those elements on the peninsula that promoted the revival of Breton language, culture, and national identity. It is true that in an unusual display of resolution in the 1890s its leaders formed a "committee for the preservation of the Breton language." They even deplored for a time the threat posed to the ancestral language of the peninsula by the French educational system and the increasing disinclination of Bretonnants (Breton speakers) to use their maternal tongue on a regular basis. "In the present grave situation," the association's annual report warned in 1897, "silence is no longer possible; it is imperative that the Association Bretonne act without delay and with energy, using all its influence in order to combat this threat."[29] But it was energy and influence that both the leaders and the membership of the Association Bretonne lacked above all else. Their committee for the preservation of the Breton language virtually died aborning.

The future of the movement for Breton revival belonged to new faces. It is symbolic that the young, impatient, and patriotic secretary of the Association Bretonne during the 1890s, Régis de l'Estourbeillon, abandoned it in despair and at the turn of the century served as the driving force behind the formation of the first avowedly Breton regionalist society.

With this society's appearance in 1898 the Breton movement embarked irreversibly on the path of self-conscious political action. Thereafter, for both Breton patriots and their French adversaries alike, it became a permanent part of Brittany's history. Before the course of that action and its place in twentieth-century Breton history is examined, however, the psychological and social dynamics that prompted numerous Bretons to identify Brittany, not France, as the anchor of their national existence and to thrust themselves into Breton national action will be explored.

CHAPTER 2

❧ The Genesis
of Breton National Feeling

Language and collective historical experience ought on
the face of it to number among the most important constitu-
tive elements in the process of nationality formation. Indeed,
since the early nineteenth century, patriotic Breton linguists,
writers, and historians have made strenuous efforts to preserve and defend the ancestral Celtic language and literature
of their peninsular homeland and to reconstruct the so-called
national history of its population as an independent people.[1]
And it is true that this labor on behalf of Breton cultural revival provided a crucial focus for both the formation of Breton
nationality and the subsequent development of Breton nationalism. But it is no less true that such cultural revivals among
ethnic minorities in the throes of nationalistic development
seldom result in the discovery of actual evidence of their
ancient existence as an independent people. Instead most
such cultural activity on the part of ethnic minority intellectuals
—certainly in the Breton case—involves the creation of "after-
the-fact" evidence in order to legitimate demands for the
present-day goal of national independence or at least to support pleas for an end to cultural discrimination.[2] Possession
of a common language and history does not in any case necessarily mean that specific individuals or groups will claim a
given nationality. It must often be accompanied, particularly
in linguistically divided regions like Brittany, by subjective
affirmations of ethnic feeling and propitious social and histori-

cal circumstances.* Only then, Hans Kohn has authoritatively argued, can "objective factors" like language and history be transformed into that "source of immense centripetal power" that lies at the heart of modern nationalist movements everywhere.[3]

Numerous Breton militants nevertheless insist that it was their discovery of and immersion in the indigenous culture of Brittany that led them to develop nationalist attitudes. The longtime nationalist leader Camille Le Mercier d'Erm was one for whom familiarity with local Breton literature was decisive. Before World War I he claimed that the Breton writers La Villemarqué, Brizeux, and Luzel and the historians Pitré-Chevalier and La Borderie were the "guilty parties" responsible for the creation of his Breton nationalist ideas. He singled out La Villemarqué's 1839 collection of Breton folk tales, the *Barzaz-Breiz (Bards of Brittany)*, for special emphasis. Reading it, Le Mercier d'Erm thought that he heard the authentic voice of his people singing and he came away from the experience convinced not only that there was a Breton nation but also that he belonged to it. Many other Bretons had the same reaction. It would in fact be difficult to overstress the importance of the *Barzaz-Breiz* in the emergence and development of Breton national feeling. So important was its role in the arousal of national consciousness among many leaders of the twentieth-century Breton movement that the nationalist historian C. Danio referred to it almost reverentially as "the breviary of the Breton patriot."[4]

In his recently published memoirs Olier Mordrel, the leading theoretician of the Breton nationalist movement after 1919, repeated Le Mercier d'Erm's point about La Villemarqué's work. He added that in his case the list of "guilty parties" ought to be expanded to include Paul Féval, Emile Souvestre, Charles Le Goffic, and Anatole Le Braz.[5] For others,

*For nearly a thousand years a linguistic frontier, running along a line from the western coast of the Bay of St.-Brieuc in the north to the mouth of the Vilaine River west of the city of Vannes in the south, has separated Breton- and French-speaking halves of the Armorican peninsula. Although French gradually came to be spoken throughout the Breton-speaking, or Bretonnant, areas west of this line, Breton in its many dialects continued to be the everyday language of the masses of the population until well into the second half of the nineteenth century. Even today Breton remains the maternal tongue of approximately one million persons living west of this line.

more popular forms of Breton culture were influential in the development of nationalist attitudes. Wearing traditional costumes of the peninsula, learning ancient local crafts and folk music, attending religious festivals called *pardons*, and listening to aged village elders recount romantic folk legends sharpened the national consciousness of many a Breton patriot. The prominent nationalist personality Yves Le Diberder once explained that love of such Breton folklore entirely accounted for the origin of his patriotic views. Its allure and influence were indeed so powerful that as a young adult he even relearned the Breton language into which he had been born, but which he had abandoned in early youth.

Learning the Breton language more commonly led to the formation of nationalist convictions rather than the other way around as in Le Diberder's case. In 1912 the separatist Job Loyant, for example, reported that a group of Bretons at Nantes became nationalists in the course of learning the ancestral language of their homeland. A half century later the nationalist leader Henri Le Lan described for an interviewer how he had undergone a similar experience. For some, the discovery of the old Celtic language was apparently a dramatic event, provoking an almost instantaneous conversion to Breton nationalism. According to his widow, the leader of the interwar Parti National Breton, Fanch Debauvais, became a nationalist when he learned that the Breton language had once been spoken in the Rennes region. The late Morvan Lebesque, celebrated contributor to *Le Canard Enchaîné* and fitful Breton nationalist, recounted in 1970 how as a young boy he first became aware of his Breton identity. One day climbing about the fortress of Dobrée at Nantes he came upon a strange inscription chiseled into a rock: "An Dianov a rog a c'hanoun." Thinking it perhaps Hebrew or Sanskrit, he made inquiries among his friends as to the meaning of these odd words. Finally he learned that the phrase meant "L'inconnu me dévore" in the Breton language, which had centuries before been briefly spoken on that part of the Armorican peninsula. It was the first time that Lebesque had ever heard of such a language and this knowledge "opened up a world" for him. He rushed to the library and, in his words, "devoured" all the books that he could find on Brittany. In the process, he recalled, "I discovered that I had a fatherland. And I realized what a fatherland was: something that makes you happy."[6]

Instantaneous conversion to Breton nationalism is a recurrent theme in the literature of the movement. The colorful interwar Breton patriot Théophile Jeusset became a nationalist at the age of thirteen when one day in 1923 he happened upon the leading Breton nationalist publication of the period, *Breiz Atao*, which carried the subtitle *La Nation Bretonne*. The contemporary leaders Lucien Raoul and Ronan Goarant report that they were instantly converted to nationalist views upon reading patriotic histories of Brittany. It was a similar chance encounter with a volume of Breton history that brought their colleague Pierre Laurent to then the nationalist movement.[7] Each stressed the revelatory aspect of his unexpected confrontation with the idea of a Breton nation and described its subsequent influence on his life in salvationist terms. Laurent explained that the entire process occurred with the suddenness and dramatic impact of a thunderclap and compared it to Saul's flash conversion to Christianity on the road to Damascus. Bretons such as himself consequently came to realize that they, like Saul, had been living in "error, ignorance, and intoxication." But in Breton nationalism they immediately found redemption both for themselves and for Brittany, which would eventually take, therefore, its "rightful place on the scale of human values."[8] One need hardly insist upon the close resemblance between these avowed instances of suddenly generated Breton nationalism and the conversion experience associated with fundamentalist and revivalist religions. Indeed, Eugen Weber has concluded that "the nationalist is a revivalist in that ancient sense in which a rich corrupted body may be brought back to perfection and rightness by being set right with the world and its own true nature."[9]

It is no coincidence that those like Laurent and the others cited above who link the origin of their Breton nationalism to a conversion experience have usually been Francophones who make the connection years after the fact. They long knew that Brittany differed somehow, at least culturally, from the rest of France. Lacking the ability to speak the Breton language, however, they had difficulty giving substantive form to this otherwise but dimly perceived difference. They grasped at anything, therefore, that concretely expressed the difference and could plausibly serve as a springboard for the subsequent elaboration of their Breton national consciousness. Chance encounters with odd inscriptions, previously unknown nationalist periodicals, or obscure history books served the purpose for many Breton patriots and eventually became lodged in their minds as decisive conversion experiences. For similar reasons many such individuals ultimately became Breton extremists as well. Without the psychological and cultural insulation provided by the Breton language, they saw themselves especially vulnerable to the encroachments of French culture. Thus they reacted with greater intensity than their Bretonnant brethren to what seemed to them a concerted assault on their relatively more precarious Breton identity. As a consequence, many a Francophone moderate became an integral Breton nationalist, while a few adopted outright separatist notions. The young men around *Breiz Dishual*, the only avowedly separatist tendency in the pre-1914 nationalist movement, were nearly all natives of Francophone eastern Brittany. It was the same with the leadership of the far more important *Breiz Atao* during the interwar period. As early as 1919 one of its founders remarked that Francophone Bretons were most sensitive to the appeals of Breton nationalism because "their lack of the language paradoxically heightens their sense of being threatened in their Bretonness."[10]

On the other hand, Francophone militants have long recognized the reinforcing value of the Breton language on nationalist convictions. In their New Year's message for 1922 the leaders of *Breiz Atao* reminded Bretonnants that they must take pride in their ancient language and that it was their duty to think, speak, and write Breton when communicating with each other. As for Francophone nationalists, they were "to try at all costs to do as the Bretonnants did," they were obliged to learn the difficult Breton language. To set the proper example, the Francophone leaders of *Breiz Atao* sought out the Breton linguist François Vallée, who taught them with the aid of his little volume *La langue bretonne en 40 leçons*. When Olier

Mordrel first met Fanch Debauvais and Yann Sohier, two leading figures in the interwar nationalist movement, neither knew a word of Breton. Both quickly learned the language, however, and Sohier went on to become one of the major participants in the effort to systematize and modernize the Breton vocabulary. Although the Breton language had come to both men after the fact of their nationalism, Mordrel reported in 1964 that each in time came to consider it indispensable to the full development of his national identity.

The relationship of language and culture to the emergence of ethnic minority nationalism in general and to its Breton variety in particular is more complex, however, than simply deciding which came first. Members of ethnic minorities do not always develop nationalist ideas because of special qualities that inhere in the language and culture of their people. Instead, they often develop such notions out of resentment provoked by discriminatory and assimilationist policies directed at that language and culture by the national majority.[11] And virtually without exception Breton patriots insist that the French government has long pursued, both officially and unofficially, such a policy of cultural persecution, particularly under the Third Republic. They do not charge that physical violence was used against Breton-speaking populations on the peninsula or that individual Bretonnants were imprisoned for speaking their maternal language. Rather the patriots argue that French authorities employed a far more subtle technique designed to diminish the value of the Breton language, to circumscribe its usage, and finally to destroy it altogether. This technique involved emphasizing at every opportunity the inherent superiority of French as a language of culture and progress. Over time, a sort of moral pressure was created that produced in the popular Breton mind an identification of the native vernacular with primitivism and, therefore, of Brittany itself with ignorance and poverty. By contrast, France was carefully presented as the antithesis of this Breton image. It was invariably pictured as a modern industrialized society that promised great rewards in the form of social advancement and personal enrichment to all those who fully embraced its language and culture. Breton parents, especially mothers who wanted their children to lead less miserable lives than they had known, often responded positively to these alluring prospects and sought to instill in their sons and daughters contempt for traditional Breton culture and language. The image of "an army of anti-Breton mothers" who in the privacy of their homes silently aided French linguistic centralizers in the campaign against the Breton language recurs in patriotic literature.[12]

The offensive against the maternal language begun in Breton homes was pursued even more vigorously in the classrooms of the state school system. Both teachers and Francophone classmates made Bretonnant students the objects of patronizing scorn. Their curious Breton costumes, rude manner, and above all else their strange-sounding language earned them humiliating nicknames as well. Many Bretons recall with indignation the countless times as children they were derisively called *pémocke*, *Mahô*, or *plouk*, terms in English roughly equivalent to "hick" or "rube."[13] Bretonnants remember most bitterly, however, the system of *symbole* used by teachers in French schools to combat the Breton language. The *symbole* was an object, usually a wornout old shoe, attached to a length of string that teachers placed around the necks of young Bretonnants overheard using the Breton language, even if at play. The only way such a guilty child could get rid of this humiliating object was to catch one of his classmates using a Breton word and then inform the teacher, who transferred the *symbole* to the new linguistic transgressor. Bretonnant students quickly developed behavior patterns that emphasized spying, informing, and duplicity, for no one wanted to be caught with the *symbole* around his neck at the end of the day. Punishments meted out to such unfortunates varied from school to school. It might mean remaining after hours to copy several hundred French composition exercises or being slapped in front of the other students. Severe beatings administered with a stick were not unknown and one Bretonnant reports that the daily *symbole* punishment at his school included cleaning the toilets. To hear the word alone, he wrote in 1966, still "evokes painful memories of my school days and provokes in me sentiments of indignation and revolt."[14]

The situation was no better in primary schools run by the church, where in fact the *symbole* first appeared, only later being adopted by lay teachers as well. In these schools instructors often devised variations of the *symbole* that amounted to refinements in cruelty. At St. Yves school in Quimper, for example, teachers each day put a little ball into the mouth of the first Bretonnant caught using his native tongue. This object was passed from mouth to mouth of successively guilty students without any regard for the most elementary rules of hygiene. The distasteful associations created in the minds of Bretonnants concerning their native language must have been overwhelming when this cruel practice was juxtaposed, as it often was, with dire warnings about the dangers involved in oral contact. Catholic teachers employed other harsh measures as well to discourage the use of Breton in their classrooms. Nuns frequently warned Bretonnants that they offended God when they spoke Breton. Priests gave lectures on "how shameful it was for true little Frenchmen to say *ya* like a common Prussian." The playgrounds of some religious schools were even posted with a sign that warned "it is forbidden to spit and to speak Breton."[15] It is hardly surprising that Bretonnants who as schoolchildren fell victim to such practices react with bitter irony to the oft-repeated formula about the Catholic faith and the Breton language being brother and sister in Brittany.[16]

It is little wonder that Breton nationalists in their protests against French cultural oppression have long aimed their bitterest attacks on the French school system, which they consider the leading agency in Brittany for the furtherance of such an allegedly hostile policy. More than fifty years ago Olier Mordrel was already denouncing it in *Breiz Atao* as an educational regime that inculcated in young Bretons "scorn for the Fatherland and the mother language" while at the same time teaching them political and social corruption. But it was the veteran nationalist figure Marcel Guieysse who launched the most telling attack on French-language schools in Brittany and in the process showed their impact on the formation of Breton national feeling.[17] He thought it "a stupid system of education that pulverized every brain and intelligence into a fine powder so that it could be poured into the same university mold," thus producing identical likenesses for all. The moral and national dimensions of these likenesses were those of French nationality and nationalism, and it was this result that so angered Guieysse. In his view French education destroyed all that was unique in Breton minds and personalities. He accordingly charged that Breton youths emerged from their French schooling intellectually diminished and psychologically troubled. But fortunately for Brittany, Guieysse went on to explain, numerous Bretons had begun at last to understand what had happened to them. Some recognized that the system of the *symbole* was a brutal means of destroying the Breton language. Others realized that the history of the Breton people had been distorted by confounding it with the general history of France. In both cases, Guieysse argued, the outcome was the same: Breton youths joined the nationalist movement out of resentment at official French teaching.

The biographies of Breton nationalists lend empirical support to Guieysse's argument. Abbé Jean-Marie Perrot, the longtime leader of Catholic-oriented Breton nationalism, once explained his career of militant Breton action in terms of an angry personal reaction to French hostility toward his maternal language. This resistance began in 1889 when at the age of twelve he was about to enroll in a Catholic school at Guingamp. Accompanied by his uncle, he chattered away in Breton during the trip to his new school. Just before entering, however, the older man warned that inside he must never speak Breton. The astonished boy asked why not. "Because if you do," his uncle replied, "you will get the rod."[18] Perrot later claimed that he never forgot this incident and devoted the rest of his life to the cause of Breton national revival. While still serving that cause in 1943 he was murdered by *maquisards*, who took him for a traitor to France. Other Breton nationalists express parallel bitterness over the alleged proscription of Breton history in French-run schools. "To think," A. Masseron complained in 1922, "when I completed my *bac* I could write ten pages on jokers [*sic*] like Agamemnon but I had never heard the name of Nominoë pronounced."[19] He joined *Breiz Atao*.

The disparaging treatment meted out to peninsular recruits, especially those from rural Bretonnant areas, in the French army has also aroused bitter resentment among Bretons. As early as the eighteenth century it is said that certain Celtic slang words—*Pétra*, *Pénôs*, and *Paour*, for example— were used by French officers to abuse Breton soldiers. Two centuries later members of the Forces Françaises de l'Intérieur, integrated after 1945 into the regular French army, were denigrated by officers of the latter as *plouks*—the derogatory term commonly used in the French military against Breton conscripts. Breton nationalists list and denounce other injurious words used in French barracks against their countrymen including—in addition to *pémocke*, *Maho*, and *plouk*—*niqousse* ("simpleton"), *bécot* ("prick"), *tête de Boche*, and *Zoulou*. "How many of us . . . have not felt," François Jaffrennou asked in 1934, "redness mount to our foreheads when as soldiers we heard our poor peasant compatriots treated with the most contemptuous and defamatory collection of names Frenchmen could dream up?"[20]

Jaffrennou's indignation had been provoked by the suicide of a young Bretonnant conscript driven to despair by the constant ridicule of his French officers and fellow recruits. Nationalists generally argue, however, that a more typical response of soldiers from the peninsula to such abusive treatment is to develop a new awareness of their Breton identity and to experience the first stirrings of Breton national feeling. The theoretical literature on psychological defensive reactions offers substantial support for such a behavioral response. On the other hand, it is well established that military service has historically played a crucial role in the integration of provincial and rural recruits into the value system of the larger national community. The integrative function of the reorganized French army after 1870, based as it was on universal male conscription, has been particularly emphasized by scholars. For every recruit from Brittany whose Breton national identity may have been awakened during French military service, therefore, many more must have found in the experience their full identities as Frenchmen. Indeed, the French sociologist Edgar Morin has argued that it was four years of army duty in World War I that completed for many Bretons the process of their integration into the

French nation.[21] Demobilized Breton soldiers who returned to the peninsula after 1918 may even, according to some nationalists, have served as agents of *débretonisation*. After having for four years "suffered insults addressed to *plouks*," one has written, many Bretonnant veterans resolved that their sons would never have to endure the same treatment.[22] They accordingly discouraged their children from speaking the Breton language and sought in every other way to prevent them from developing conscious Breton identities. To the army of anti-Breton mothers so much deplored by nationalist writers there was thus joined at least a division of anti-Breton fathers.

Yet, military service may have encouraged the growth of Breton nationalism in another sense. Lord Acton once observed that "exile is the nursery of nationality." Since it has long been the practice of the French state to post army inductees to garrisons far from their native regions, conscription amounted to a kind of internal exile for many young men from Brittany. Made anxious and frightened by their new and unfamiliar surroundings, Breton soldiers banded together for moral support in a common effort to cope with these and other problems produced by the abrupt change in their lives. While exchanging views and impressions some of them, according to the nationalist writer Job de Roincé, for the first time discovered their love for Brittany. Thereafter they began to attach greater significance than ever before to the fact of their Breton identity and origin. It was in such circumstances, de Roincé added, that the group of young Bretons who eventually formed the nucleus of *Breiz Atao* first became acquainted with each other.[23]

Prolonged absence from their Breton homeland, besides the French military service performed by all able-bodied males, has been a recurrent pattern in the lives of Breton nationalists. Some were the children of French military officers or high-ranking civil employees of the war department posted outside Brittany. Olier Mordrel himself was born the son of a general from St.-Malo who spent most of his career in the French colonial regiments. Ned Urvoas, the reputed leader of the contemporary terrorist movement, fought in the Spanish civil war as a member of the International Brigade and subsequently lived for many years in South America. Ronan Goarant had a long career in the French navy before retiring to Brittany, where he joined the nationalist movement. His colleagues Yann Poilvet and Paul Morin, although born in Brittany, spent most of their lives far from the Breton peninsula and rallied to the ranks of the nationalists only as mature adults. Two other prominent figures in the current movement, Yann Poupinot and Henri Le Lan, lived for a while in Germany during World War II as conscripts in the notorious Service de Travail Obligatoire. It is also worth noting in this respect that the militant separatist wing of the contemporary movement is directed from Ireland. It is led by Yann Goulet and Alan Heussaf, who found asylum there at the end of World War II after having been condemned—the former to death—by French courts for collaboration with the Nazis.

Residence in the French capital has been the most common form of non-military-related exile undergone by Breton patriots and nationalists. The revival of Breton culture in the nineteenth century took place in large measure against a Parisian background, since Le Gonidec, La Villemarqué, Le Braz, and Le Goffic did their most important work in that city. Various reasons brought subsequent generations of young Bretons to Paris. Some came to pursue their professions more advantageously. Others belonged to families that had abandoned Brittany in the hope of finding jobs and more comfortable lives in the national capital. But the largest group of young Bretons who experienced a Parisian exile had gone there to continue their education. So it happened that the pre-1914 Breton nationalist movement was largely a Parisian affair of young students originally from Brittany. The largest, richest, and most militant section of its interwar successor was similarly composed of Breton students living in Paris. They eventually operated out of Ker-Vreiz (Brittany House), a meeting hall for Breton militants established in the 1930s near Montparnasse station. The hall still exists in the original location and today remains the hub of nationalist action brought by the Breton student population of the capital.

Still, it would be rash to conclude that Lord Acton's formula concerning the relationship between exile and nationality formation generally applies in the Breton case. On the contrary, Breton writers have long deplored the denationalizing consequences on local populations of residence outside Brittany. The patriotic press is particularly full of the deleterious effects of Parisian sojourns on young Breton students. Already in 1899 François Jaffrennou was complaining that after a year in Paris such young people developed attitudes of superiority toward their families and learned to scorn their homeland. "Very few young persons who take their degrees at Paris," he remarked, "return here imbued with the importance of local action, the leading role of agriculture or anything that has to do with regional affairs."[24] To explain the development of Breton national feeling in terms of collective response of natives of the peninsula to separation from their homeland in any case runs up against the familiar "chicken-and-egg" problem. It is not clear which came first, departure from Brittany or nationalist attitudes, and thus whether or not it was simply a matter of the former intensifying the latter.

All the explanations of why Frenchmen of Breton background developed ethnic Breton feeling thus far discussed have proved inconclusive because they either depend too heavily on the personal testimony of nationalists themselves or concentrate too narrowly on incidental elements in their life situations. The consequence is to emphasize particular circumstances at the expense of broad-based causal factors. Instead of leading to the formulation of a theoretically consistent general argument, this procedure permits little more than the assembly of a series of discontinuous ad hoc explanations. In order to arrive at the more desirable former outcome, the emergence of ethnic minority nationalism in contemporary Brittany must be related to underlying processes of dynamic social and historical change. Thus the social composition of the Breton nationalist movement and its relationship to the rapidly changing patterns of social relations in nineteenth- and twentieth-century Brittany should be examined.

The most striking aspect of the social composition of the Breton nationalist movement, especially at the beginning, is how few of its members come from the top and bottom of the Breton social structure. Virtually no representatives of the landed aristocracy or the wealthy upper-middle classes, particularly those associated with modern forms of trade and commerce, financial management, and industrial activity, have joined the nationalists. The sociological correlates of these two groups—impoverished peasants and landless agricultural laborers on the one hand and factory workers on the other— have generally been absent from the ranks of Breton nationalism as well. Instead, the overwhelming majority of nationalists has had its origins in that part of the Breton social structure located between these extremes. Breton nationalism has accordingly been a movement composed mostly of shopkeepers, commercial employees, artisans, rural craftsmen, small-scale independent farmers, priests, and members of long-standing professional occupations, such as lawyers, teachers, physicians, and notaries.

Those who became Breton nationalists thus had their roots plunged deeply in and depended for their continued survival on the traditional social structure of the peninsula. They were persons of some status, prestige, and respectability as well. Yet, menaced by disruptive modernizing influences coming into Brittany from the outside French world, their future prospects were not bright. In the twentieth century they faced, if not outright extinction, at least progressively marginal existences at the exposed periphery of a transforming Breton society. Strongly individualistic in ethos and hostile to the notion of collective organization, such people lacked the institutional means either to defend their interests or to voice their complaints. It is striking how much these modern Bretons, both in their social position and in their behavior, resemble the marginal elements of medieval society, which Norman Cohn described as pursuing the millenium. Caught in a technologically backward society and confronted by the prospect of radical social change, these medieval populations tried to deal with their common plight by forming salvationist movements on behalf of assorted millenarian ideas under the leadership of charismatic personalities called *prophetae*.[25] Twentieth-century Bretons who found themselves in similarly exposed and defenseless circumstances reacted in an identical fashion. Breton nationalism was their salvationist movement. The restoration of Brittany as an independent nation was their millenarian idea. Charismatic leaders like Olier Mordrel and Fanch Debauvais were their *prophetae*. Examination of the social function of such Breton *prophetae* and identification of the strategies available to them in their struggle to stave off the threatened destruction of their entire social group are crucial to a full understanding of the appearance of ethnic minority nationalism in twentieth-century Brittany.

According to Cohn's definition, medieval millenarian *prophetae* were intellectuals or half-intellectuals. The leading promoters of Breton nationalism have generally fitted that description as well: writers like Mordrel and Loeiz Herrieu; linguists like François Vallée and Roparz Hémon; journalists like Morvan Lebesque and Léon Le Berre; poets like Camille Le Mercier d'Erm and J.-P. Calloc'h; professors like Fanch Eliès, Emile Masson, and Yann Sohier; architects like Maurice Marchal and Pierre Lemoine; engineers like Erwan Gwesnou, Charles Laîné, and Pierre Laurent; artists like Jeanne Malivel and Théophile Jeusset; sculptors like R.-Y. Creston and Yann Goulet; and even a music critic Maurice Duhamel. In this respect Breton nationalism has differed little from earlier varieties of European nationalism that, especially in central, eastern, and southeastern Europe, were largely the work of literary figures and other assorted intellectuals. This recurring pattern has led the British scholar Anthony D. Smith to theorize that a leading historical function of nationalism has been to resolve "the crisis of the intelligentsia."[26]

Such a crisis arises out of the threat to the social dependencies of a traditional order that is being undermined by modernizing currents. Among these dependencies the intellectuals, by virtue of their superior educational attainments and their broad cultural experience, are particularly cognizant of the peril in which they are placed by the conjunction of the old and the new. Indeed, their vulnerability is perhaps greater than that of any other dependent group. Long the most articulate exponents of the ideological world view that gave the traditional order its theoretical legitimacy, they had received substantial moral and material rewards from those whose interests they served. Such intellectuals thus find themselves doubly threatened: from above by the collapsing debris of the old order and from below by the builders of the new one, who are determined to sweep away all those whose fortunes are tied to the traditional holders of power. According to Karl

Mannheim, the social thinker to whom Smith is most heavily in debt, these intellectuals may extricate themselves from their dangerous situation by following either of two courses of action. They may seek affiliation with one of the various groups that are struggling to dominate the emergent social order or, through scrutiny of their social moorings, they may seek to rise above their particular class interests and forge a new mission for themselves as the detached guardians of the moral and material objectives of the people as a whole.[27]

For the menaced nineteenth-century intellectuals of the peninsula this decision amounted to a choice between varieties of evil. Affiliation with either of the two major competitors for Brittany's historical succession—the urban proletariat on the one hand and the industrializing middle class on the other —seemed out of the question, since both were committed to and had an interest in the wholesale destruction of the existing Breton social order. These intellectuals had no other alternative, therefore, except to embark on the second course of action outlined by Mannheim. But scrutiny of their social moorings only reconfirmed for them how much they had their origins in and still functionally depended on the old authority structure of the peninsula. This situation seemed unlikely to improve their prospects, since it was the threatened disintegration of that structure that had precipitated their crisis in the first place. Moreover, in the process of examining their social moorings, the intellectuals had been thrown back on the reactionary ideas and authoritarian values, especially those associated with intransigent Catholicism and monarchism, that had long been promoted by Brittany's entrenched clerico-aristocratic class. These materials were hardly the most promising ideological fabric out of which a new role as the disinterested defenders of the whole community could be fashioned.

Yet there seemed a way out. During the second half of the nineteenth century the peninsula's traditional rulers had increasingly come to demand from Paris a system of administrative decentralization and regional autonomy for their homeland. Advocacy of these doctrines had the effect of narrowing from France to Brittany the moral and political vision of the old order in which endangered Breton intellectuals had just rediscovered their social moorings. This historic contraction unexpectedly furnished a means by which Brittany's traditional intelligentsia might resolve the crisis by providing its members a new, although restricted, arena in which they could credibly press their claim to be the guardians of the interests of the *Breton* people as a whole. At the same time a regionally reorganized Brittany offered a chance that the long-standing social order on the peninsula could be preserved intact, thereby removing the mortal threat that hung over the heads of its intellectual class. On the eve of the twentieth century, therefore, elements of the latter emerged as the foremost advocates of and leading theoretical spokesmen for administrative decentralization and regional reform in Brittany.[28]

Realization of these objectives depended on the active cooperation of the French political class in Paris. It became clear very early in the twentieth century, however, that Parisian central authorities had no sympathy for regionalist ideas. Instead, refusing to concede even the most innocuous demands of the regionalists, the authorities stood more and more in a militantly antagonistic relationship to them. Before long this hostile attitude provoked among the latter a sense of aggrieved goodwill and exasperated local patriotism, sentiments that in time took the form of self-conscious Breton nationalism.[29] Indeed, the emergence of ethnic minority nationalism in modern Brittany must be viewed against the prior appearance of regionalism on the peninsula and the subsequent failure of its promoters to win concessions from the French government. Thus it is crucially important to understand why Brittany's traditional ruling class at the end of the nineteenth century came to embrace regionalist convictions and thereby set the stage for the development of Breton nationalism after 1900.

Until well into the nineteenth century the social structure of Brittany generally retained its ancien régime character. On the one side were the landed nobility and its clerical allies who together wielded a virtual monopoly of social, economic, and political power on the peninsula. On the other was the Breton peasant mass, which felt pressed down under the full weight of that monopoly. Between the two was interposed a rudimentary Breton middle class that did not rest on modern capital accumulation and industrial structures and functions. Instead it was composed of *notables de fortune* whose wealth and social position were long-established and *hommes de compétence* who owed their social standing to the exercise of liberal professions rather than to expanding economic roles. Characteristic members of the middle class were men of law, physicians, bureaucratic officials, and what Henri Sée once called *gens de finance*.[30] Like the intelligentsia, this Breton middle class consequently existed as little more than an appendage of the clerico-aristocratic elite, entirely dependent on that elite for its functions and livelihood. There was a merchant and industrial element, but it was extremely small and played a minor role. Merchants existed primarily to furnish goods to the ecclesiastic, aristocratic, and wealthy professional classes. As for the Breton industrial structure, it was composed of a small number of widely dispersed establishments whose limited labor force produced articles for mostly local consumption.

The preponderant position of the clerico-aristocratic elite in Brittany before 1900 could hardly be exaggerated. The enormous power of the clergy derived from its absolute monopoly over the spiritual lives of Bretons. In the final analysis fear lay at the base of this discretionary authority. Like their forbears in the Middle Ages, Breton priests until very recently claimed to hold in their hands the keys to heaven or the sentence of hell. They alone placed under interdiction "bad" Christians unworthy of the sacraments. They even exercised the right to designate to the local landed noble which erring peasant farmers he must evict or which freethinking artisans he was obliged to boycott. According to Yann Brekilien, the priest functioned as the "absolute sovereign" of the Breton village and directly intervened in all its affairs.[31] He expected, moreover, and received the obedient regard of all its inhabitants. Some have explained this popular submission to priestly authority in terms of an alleged Breton weakness for mystical power. More likely, it was a mass response to the imposition of raw power on superstitious and ignorant populations hardly able to distinguish a priest from a sorcerer. Against possible resistance from less credulous members of the upper classes, the local priest stood secure behind the immensely powerful and wealthy ecclesiastical hierarchy in Brittany and his own relative financial independence.[32]

Fear also lay at the bottom of the Breton landed aristocracy's domination of the peasant masses. Since the economic survival of the latter narrowly depended on the local château, a great Breton landowner easily made good his claim that he belonged to a class whose members were born to rule. Thus he dictated to "his" peasant tenants how they ought to vote. Thus he imposed on peasant families religious schools for their children. On both sides it was understood that resistance on the part of the peasant meant loss of his farm and with it the only means of livelihood for his family. The ascendancy of the château extended far beyond the confines of its tenant farms, however. The village merchant feared being boycotted by the local noble, his best and perhaps only real customer. The notary feared loss of his one important client with legal business to assign on a regular basis. Since he was often in debt to the local noble or needed passage for his cattle across the noble's domains, even the small independent proprietor who lived on his own land shrank from alienating so powerful a benefactor and potential enemy. The prudent course in all these cases was submission before the overweening power of the local château.[33]

Wealthy by inheritance and tenant income, the numerous Breton landed aristocracy lived in the countryside where its members supervised their vast estates and generally looked after the maintenance of public order. Many had ample time left over to play an active and disproportionately large role in local politics. Indeed, the power of the Breton landed class was long manifested in its domination of the political life of the peninsula. As late as 1870 nobles still held 40 percent of the 179 seats on the five Breton departmental councils, while another 40 percent of the seats belonged to various of their traditional professional and middle-class dependencies. Even in Loire-Inférieure, the most economically advanced of the five departments, no more than 10 percent of the councillors were drawn from modernizing socioeconomic structures. Four decades later, members of the Breton nobility continued to occupy more than 30 percent of these posts and 216 of the peninsula's 1500 communal mayors belonged to the local aristocracy.[34]

Landed aristocrats also accounted for a significant part of Brittany's delegation to the Chamber of Deputies in Paris. Between 1879 and 1914 Breton voters elected a steady third of their deputies from among this class. Certain noble families enjoyed what amounted to parliamentary fiefs and were thus able to participate in French political life with greater continuity than any other Breton group. Ideologically, Breton nobles were almost uniformly hostile to the republic. Monarchists until 1885 when they began to call themselves conservatives, their parliamentary representatives numbered among the most ardent defenders of the interests of the Catholic church. This surely reflected their private religious beliefs but it was also politically expedient, since the nobility was thus guaranteed the powerful aid of the Breton parish clergy during electoral campaigns. Thus was reinforced the clerico-aristocratic alliance that traditionally stood at the summit of the social, economic, and political structure of the peninsula.

The small and dependent Breton middle class did not offset the intense conservatism that Brittany's clerico-aristocratic elite continued to stamp on local public life during the early decades of the Third Republic. On the contrary, its members emulated the Breton nobility in manners, political ideas, and religious convictions. This identification meant in practice that the established bourgeoisie was rootedly hostile to anticlericalism and most forms of political and social liberalism. Even those middle-class officials who gradually replaced landed nobles in responsible posts of the public administration and in the political life of the peninsula were little inclined to modify the conservative outlook and policies of their predecessors. Thus André Siegfried was led to observe many years ago that within the framework of an increasingly bourgeois, anticlerical, and republican France, Brittany in 1913 remained predominantly "Catholic, clerical, conservative, scarcely republican in spirit."[35]

Throughout most of the nineteenth century Brittany thus existed as a land of fundamentally static social organization and authoritarian political culture. These conditions flowed naturally from the preindustrial economic structure of the peninsula. Traditionally an agricultural and maritime society, the region in 1881 still had two-thirds of its active population engaged in farming and fishing occupations, while only 15 percent worked in industry. The rural character of nineteenth-century Brittany was even more pronounced than these figures suggest. By mid-century no Breton city had yet reached a population of one hundred thousand persons. The three largest—Nantes, Brest, and Rennes—together accounted in 1851 for slightly less than 7 percent of the peninsula total. In fact fewer than fifty of Brittany's fifteen hundred communes at this time counted more than two thousand inhabitants, the official definition then used in France to designate an urban agglomeration. In 1881 the nonurban share of the Breton population stood at 78.5 percent of the total, a figure approximately one-fifth higher than that for the rest of France. Scarcely touched by modern urban and industrial culture, these teeming rural masses in the second half of the nineteenth century lived in virtually the same ignorance and grinding poverty as had their ancestors during the old regime. In the words of a specialist of the period, Brittany in 1880 accordingly displayed "an almost indecent fecundity in an otherwise Malthusian France, a congenital incapacity to stimulate the growth of large-scale industry and all the other traits characteristic of a deliberately peasant society still tied to the rectory and the château."[36]

During the twenty years before 1900, however, a constellation of social changes began to appear that presaged the eventual transformation of the rural face of Brittany as well as the undermining of its clerico-aristocratic ruling elite. The first of these changes was a quickening of industrial activity. New industries were established throughout the peninsula while older ones were consolidated and modernized. Stimulated by tourism, the famous laceworks of Quimper experienced significant expansion. Paper manufacturing in Finistère, Côtes-du-Nord, and Morbihan exhibited new vigor. Rennes became a center of the dairy and tanning industries, while food-processing enterprises were established in various maritime cities. The forges of Hennebont continued to produce high-quality iron and steel that in turn were fabricated into farm implements at small manufacturing centers like Redon, Guingamp, Châteaubriant, and Quimperlé. Much of the metal was also fashioned into the tools of war at government arsenals in Lorient, Rennes, and Brest. At the extreme eastern frontier of Brittany Fougères remained the leading shoe manufacturing city in France; in 1900 more than eight thousand persons were employed there in the production of footwear and other leather goods.

It was in the basin of the lower Loire valley around Nantes and St.-Nazaire that the tempo of Breton industrial activity was quickest. The long-established cane sugar industry at Nantes survived the challenge of the newly introduced sugar beet and went on to greater development. The commercial baking industry became an important source of economic activity, along with new chemical works based on the manufacture of soaps and fertilizers. Nantes also consolidated its traditional position as a shipbuilding center with the creation of the Société des Chantiers de la Loire in 1881. These various industrial advances in turn stimulated the development of a basic metallurgical industry. The Couëron lead and copper foundry became one of the most important in France, while the manufacture of tinplate by the firm of J.-J. Carnaud was second only to that of Hennebont. Meanwhile, economic activity was so vigorous at nearby St.-Nazaire that it emerged as the fastest-growing city on the Breton peninsula.[37] Between 1872 and 1913 its maritime traffic nearly tripled, while its metals industry based on the Usines Métallurgiques de la Loire employed some twelve hundred workers on the eve of World War I. But it was the shipbuilding industry organized around the Chantiers de la Loire and the Chantiers de Penhoët, both founded in 1881, that made St.-Nazaire one of the leading industrial cities in all of France.

Industrialization had advanced far enough in Brittany by 1913 that 23 percent of the active Breton population was engaged in manufacturing trades, half again as many as had been so employed in 1881. Corresponding to this increase in the size of the industrial working class was a decline in the share of the active population engaged in agricultural and maritime pursuits. During the decade 1881–91 alone this proportion dropped from 67.6 to 62.5 percent; by 1914 it stood at 57.6 percent. Decline of the agricultural population and consequent desertion of the countryside acted as a major dissolvent of the hitherto stable Breton social structure. Released from their traditional attachment to the soil, newly mobile Breton peasants migrated to the cities where they were exposed for the first time to new and more modern ideas and styles of life. Thousands of them discovered the possibilities for better lives provided by electricity and steam-powered machinery, marvels they had neither possessed nor indeed known anything about in the country. They also realized that it was possible to lead lives free of the constant interference of prepotent local nobles and priests. These new discoveries were communicated back to relatives who remained on their farms, and who thus also saw their horizons widen to some degree beyond the shadow cast by the local château and rectory. This development had historic significance for Brittany, for what the movement from farm to city meant most of all was a decisive breach in the wall of ignorance behind which the peninsula's clerico-aristocratic ruling elite had always enjoyed unchecked dominion over the Breton masses. With this change the elite began to lose perhaps the most effective negative instrument for the maintenance of its ascendancy in Brittany.

Yet the rate of urbanization was not so rapid that Breton society was immediately and radically transformed. From 1876 to 1911 the proportion of the Breton population that lived in urban agglomerations rose only from 20 to 27 percent. The population of the largest cities in fact increased very slowly while the smaller towns grew relatively faster. The exodus of rural Bretons to the cities was then clearly not a response to the irresistible appeal of powerful industrial centers. In any case, the natural increase of the prolific Breton people would have more than doubly accounted for the expansion of Brittany's urban population.[38] Surplus Bretons were obviously going somewhere, but it was not to other Breton farms or even in large numbers to Breton cities. Instead, they were leaving Brittany altogether, forming one of the great intra-European migrations in modern times. By 1911 more than 411,000 Bretons lived elsewhere in France. Nearly 160,000 settled in the department of the Seine alone, making Paris's Breton population larger than that of any Breton city. Thus, during the three decades before 1914, hundreds of thousands of Bretons "voted with their feet" against the clerico-aristocratic masters of the peninsula who meant to keep Brittany's masses firmly anchored to the mentality and social isolation associated with the ancien régime.

The exodus of so many Bretons at first may have actually seemed to strengthen the local position of the Breton ruling class. Paris and other French cities naturally attracted the most youthful, vigorous, and adventuresome members of the Breton population. Since it was these who were most likely to offer resistance to the authority of local priests and nobles, their departure must in many cases have been welcomed by the latter. Yet mass outward migration of Bretons posed a far more serious and immediate threat to the supremacy of the peninsula's ruling elite than did either of the parallel and slower processes of industrialization and urbanization. This was true whether the emigration was temporary or permanent. In both cases the effect was the same, much like that of intra-Breton migration from farm to town: It was to broaden the customarily narrow horizons of the Breton population and thereby breach further the wall of ignorance that had so long shielded the authority of the peninsula's entrenched ruling class from challenge from below.

Two factors generally lay behind these decisions for flight. In the first place, salaries were much lower in Brittany than in many other parts of France. In the departments of Seine-et-Oise and Meurthe-et-Moselle and at Lyon the average daily wage in 1911 exceeded six francs. In the Breton departments of Finistère and Morbihan the corresponding figure was less than four francs. Second, extremely inflated real estate prices in Brittany meant little chance for surplus Breton populations to acquire real property and thus remain on the land. So it happened that agricultural laborers, servants, small proprietors, and even petty merchants emigrated and found jobs as factory hands, housemaids, seamstresses, railroad employees, clerks, and postal workers. But if physically separated from their homeland, these emigrants maintained —through a steady stream of letters, newspapers, and manufactured goods they directed to Brittany—regular liaison with friends and relatives who stayed behind. Before 1914 André

Siegfried hence found everywhere on the peninsula families who spoke of their "representatives" living elsewhere in France from whom they learned that "an external world existed where people lived, acted, and thought differently than they did."[39]

The growing presence and authority of the French state in Brittany simultaneously familiarized local populations with the wider world outside their homeland. Not only did this threaten to disrupt the long-standing pattern of social relations in Brittany, but it augured as well the eventual transfer of full decision-making responsibility for local affairs to Parisian bureaus far removed from the influence of the traditional rulers of the peninsula. Nothing better illustrated these trends than the burgeoning French naval and military installations on the peninsula. Naval ports and shipyards, military schools, army bases, and fortresses all concretized for Bretons the existence of the French state and accustomed them to the increasing frequency and range of its intervention in their lives. Through its gendarmerie the state assumed more and more responsibility for the maintenance of public order. It employed thousands of workers at various arsenals, who found their regular wages unaffected by the vagaries of the economy and a secure pension upon retirement. It also provided pensions for thousands of Breton sailors, who usually retired from the French fleet to their native province. In Siegfried's terms, the state emerged as a king of deus ex machina whose sovereign intervention was solicited by Bretons in widely disparate ways. It was the rich and powerful benefactor who provided money and assistance when these were needed. It served as the arbiter everyone called in to resolve the slightest conflict. The state, in short, was becoming in Brittany what the clerico-aristocratic elite on the peninsula had always claimed to be but seldom was. Once the Breton masses came to realize that, the conclusion that they ought to rid themselves of their longtime masters was not long in coming.

The instrument for accomplishing this task of social surgery existed in the form of universal manhood suffrage. The growing size of the republican vote in successive parliamentary elections after the fall of the Second Empire in fact revealed the emerging determination of the Bretons to cast off their old rulers. At first, however, candidates sponsored by the clerico-aristocratic class under the banner of legitimism secured huge majorities. In 1871 their majority approached 80 percent in Côtes-du-Nord, Ille-et-Vilaine, and Morbihan, while it was only slightly smaller in Loire-Inférieure and Finistère. These ultra-conservatives continued to dominate most constituencies on the peninsula during the first several parliamentary elections held under the Third Republic, although with substantially reduced majorities. Indeed, legitimist candidates were able to win an absolute majority of votes only once after 1871, in Loire-Inférieure in 1876. Otherwise, even if relative majorities enabled them to hold on to their seats, they faced after 1871 a negative majority of republican and abstentionist voters in most Breton parliamentary constituencies.[40] In the department of Ille-et-Vilaine the legitimist right actually received fewer votes than the republican left in the elections of 1876, 1877, and 1881.

The clerico-aristocratic right endeavored in the early 1880s to stabilize its obviously contracting electoral base by dropping its association with legitimism. The problem was, the prefect of Finistère reported later in the decade, that the fate of the royal pretender "left the population perfectly indifferent."[41] The conservatives thus sought more propitious ground and chose to present themselves as the staunchest defenders of the Catholic church and its educational system based on the *école libre*. This new emphasis at first seemed extremely popular in devoutly Catholic Brittany, especially since official policy in Paris under the leadership of men like Jules Ferry was so provocatively anticlerical. The consequence was a decisive upswing in the electoral fortunes of the right in 1885 when its candidates won absolute majorities in Côtes-du-Nord and Finistère, commanded relative majorities in Loire-Inférieure and Morbihan, and virtually split with the republicans in Ille-et-Vilaine. Four years later the Breton clerico-aristocratic party improved its position vis-à-vis the republican left throughout the peninsula. Its candidates scored a particularly impressive victory in Loire-Inférieure, where they outpolled their republican opponents by more than six to one.

The results of the elections of 1885 and 1889 confirmed

for many that Brittany was a politically reactionary region adamantly hostile to the republic. This reputation was undeserved insofar as it rested on the notion that the defense of the Catholic church and allegiance to the republic were mutually exclusive. The religious issue in fact masked during the 1880s the continuing contraction of the electoral base of the extreme right in Brittany just as it simultaneously obscured the steady growth of republican sentiments among Breton voters. Were it possible to remove this factor from Breton politics, then the parallel trends of conservative decline and republican advance would stand revealed. At the same time the apparent revival in the electoral fortunes of the Breton clerico-aristocratic right in 1885 and 1889 would be shown to be a temporary phenomenon of limited political significance.

To the consternation of Brittany's ultraconservatives, the religious issue was unexpectedly removed from Breton politics in the early 1890s by none other than Pope Leo XIII himself. Advising the faithful that there was no necessary contradiction between Catholicism and republicanism, he specifically urged French Catholics to rally to the Third Republic in order to counteract the growing strength of the socialists. This papal initiative, accompanied as it was in Paris by the generally moderate orientation of the Méline period concerning the church issue, had the effect in Brittany of cutting the ground from under the clerico-aristocratic conservatives. This result was apparent already in 1893 when new parliamentary elections witnessed a dramatic drop in the vote for candidates of the extreme right and a parallel recovery by those of the republican left in all five Breton departments.[42] With the partial exception of Ille-et-Vilaine, these trends were emphatically confirmed in the next general election for the Palais-Bourbon held in 1898.

Clerico-aristocratic conservatives in Brittany were deeply disturbed by the local outcome of the last two French parliamentary elections of the nineteenth century. It was clear, moreover, that the twentieth century had even worse surprises in store for them if something were not done, and soon, to reverse their declining fortunes. It was not readily apparent to these frightened conservatives how such a reversal might be accomplished so that they would not be definitively pushed from their privileged positions atop the Breton social structure. A return to legitimism was unthinkable; support for the pretender had already proved by the late 1870s a political dead-end. The religious issue had also turned out to be a slender reed on which they might rely for long-term political success. Recent experience had shown only too well that uncontrollable external factors such as Vatican or Parisian policy could at any time define the issue out of existence.

Linking their political fortunes to any French national issue in fact involved great risks for Brittany's pressed clerico-aristocratic class. Such a tactic virtually guaranteed that Paris-based French political parties would extend to or significantly expand their activities on the Breton peninsula, which in turn was certain to hasten the spread of even more modern ideas among the Breton people and foster the political education of its voting population. But it was precisely the further development of these processes that embattled Breton conservatives most needed to halt in order to preserve their dominant position in Breton society. On the other hand, participation in French electoral politics, distasteful as it was for haughty Breton aristocrats, was a practical necessity that could not be avoided. They thus had to find a way to mobilize the Breton masses politically so that particular conservative objectives could be achieved without at the same time fundamentally altering the paternal relationship that traditionally kept them subservient to Brittany's old ruling class.[43] In regionalism and the defense of indigenous Breton culture many conservatives found what they hoped would be the basic elements of such a strategy.

The conversion of the Breton clerico-aristocratic right to regionalist ideas was motivated above all by the desire of its members to shield Brittany from the modernizing influences of French culture. In this manner the constant erosion of the wall of mass ignorance of modernity, which had long been the surest bulwark of conservative supremacy on the peninsula, could be checked. Regional self-government based on a local assembly endowed with sole legislative responsibility for the determination of domestic Breton policies seemed to provide an appropriate mechanism for the achievement of this overriding goal. Despite the inroads of republicanism and other modern ideas in Brittany, conservatives calculated that they remained sufficiently entrenched to dominate a locally chosen parliament without great difficulty. Their control of the internal affairs of the peninsula thus assured, they would be excellently placed to enact a set of regional measures designed to freeze, or even to reverse, the social, economic, and political development of Brittany as it stood at the close of the nineteenth century.

Breton conservatives hoped that in the defense of local Breton culture they had found a means to achieve their regionalist end. Defense of throne and altar had both come up nonstarters. Perhaps the defense of a uniquely Breton culture and society would prove better suited to spark a sympathetic response among the masses of the peninsula. The conservatives further hoped that this response would be strong enough to persuade Paris to concede, in order to maintain social peace in the west, a regime of regional autonomy to Brittany on condition that the integrity of France's national territory be preserved. Once they secured formal power inside Brittany, moreover, Breton conservatives were confident that they could easily deal with any potential domestic disorder engendered by their previous mobilization of the Breton masses. With such heady projects in mind, a group of Breton notables drawn largely from the peninsula's clerico-aristocratic right met in 1898 to organize the Union Régionaliste Bretonne. Subsequent events were to show, however, that it was the failure of this society either to mobilize the Breton masses or to win for Brittany a statute of regional autonomy that provoked a nationalistic response from so many Breton patriots.

CHAPTER 3

❧ *The Regionalist Initiative and Its Failure*

During the early summer of 1898 a group of Breton intellectuals circulated an appeal throughout the peninsula calling on members of Brittany's upper classes to assist them in the creation of a Breton regionalist society. French provincial life, the authors of this document argued, was suffocating under Parisian centralization and being corrupted by modern urban culture. Bretons who wished to protect their homeland from these evil influences were urged to join in a common effort to work for the decentralization of the French political and administrative system. The group hastened to add that their action was in no way meant to undermine French unity; to do so would be "a calumny and an insult." On the contrary, they insisted that their desire "to recreate regional life in Brittany" was inspired above all else by the hope that it might lead to the building of a better and more healthy France.

Several Bretons who saw merit in the above ideas gathered at Morlaix in August 1898 and under the chairmanship of the deputy Emile Cloarec drafted bylaws for the Union Régionaliste Bretonne (URB). Avowedly nonpartisan and nonsectarian, the sole purpose of the new organization according to Article III of its charter was "to develop by the revival of Breton sentiment all forms of Breton activity." The URB founders meant, however, that their new society would be something more than just a vehicle for the defense of the economic, political, and cultural interests of the peninsula. A declaration of principles appended to the bylaws thus explained that the URB was intended to serve as "a barrier to the invasion of Parisianism." The Morlaix assembly even hoped that in time the new regionalist society would constitute the foundation on which the edifice of administrative decentralization and regional autonomy for Brittany would eventually be built.[1]

The final act of the Morlaix meeting was to elect the well-known Breton writer Anatole Le Braz as the first director of the Union Régionaliste Bretonne. The real leader and moving force behind the creation of the new organization, however, was the Marquis Régis de l'Estourbeillon, the restless secretary of the lethargic Association Bretonne. Born at Nantes in 1858, he later moved with his family to Vannes where he led the life of a leisured aristocrat, dabbling in journalism and historical research. In 1893 his royalist neighbors sent him to the Palais-Bourbon where he served continuously until 1919. Named delegate-general of the URB in 1899, three years later he was elected to the newly created office of president, a post he held until his death in 1946. Olier Mordrel was thus not far wrong to conclude that Estourbeillon *was* the URB and as such acted like "the Pope in his Church."[2]

Authoritarian in temperament and Catholic and monarchist by background and conviction, Régis de l'Estourbeillon sought to impose his views on the URB. He immediately encountered resistance from those members whose religious and political ideas were less traditional. Thus from the outset the URB was beset by internal dissension. Even as early as its second annual congress in 1899 the URB began to manifest a tendency toward intramural quarreling. At that time one of Estourbeillon's ultraconservative allies violently attacked the Third Republic. The official minutes of the meeting record that not all those present shared his views. Later in the day Anatole Le Braz formally disassociated the regionalist society from these "provocations" and resigned his post as director. He was a loyal republican and suspected that the avowed nonpartisan stance of the URB actually disguised a general antirepublican attitude on the part of most of its membership. Yet Le Braz was content merely to resign his post and to withdraw into the background. Others who thought as he did were less complacent and quit the fledgling regionalist society altogether. Thus as early as 1900 the first schism of the

URB occurred when several left-leaning Breton republicans revolted and formed a short-lived rival group, the Bleus de Bretagne. Its organ was *La Pensée Bretonne*, whose director, Yves Le Febvre, ultimately became the most hated adversary of the prewar Breton nationalist movement.

The core of Estourbeillon's political philosophy was advocacy of regionalism and administrative decentralization for Brittany. These ideas were unanimously shared by the URB membership and hence served to neutralize divisiveness on other issues. In any case, the common objective of the various decentralizing schemes that were discussed within the URB was, according to the minutes of the 1902 congress, to defend Brittany's "mores and local traditions against the cosmopolitan spirit that tends more and more to make everything uniform." The URB membership went on to assert that Bretons were ethnically different from other Frenchmen and hence required "internal rules and laws" adapted to their particular needs and traditions. "We want," the regionalists declared, "decentralization as broad as our present mores and loyalty to France can permit."[3] The following year at Lesneven the URB adopted the first of many formal resolutions urging on the Chamber of Deputies the desirability of administrative decentralization. Estourbeillon and "twenty representatives of the Breton people" were designated to deliver the resolution to the Parliamentary Commission on Decentralization. Ironically, therefore, even as they protested Parisian centralization, the URB regionalists looked to the French capital for relief and redress.

They looked in vain, for the Lesneven resolution on decentralization and all those that the URB routinely adopted each year after 1903 failed to have the slightest impact on Paris. Not surprisingly, many members came to believe that such resolutions amounted to a waste of Breton time and energy. Instead they urged the URB to take its case directly to the Breton people in order to build a mass-based movement powerful enough to compel Paris to action. Some saw in the defense of the Breton language, which many favored on principle anyway, a ready means for enlisting popular support behind the decentralizing program of the URB. This strategy involved a certain risk, however, since its focus on the cultural division of Brittany between those who could and those who could not speak Breton was likely to provoke quarrels within the regionalist society. Indeed, a URB resolution of 1909 that called for bilingual instruction in Brittany's schools had already embroiled Bretonnants and non-Bretonnants over the related issues of what constituted Breton nationality and whether or not Francophone inhabitants of the peninsula truly possessed it. Charles Le Goffic, for one, thought they did not; he resigned from the URB in 1901 because he felt that the regionalists were not paying sufficient attention to the language question.[4] The druidic leader Yves Berthou left for the same reason four years later.

These Bretonnant withdrawals highlighted the reluctance of the URB leaders to embrace the language question with enthusiasm and seek to build a mass movement on it. The upper-class background of many led them to view with horror the prospect of direct contact with the Bretonnant masses that this policy necessarily entailed. The Francophone heritage of most meant that they had no real sympathy for the cause of the old Celtic language in the first place. For two reasons, therefore, Estourbeillon and his colleagues were unwilling to go beyond sponsoring resolutions on behalf of bilingual instruction that would have no more impact on Paris than those in favor of decentralization. As a result of this circumspection at the top, after a few years the URB lapsed into a state of lethargy not unlike the inaction that had originally caused Estourbeillon and his friends to bolt the ranks of the apparently moribund Association Bretonne.

The URB's lack of vitality was manifested in the increasingly stereotyped character of its annual congresses. They always began with a florid speech by Estourbeillon during which he paraded his attachment to his Breton *petite patrie* and his loyalty toward his French *grande patrie*. Invariably he assured his listeners that he secretly harbored no separatist mental reservations. To have such thoughts, he must have repeated a hundred times, would be both "chimerical and culpable." After the presidential discourse there typically came "progress" reports from spokesmen for the various sections into which the URB was divided: administrative decentralization, language, local history, agriculture, and commerce. These were followed in turn by the ritual and unanimous endorsement of an ever-longer list of resolutions, with those on decentralization and the defense of the Breton language always in the lead. Behind these resolutions the URB leaders then called for the formation of a so-called Breton front, by which they meant a union of all Breton patriots in order to further the cause of Brittany even, as the annual report for 1908 put it, at the expense of dearly held "personal political, social, and economic preferences."[5] To these appeals for union the regionalists usually joined a declaration reaffirming the avowed nonpartisan character of the URB. Given the notorious conservative bent of its membership, these naive gentlemen probably reasoned that only modern ideas were political and thus that their own traditional social notions were the same thing as ideological neutrality.

The conservative and antimodernist orientation of the URB deepened throughout the years after the turn of the century, an evolution that was expressed in manifold ways. There were, for example, repeated attacks on Paris as the site of all that was vicious in modern life. Estourbeillon's vivid description of the French capital in 1909 as "a city of gold and mud, grandeur and villainy, beauty and hideousness" is typical.[6] Then there were endless complaints that the origin of the alleged crisis in Brittany lay in the progressive neglect of its traditions: language, faith, and native costumes. For this the never-ending flight of the young from the peninsula was held chiefly responsible, for once having left Brittany these youth, even if one day they returned, tended to forget the "true nature of their real fatherland."[7] In 1908 Leon Le Berre argued that the only way to stem this Breton exodus was to imqrove the quality of life on the peninsula. He specifically recommended that industry be established, agriculture modernized, and educational opportunities for the young in Brittany expanded. Such ideas could evoke little sympathy inside the URB, since it was exactly the industrialization and modernization of Brittany that its leaders most wanted to halt. Their ideal, as the URB annual report for 1908 made clear, was instead to keep young Bretons tied to the soil.[8] This goal was the same as to argue for the perpetuation of a social system that gave virtually all of its advantages to the class from which most of the membership of the URB was drawn. Even if they were only dimly aware of it, emigration for the URB conservatives meant mobility, and mobility spelled contact with modernizing influences outside the peninsula. Since they feared that modernity was likely to bring a radical alteration in their preponderant position in Brittany, URB members vehemently attacked emigration as one of its primordial carriers.

The conservative hue of the URB was also heightened by the evident Catholic bias of its members and their parallel hostility for socialism. After 1907 its annual congresses began with the celebration of a mass. This change was made because a majority of the URB members agreed with the Comte de Laigue that "since the old Catholic faith is an integral part of the Breton idea, it would be an error to exclude it from the official program of a meeting of Bretons."[9] The URB regionalists expressed their opposition to socialism in frequent and vigorous defenses of private property as well as in attacks on the demoralizing effects of materialistic collectivism. They particularly disliked the internationalism implicit in socialist ideology and interpreted it as a threat to the right of the Breton people to a distinct ethnic identity and existence. The antisocialist slant of the URB regionalists came in time to characterize the Breton movement as a whole and consequently discouraged left-leaning Bretons from rallying to the cause of Brittany, diminishing in the process the possibility that the united front demanded by so many Bretons would ever be built. Especially during the interwar years many Breton socialists found it difficult to function simultaneously as Breton nationalists. That some of them sought to escape the dilemma by adopting the German solution and styling themselves national socialists does not in retrospect seem particularly surprising.

The exaltation of race, another theme that loomed large in the interwar Breton nationalist movement and encouraged the development of Breton extremism, actually had its origins in the URB. Individual regionalists often claimed that Bretons constituted a distinct racial grouping, and Estourbeillon himself in 1907 remarked that everywhere in Brittany "racial sentiment remains vigorous."[10] No specific racialist doctrines were elaborated during these early years, however, and Breton patriots confined themselves to vague statements about Brittany's membership in a larger Celtic culture dispersed over western Europe, an approach that served to stimulate interest in other Celtic nations. Annual URB congresses accordingly heard reports concerning the activities of other Celtic peoples. In 1907 the URB even voted to cosponsor a proposed interceltic exposition in order to show to the rest of the world the contributions of the Celts to human civilization. Another indication of the growing interest in Celtic culture came in 1907 with the founding at Lorient by two leading members of the URB, André Mellac and Loeiz Herrieu, of the periodical *Le Réveil Breton*, whose masthead proclaimed it to be a "regionalist journal of information for Bretons and other Celts." All these things together signaled the emergence in the first decade of the twentieth century of the pan-Celt idea, which still remains a major article of faith among many contemporary Breton nationalists.

The introduction of racialist and Celtic ideas into the URB accentuated the contrast between Bretonnants and Francophone Gallos from eastern Brittany. These notions had obvious attraction for those regionalists who believed that ability to speak the old Celtic language of the peninsula was an essential part of being Breton. This requirement created some difficulty for many leaders of the URB, beginning with Estourbeillon himself, who hailed from the Francophone east. To defend themselves from the strictures of linguistic exclusivists, these leaders began to emphasize the common historical heritage of the two Brittanies, a heritage, they proclaimed, that showed clearly that "Brittany has only one soul and only one race, the Celtic race."[11] To symbolize this intrinsic unity, the URB voted in 1906 to hold a second annual meeting in Francophone eastern Brittany in addition to the regular congress, which had always before been held in the Bretonnant west. At the same time the URB regionalists took particular care to stress the existence of Breton feeling at Nantes, the ancestral home of the dukes of Brittany, but in recent centuries a city virtually indistinguishable from all the others in the French provinces. These developments represented a victory for Francophone regionalists since by acquiescing in them, for a time at least, Bretonnants implicitly admitted that Breton identity was not exclusively a matter of language. Beneath the surface, however, the incipient clash between Bretonnants and Gallos continued to build until it burst into the open in 1911.

Meanwhile, despite its general lack of vigor and the growing dissension that threatened to destroy what cohesion it possessed, the URB grew steadily for more than a decade. The regionalist society published an official roster in 1901 that counted almost 150 members. Six years later Estourbeillon confidently anticipated that the regionalists would soon boast 1,000 adherents. Although the URB never attained that size, it had been able to enroll 689 members by the spring of 1911 when its maximum expansion was reached. After the rupture of September 1911, however, the URB began what turned out to be an irreversible decline. Already by the end of that year its membership had been reduced to fewer than 300 persons.

URB membership lists give a general idea of the social composition of the prewar Breton regionalist movement. The largest number of members belonged to the professions; in 1911 this group accounted for one-fifth of the entire URB membership. Eight percent more came from established non-industrial middle-class strata—shopkeepers, artisans, and other self-employed persons. Ecclesiastics made up another 11 percent of the total. Members who belonged to the aristo-cratic and landed classes were considerably less numerous in the URB than in the older Association Bretonne. At the turn of the century the latter organization recruited half of its members from this group, while the corresponding figure for the URB in 1911 was 17 percent. On the other hand, the URB leader-ship was drawn almost completely from the Breton landed aristocracy and its retainers. Moreover, all the above groups —in the aggregate amounting to 56 percent of the URB mem-bership in 1911—had their roots in and interests tied to the clerico-aristocratic elite that had for so long stood at the top of the Breton social structure. By contrast, only 2 percent of the 1911 membership belonged to modernizing industrial and entrepreneurial business sectors of Breton society. The con-clusion is inescapable. In terms of its social composition, the prewar regionalist movement in Brittany looked not to the future, but steadfastly to the Breton past for its moral compass. Before the year was out events were to show that the Union Régionaliste Bretonne had no future at all in the Breton movement.

The almost somnolent tranquillity of the URB was disturbed at intervals before 1911 by its more ambitious, militant, and generally Bretonnant members. The protest resignations of Charles Le Goffic and Yves Berthou have already been noted. In 1908 it was the turn of Léon Le Berre, Loeiz Herrieu, and Jos Parker to castigate what they called the pointless *biniouserie* of the URB. At the same time they charged that Estourbeillon was too much influenced by a Paris-based coterie of Breton émigrés who gathered around the newspaper *Le Breton de Paris*.[12] The resignations of Le Berre and Herrieu two years later over Estourbeillon's alleged autocratic direction of the regionalist society indicated that the URB was on the verge of a major crisis. For a while Estourbeillon sought to head it off by conciliating the dissidents. In 1908 he therefore acknowledged that the URB might in the past have been too much preoccupied by "superannuated archeologism" and promised that this emphasis would cease. He spoke freely of "the Breton nation" and hoped that the entire URB membership would devote all its strength "to the resurrection of Breton national life." He also endeavored to reassure his critics that the URB was genuinely nonpartisan; "the Regionalist Union," he insisted, "is not a politico-religious association. We are all good Bretons and each of us remains entirely free to hold any political opinion whatever."[13] Estourbeillon's efforts were unavailing, however, and at its summer congress of 1911 the URB fell into full crisis.

The site of this meeting was the picturesque little town of St.-Renan in Bretonnant Finistère. Ninety-four members of the URB were on hand. The first order of business was the triennial election of the president and his slate of officers. Since 1902 this proceeding had always ended in the perfunctory reelection of Estourbeillon and his personally selected nominees. At St.-Renan, however, Estourbeillon found that his nominees of 1908 had become his adversaries three years later. Supported en bloc by the Bretonnants, they were united behind the presidential candidacy of the sitting vice-president

Jos Parker. After unsuccessful attempts to remove Estourbeillon as presiding officer during the vote and to register a formal protest to this procedure, the harried URB leader imperiously ordered that the poll be taken. Amid the shouting, jeering, and foot-stamping of dissident members, the votes were counted and Estourbeillon was reelected by a three-fifths majority. The defeated Bretonnants angrily marched out of the meeting hall singing "Sao Breiz-Izel" ("Long live lower Brittany") and out of the URB as well.

The events of September 1911 left the Union Régionaliste Bretonne in a state of paralysis and its approach to the cause of Breton revival repudiated by the most determined and nationally conscious Bretons. After St.-Renan, it is true, Estourbeillon tried several expedients to revive the shattered society. He sought to turn its annual *Bulletin* into a monthly. He sponsored a public subscription to raise money for the construction of a statue to Nominoë. He attempted to organize a so-called Institut National de Bretagne patterned after the Institut de France. All of these were abortive projects, soon abandoned. The fund drive for Nominoë's statue, for example, was suspended after collecting only 1,815 francs.[14] Otherwise, under the dithering direction of Estourbeillon the URB simply frittered away what little credit it still possessed after 1911. By 1913 its prestige had fallen so low that the municipal council of Guéméné-sur-Scorff would not allow the URB to use any public facilities for its summer congress, which had been scheduled there the previous year. Although Estourbeillon and his remaining colleagues refused to recognize it, the unhappy truth was that the URB was moribund and leadership in the Breton movement had passed out of their hands.

At first it appeared that this leadership would be taken up by the breakaway dissidents who had opposed Estourbeillon at St.-Renan. After stalking out of the 1911 congress they moved quickly to set up a rival regionalist organization. Thus appeared the Fédération Régionaliste de Bretagne (FRB), founded at Rennes on 29 October 1911 by twenty-two former members of the URB. Jos Parker became its first president and Jean Choleau, François Vallée, Leon Le Berre, Loeiz Herrieu, and Joseph Duchauchix held lesser offices. These men supervised the drafting of bylaws and the formation of six sections within the FRB that dealt with economics, history, language, agriculture, fine arts, and emigrant problems under the direction of specialists in those areas.[15] A *conseil de direction* completed the structure of the new regionalist society. Composed of fifty persons who were trained in Breton and Celtic studies, this body possessed final authority in all decisions concerning the affairs of the FRB. The president and his fellow officers were by statute responsible to it for all their acts, a provision designed to prevent one-man rule such as Estourbeillon enjoyed at the URB. In an even more obvious slap at Estourbeillon, the founders of the FRB expressly denied leadership positions in their new society to members of parliament.

The first congress of the FRB was held in July 1912 at Douarnenez in Finistère. Its organizers chose this site in order to emphasize the Bretonnant character of the new regionalist society, most of whose members came from Breton-speaking areas of the peninsula.[16] Indeed, the FRB intended to give far more attention to the protection and development of the Breton language than the URB had ever done. The leaders of the FRB nonetheless linked the language issue to that of regional reorganization for Brittany. Several speakers at Douarnenez thus emphasized that local self-government in Brittany constituted the best line of defense for the peninsula's old Celtic language. In his inaugural address as FRB president, Jos Parker accordingly stressed that the aim of the new regionalist federation was to win for Brittany a system of "decentralization and autonomy that will permit the full development of our interests and the qualities of our race as well as respect for our ancestral traditions." He insisted on the religious and ideological neutrality of his organization and in so doing implicitly contrasted it with the conservative and Catholic orientation of the URB. Nothing he said made the point better, however, than the presence behind him on the dais of a priest and a well-known member of the anti-clerical Radical-Socialist party. Parker also noted that the FRB counted among its membership representatives of all social classes, professions, and political opinions in Brittany. This he obviously thought made the regional society he headed better equipped than the URB to defend the vital interests of the peninsula. He ended by urging all those who "approved our patriotic objectives and liberal organization" to join the FRB so that together they could defend their "disintegrating sacred heritage and traditions, sapped alike by hatred or blind disdain of all that which is not yet levelled by modernity."[17]

The prospects of the FRB initially seemed bright enough. More broadly representative of Breton social structure and opinion than the URB, it attracted nearly two hundred members within a year, including many of the most intelligent and prominent figures involved in Breton action. In *Le Pays Breton*, moreover, the newly formed regionalist federation had its own weekly newspaper. In actuality, however, the FRB never really got beyond statute-building and wishful thinking. To the chagrin of its promoters it, even more than the URB, existed largely on paper. There was, it is true, the FRB-sponsored Breton Week at Hennebont during the late summer of 1913. But this affair consisted mostly of monotonous speeches by Parker and his colleagues, livestock-judging contests, needlework exhibits, displays of preserves and local wines, and an outing to Larmor. This was the stuff of country fairs, not the determined Breton action so many patriots had hoped to find when they broke with the URB and rallied to the FRB. Quickly disenchanted with the new regionalist society, these men began to join more self-consciously Breton nationalist groups that emerged on the eve of World War I. Yann Poupinot thus did not go far enough when he once wrote that the outbreak of hostilities in August 1914 killed the Fédération Régionaliste de Bretagne.[18] In fact, only two years after its formation it was already dead.

Given the history of the regionalist organizations, it seems hardly an exaggeration to conclude that the impact of the Breton regionalist movement before 1914 was extremely limited. The heady optimism of François Jaffrennou who declared that "no human force can henceforth stem the flow of the Breton movement" appeared little more justified on the eve of World War I than when he had originally made the statement a decade before.[19] Yet, efforts on behalf of Breton revival were nevertheless beginning to modify the shape of public opinion in Brittany. The Breton themes and positions of the regionalists particularly found reflection in the changing attitudes of the political elite of the peninsula. The electoral manifestos of deputies elected to the French Chamber from Breton constituencies reveal this development. In the first parliamentary elections of the Third Republic successful candidates rarely claimed a specific Breton identity and seldom used the words "Breton" or "Brittany" in their electoral propaganda. Few even bothered to refer to themselves as *enfants du pays*. Instead, they concentrated on the major French political controversies of the time, especially church-state relations, and pledged to look after such local interests as agriculture and shipping. Language that identified candidates as Bretons or at least as *enfants du pays* became, however, increasingly common in electoral manifestos issued on the peninsula during the two decades before World War I, culminating in the 1914 parliamentary election, when more than one-third of all successful candidates in Breton constituencies used such language. Similarly, advocacy of decentralizing schemes like those advanced by the regionalists, seldom endorsed by Breton deputies during the early years of the republic, had by 1914 been embraced by nearly a quarter of Brittany's representatives at the Palais-Bourbon.[20]

Candidates in Bretonnant constituencies were most likely to give a Breton character to their electoral manifestos. Even as early as 1881 Louis Hémon in Finistère thus spoke of the traditional qualities of the Breton race. Four years later the "conservative union" list in Côtes-du-Nord circulated its manifesto in Breton translation. Altogether during the period 1889–1914 ninety winning candidates stressed their Breton identities and origins; of these, seventy-five hailed from Bretonnant constituencies. During the same period thirty-four successful candidates publicly advocated administrative decentralization for Brittany; twenty of these came from Breton-speaking areas. Numerous electoral manifestos circulated in Bretonnant constituencies during the last three elections before World War I displayed a genuinely militant Breton tone. Thus in 1906 a winning candidate from Finistère described himself as "a true Breton from lower Brittany, faithful to our traditions and strongly attached to the paternal soil." He went on to advise his electors to give their votes "only to a Breton like yourselves in whose veins flows the blood of your ancestors." One of his colleagues in Côtes-du-Nord contemporaneously made a point of his ability to speak Breton, while four of eight deputies elected in Morbihan emphasized their Breton identities. Eight years later a successful candidate in Finistère named Corentin-Guyho perhaps went furthest of all when he declared himself a "Breton in name, in fact, and above all in heart."[21]

The European war that erupted in 1914 cut short this evolution and dealt a near-mortal blow to Breton regionalism. Indeed, World War I is significant insofar as the Breton movement is concerned primarily because it swept away the remaining debris of regionalism and left the field clear in Brittany for the militant action of a new generation of young and determined Breton nationalists. Thus most of the specialized Breton press ceased publication in the summer of 1914. Those periodicals that continued to appear felt the heavy weight of the French military censor. All references to the proposed formation of Breton regiments displaying Breton flags in *Le Breton de Paris*, for example, were blanked out. Fanch Vallée could publish in his Breton linguistic review *Kroaz ar Vretoned* only those articles that had previously appeared elsewhere. Even then censorship authorities blue-penciled any allusion to the existence of a separate and distinct Breton culture in such old pieces. The Breton regionalist societies responded to the outbreak of war by halting their Breton action and urging their members to join with other Frenchmen in a *union sacrée* against the German adversary. The elderly leaders of the Association Bretonne and the URB accordingly spent the next four years aiding the war effort as home-front patriotic drumbeaters, recruiting officers, and war bonds salesmen. At the same time many of their younger compatriots in the FRB were mobilized into the French army and saw combat service on the western front.

In short, the coming of war in 1914 meant for Breton regionalists a total interruption of what had been for most of them a decade or more of sustained Breton action. Many hoped, however, that this would turn out to be only a short pause and that they could resume their efforts on behalf of Brittany once hostilities had come to an end. Events were to show that Breton regionalism as it had existed before 1914 could not be so easily revived. The FRB was reconstituted immediately after the war, with Fanch Vallée as president. He resigned in 1921 after failing to resolve the growing differences that separated the FRB's original Bretonnant majority from a large postwar influx of new Gallo members. Until well into the 1930s the FRB was in fact paralyzed by uncompromising hostility between almost equally balanced Bretonnant and Gallo factions, led respectively by Leon Le Berre and Jean Choleau. Since neither man could muster a clear majority of votes behind his candidacy for leadership of the regionalist federation, the FRB presidency actually stood vacant for a half-dozen years after 1928. Choleau and Le Berre ultimately composed their differences in 1934 and thereafter the former took in hand the affairs of the FRB. His was an empty victory, however, for it was soon apparent that Jean Choleau was about the only flesh-and-blood reality the regionalist federation still possessed. The indefatigable regionalist leader nonetheless continued for three decades more to organize annual congresses, to arrange public lectures on Breton topics, and to bring out slender issues of *Le Pays Breton* for an ever-diminishing Breton audience. All three—president, publication, and regional society—finally succumbed together in 1964.[22]

It can hardly be argued that the Fédération Régionaliste de Bretagne compiled an impressive record of achievement during its half century of existence. The organization never attracted a significant following in Brittany and its impact on decision-making processes in Paris was negligible. Yet, despite this paucity of accomplishments to its credit, the FRB still merits a notable place in the history of twentieth-century Breton action. Above all else, its promoters performed the crucial task of releasing the Breton movement from the suffocating embrace of the clerical and reactionary Union Régionaliste Bretonne. At the same time they demonstrated that a Breton action society could be genuinely apolitical, nonsectarian, republican, democratic, and, in tone at least, vaguely nationalist. In practice this orientation meant that the essential historical role of the FRB was to serve as a bridge between the conservative Breton regionalism of the prewar URB variety and the militant Breton nationalism exemplified by *Breiz Atao* after 1918.

Immediately after World War I, however, the aging conservatives of the URB seemed to exhibit more vigor than either their counterparts in the FRB or the young nationalists of *Breiz Atao*. Régis de l'Estourbeillon resurfaced in 1919 and sought to ventilate in an open letter to Woodrow Wilson the so-called Breton question, which he called "the right of languages and the liberty of peoples."[23] The crux of this document was an appeal to the American president to exert his influence so that all peoples would enjoy the right of self-determination. Estourbeillon hoped in particular that the eventual peace treaty would guarantee "the imprescriptible rights of peoples to speak and teach their languages and to preserve their traditions and beliefs." In order for his cause to receive the widest possible publicity, the URB president sent a copy of his letter to Wilson to each of the delegates to the peace conference at Paris. This undertaking failed to have even the slightest impact. All that Estourbeillon could show for his trouble were polite acknowledgements from several of the assembled conferees that they had received his appeal for Breton self-determination. The matter went no further, Breton nationalists have since liked to argue, because French representatives made abundantly clear to the other delegates their hostility to the notion of national revival in Brittany.

Estourbeillon was not daunted by his initial failure to win support for the Breton cause at the Paris peace conference. Instead he turned his attention directly to the Commission for the League of Nations and called on that body to proclaim the rights and liberties outlined in the Covenant henceforth inviolable for all peoples. He cast this appeal in the form of a petition and circulated it throughout Brittany for signatures.[24] More than eight hundred Bretons, including many of the most important political and ecclesiastical figures on the peninsula, immediately signed the document. The most prominent personalities involved in the prewar Breton movement, as well as many of those who would subsequently make their mark in the nationalist movement associated with *Breiz Atao*, also supported Estourbeillon's petition. All the leading Breton action groups endorsed it, as did the entire Breton regionalist and nationalist press. Estourbeillon himself recognized, however, that his petition would carry little weight unless it received the backing of additional thousands of Bretons. This support never materialized and the second postwar effort of the longtime URB leader on behalf of Brittany remained as dead a letter as had his original appeal to President Wilson.

Many Bretons who had vainly supported Estourbeillon in these efforts soon concluded that something more substantial than open letters and petitions was needed if their cause were to prevail. Thus they sought to concert the action of all Breton groups and militants in order to create a powerful current of peninsular opinion before which they hoped Parisian centralizers would have to yield. Delegates from the URB, the FRB, the Gorsedd des Bardes, and the newly formed Groupe Régionaliste Breton accordingly met in September 1919 and established the Committee for the Defense of Breton Interests (CDIB). Its organizers set their sights on participation in electoral politics. In November a CDIB manifesto therefore urged Breton parliamentary candidates to act as "the defenders and protectors of Brittany." Those who wanted CDIB backing in their campaigns were specifically called upon to support publicly a system of regional autonomy for Brittany and to pledge themselves to work for the official recognition of the Breton language and its right to be taught in the schools of the peninsula. CDIB-backed candidates also agreed, in the event of their election, to sponsor the formation of a Breton parliamentary group in the new Chamber.[25]

Thirty-five candidates in Breton constituencies for the 1919 legislative elections ultimately subscribed to the CDIB program, or at least indicated their general sympathy for it. Sixteen of these finally won election. It quickly became apparent, however, that in every case endorsement of the CDIB proposals amounted to no more than an empty campaign gesture. Once safely in their seats at the Palais-Bourbon, all sixteen delegates promptly forgot both the CDIB and their promise to help organize a parliamentary group of Breton deputies. The irresistible movement of opinion capable of engulfing all of Brittany's political representatives that so many CDIB leaders hoped their ideas would precipitate had obviously turned out to be a phantasm. The reason for this outcome had a lot to do with Régis de l'Estourbeillon's refusal to have anything to do with the CDIB. Many of its leading personalities had opposed him at St.-Renan in 1911 and the stubborn old URB president was still not willing to forgive and forget. Although he claimed to endorse the notion of solidarity among all Breton regionalists, Estourbeillon nonetheless insisted that erring FRB members in the CDIB must return to the fold of the parent URB. All refused to bow to his peremptory demand. Estourbeillon had the last word, however, when he learned that the organizers of the CDIB had failed to register the statutes of their committee with the local prefecture in Rennes, as required by the 1901 law on associations. Late in 1920, he filed bylaws for his own Committee for the Defense of the Interests of Brittany and legally enjoined the original founders of September 1919 from using the abbreviated title "CDIB."[26]

The animosities born at St.-Renan nearly a decade before clearly remained too strong to permit the reunification of the two principal branches of the Breton regionalist movement. The consequence was to reduce substantially any possibility that regionalism would have an important place in the interwar Breton movement. Division into quarreling URB and FRB factions was not, however, the only reason for the ineffectiveness of Breton regionalism after 1919. Dissension among those Breton patriots who took their lead from Estourbeillon also contributed to the weak position of the interwar regionalists. This disagreement arose primarily because the movement over which he presided wore two faces. In addition to the Union Régionaliste Bretonne itself there were also the new CDIB and its monthly organ *La Bretagne Intégrale*. Both were formally subject to the authority of the Marquis de l'Estourbeillon and this meant, in the beginning at least, that their action and *prises de position* on the Breton question were identical. But since François Simon—a man of generally more advanced Breton views than the veteran URB president—ran the day-to-day affairs of the CDIB, it was always possible that the paths of the two functionally separate regionalist organizations might diverge. This possibility became a reality in 1922 when Simon increasingly sought to act independently of Estourbeillon.

From the outset Simon made parliamentary and electoral politics the stock-in-trade of *La Bretagne Intégrale*. He especially directed the critical attention of the CDIB organ toward Brittany's elected representatives in Paris. It complained editorially that all of them were only "lip-service Bretons" and laid the deepening poverty of Brittany's population to their long-standing neglect of the vital economic interests of the peninsula. Simon was hardest of all on those Breton parliamentarians who had been elected in 1919. In particular he accused them of standing idly by while Paris systematically deprived Brittany, although it had given more blood to France than any other region during the recent war, of its just share of reparations. This Parisian attitude amounted to a "contemptuous challenge," which Simon predicted Bretons would answer electorally. Indeed, for some time he had been calling for the creation of a broad-based, nonideological Breton party. His idea was that Bretons should learn from the Irish experience and emulate the political strategy of their overseas Celtic brothers. He thus counseled Breton voters to ignore party labels and ideological appeals during parliamentary elections. Instead he urged that they should send to Paris only the most determined Breton patriots whose sole political objective was to free their homeland from subjection.

By the early fall of 1922 François Simon was insisting that the Breton question had become "acute and burning." His patience clearly wearing thin, in September he declared that Brittany had "made a gesture—250,000 dead—and we wait for an outstretched hand. There is no reply." No wonder, he concluded, that "some among us want to separate themselves from you [France]. . . . It is the inevitable result of your attitude."[27] For Simon to imply that separatism could in any way be an understandable position for a Breton to take was too much for the scrupulously loyal Estourbeillon. He intervened, temporarily suspended the publication of La Bretagne Intégrale, and ousted Simon from his leadership of the CDIB. He then took the committee presidency for himself and resumed publication of its organ in May 1923 with the obedient Henri Quilgars as editor-in-chief. Henceforth both the CDIB and La Bretagne Intégrale, according to the announcement of these changes, would have their entire program comprehended in the longtime slogan of Estourbeillon: "La plus grande Bretagne dans la plus glorieuse France."[28] Caution and conservatism returned to the CDIB.

Though Simon had been eliminated from the CDIB, his successors retained his strategy of organizing a Breton political party to fight parliamentary elections. The immediate problem before them was the approaching election of 1924. Estourbeillon and Quilgars therefore urged that the various Breton societies should coalesce into a Breton National party to field candidates. That such a party must be ideologically conservative and nonseparatist was made clear in the December 1923 issue of *La Bretagne Intégrale*. That it would also be clerical was indicated in early 1924 when its sponsors invited the intensely Catholic regionalist society Bleun-Brug to join the URB and the CDIB in a formal entente. On the eve of the election a hasty attempt was made to clothe the as-yet-nonfunctioning Breton party with a program that, far from innovative, consisted simply of positions that the URB regionalists had been advocating since 1898. Thus the party called for administrative decentralization in Brittany, respect for its ancestral faith, language, and traditions, and repudiation of any thought of separatism.

All these projects of ententes, Breton parties, and parliamentary candidates were to hanker after impossible dreams. The entente uniting Bleun-Brug, the URB, and the CDIB never got beyond the proposal stage. The so-called Breton National party was never organized. Breton candidates were not presented in the 1924 parliamentary election. True enough, time and funds to mount these efforts were generally lacking. Nor did it much help that influential conservatives on the peninsula, many of whom had sympathized with the Breton cause before the war, after 1919 opposed the formation of an electorally oriented Breton Regionalist party. Preoccupied as they were by the threat of Bolshevism, they feared that such an undertaking would draw votes from the right in Brittany and thus jeopardize the electoral chances of their anticommunist "party of order." But the most important reason for the failure of all these CDIB-sponsored projects was lack of support among the Breton public. However novel regionalism and its proponents might have seemed in 1898, after a quarter of a century both had acquired that well-known familiarity that first produces contempt and then ends in indifference. Estourbeillon and Quilgars nevertheless managed to keep the

CDIB and *La Bretagne Intégrale* afloat for a few more years. Both finally passed into oblivion at the end of 1928 after a last-ditch effort to influence the outcome of parliamentary elections that year through a policy of obstructionism and abstention failed to have any impact whatever on Breton voters.

The record of the older Union Régionaliste Bretonne during the 1920s was hardly more impressive than that of the CDIB. Under the leaden direction of Régis de l'Estourbeillon, its members confined their regionalist action to annual URB congresses and the preparation of its publications. In 1922 the URB observed its twenty-fifth anniversary, but it was not exactly an occasion for celebration. Even the editors of its yearbook, after surveying this quarter century of efforts, admitted that the results thus far obtained were minimal.[29] They went on to suggest that past URB efforts had been too much directed toward elite formation, thereby implying that if Breton regionalism were ever to be successful it must be carried to the masses. But that was the problem, for the upper-class Bretons who increasingly dominated the membership of the URB still were not particularly eager to mingle with the common folk. True, the leaders of the URB did concede in 1922 that in the past they had depended too heavily on the aristocratic element among them and were careful to insist that in the future their society was open to all Bretons regardless of class. All that they required was that prospective members be *bien élevé*.[30] But since to be *bien élevé* meant in Brittany to belong to the upper classes, especially to the landed aristocracy, this provision made a mockery of their assurances concerning the classless character of the URB.

It is scarcely surprising then that the relevance of the URB to the realities of postwar Breton action grew steadily more problematical after 1919 and that its membership dwindled to a few score isolated individuals. Throughout the 1920s the organization therefore seldom attracted more than sixty persons to its annual congresses. These meetings themselves were little more than excuses for summer vacation family outings. All that they ever accomplished was to register a yearly vote of confidence in the leadership of Estourbeillon and his fellow officers and to provide them with a platform for the expression of their by now monotonously familiar views on Breton revival. Indeed, it was only by pursuing petty internal quarrels to the point of absurdity that the URB could give even the semblance of life. In 1923, for example, what remained of the regionalist society nearly destroyed itself in an angry dispute over the outside activities of certain of its members and the procedure used to select the Breton city for its annual congress.

Internal disarray, inability to discover effective means of action, the growing strength of rival nationalist movements— all combined by the late 1920s to relegate URB-style regionalism to the very margins of the Breton movement. The druidic strand of interwar Breton regionalism suffered a similar fate. For some time after the war its grand druid, Fanch Jaffrennou, did not even trouble to reconstitute the Gorsedd des Bardes. He finally revived it at the end of the 1920s in order to stabilize a shaky publishing venture he had undertaken in 1926 with an obscure but wealthy Breton aristocrat named Jean de Saisy de Kerampuill. His plan was that this publication, eventually known as *An Oaled* (*Le Foyer*), would serve as the official voice of the Gorsedd and that subscriptions to it would be required of all members of the opportunely revived druidic society. So successful was the maneuver that *An Oaled* remained in healthy financial shape until Jaffrennou voluntarily suspended its publication on the eve of World War II. As for its Breton content, *An Oaled* had little to offer. Its editors were content to promote a mild nonsectarian regionalism indistinguishable from that of the Fédération Régionaliste de Bretagne. Beyond that, the slender little periodical often seemed to exist only to bait the young nationalists of *Breiz Atao*, whom the loyal Frenchman Fanch Jaffrennou thoroughly despised.[31] They were not slow to reciprocate this enmity by covering the longtime Breton druidic leader with the same scorn that communists usually reserve for democratic socialists.

Breton regionalism of Catholic inspiration fared little better during the interwar period than did its pagan counterpart in the Gorsedd des Bardes. Immediately following the war Catholic regionalists first rallied to the banner of *Buhez Breiz* (*La Vie de Bretagne*), a monthly that began to appear in January 1919 under the editorial direction of Pierre Mocaër. Recognizing that "the world at the end of 1918 was not the one of the summer of 1914," Mocaër urged like-minded Bretons to concern themselves with the real moral and material needs of Brittany's people. Thus he called on them to help build factories that were not "sad and inhuman prisons," farms that were not "humid slums and breeding-grounds for tuberculosis," and schools that would "no longer be places in which our children are taught to scorn their native land and are punished for speaking their maternal tongue." Mocaër hoped in short for a reborn Brittany where "all Bretons can live better lives [and] where there will be intellectual life worthy of a civilized people."[32] But neither he nor any of the other enlightened Catholics of *Buhez Breiz* knew how to translate these eminently desirable aspirations into living realities. It probably made little difference anyway, for from the outset *Buhez Breiz* exhibited the same internal bickering that has so often afflicted the rest of the Breton regionalist movement. So serious did the disagreements become that Mocaër had to suspend publication in late 1919 and the periodical lay silent for nearly two years. He was able to revive it at the end of 1921 and for the next three years he and a shrinking band of colleagues battled lengthening odds to keep *Buhez Breiz* alive. They finally abandoned the unequal struggle in December 1924 and advised their readers that the forty-eighth issue of the Catholic regionalist journal would also be its last.

Buhez Breiz linked the cause of the church in Brittany only indirectly to that of Breton revival. By contrast, the Catholics of Bleun-Brug unambiguously insisted that Breton revival must have its moral base in the defense of traditional Catholic dogma and values. This attitude reflected their nostalgic affection for Breton society as it had existed before 1789. Since they believed that the moral integrity of ancien régime Brittany was owed to the morally cohesive influence of the church, they were led to make defense of traditional Catholicism an essential part of their Breton patriotism. Defense of the Breton language—the medium of daily intercourse in eighteenth-century Finistère—for similar reasons occupied an important place in their Breton program. In time Bleun-Brug leaders like Abbé Perrot and his protégé Yves Le Moal began to express their Breton views in far more militant terms than did the Catholic moderates of *Buhez Breiz*. Indeed, during the 1920s

Bleun-Brug took on a distinctly nationalist flavor that had its origin in a series of articles published after 1923 by Le Moal in *Feiz ha Breiz* (*Foi et Bretagne*), the monthly organ of Bleun-Brug. Le Moal based his nationalist convictions on the presumed validity of the 1532 treaty of union and its alleged violation in 1789. These events plus the manifest national traits of the peninsula's people, Le Moal concluded, made legitimate Breton demands for a system of genuine autonomy within the framework of the French state.

Le Moal's arguments greatly resembled those of the youthful militants of *Breiz Atao*, who also made violation of the 1532 treaty the legal point of departure of their Breton nationalism. Ecclesiastical authorities in Brittany soon became alarmed that Bleun-Brug served as the stalking-horse for (or at least unwittingly played the game of) these young men whom many on the peninsula suspected of being separatists at heart. At first Le Moal and Perrot were able to still such fears by denying that they intended in any way to encourage the *Breiz Atao* nationalists. In a letter to the religious censor of *Feiz ha Breiz* Le Moal even argued that his original reason for writing the 1923 series on the Breton question had been preemptive; he hoped "perhaps to bring the best of them over to us."[33] This reassurance so placated church officials that they were not troubled by the reorganization of Bleun-Brug in 1925 under the name of Société d'Education Nationale and the extension of its activities outside Finistère for the first time. Their equanimity vanished, however, with the election of Abbé François Madec as secretary-general of Bleun-Brug in 1926.

It was bad enough that Madec was an outspoken democrat. Worse still, he was a clear-cut Breton nationalist. He made this obvious when a new monthly he created for use in French-speaking eastern Brittany called *Foi et Bretagne* announced in its second issue that "inspired by our history Breton nationalism is for us a means of protection, a reaction against all that threatens the integrity of our homeland."[34] This statement generated a protracted correspondence between Bishop Duparc of Quimper, who became increasingly menacing in his language, and Perrot, who on behalf of Madec grew more and more disingenuous in his replies. The end came in late 1927 when Madec sought to align Bleun-Brug with the movement organized by *Breiz Atao* in Brittany to protest the arrest and trial of the leaders of Alsatian autonomism. Hence, on 27 October Duparc formally ordered Bleun-Brug to desist from political activity and return to its original program of defense of the church and the Breton language on the peninsula. There was nothing for Perrot and Madec to do but submit. The brief involvement of the Catholic regionalists of Bleun-Brug with ethnic minority nationalism in Brittany thus ended in total failure.[35]

Indeed, the history of Breton regionalism during the decades immediately before and following World War I may be fairly characterized as one of failure. Several factors contributed to this negative result. One of the most important was the chronic inability of individual regionalists to put aside private social, political, and ideological convictions in favor of common action on behalf of the presumably greater interests of their Breton homeland. Instead of uniting solidly against Parisian centralization, which all deplored as the gravest threat to Breton patriotic feeling, conservatives and progressives, Bretonnants and Francophones, Catholics and freethinkers within the regionalist movement exhausted themselves in endless and paralyzing internal conflicts. The innumerable calls for unions and common fronts that regularly issued from the various regionalist organizations after 1898 may therefore be taken for the exercises in hypocrisy and bad faith that they usually were.[36] Such indulgent behavior did not come cheaply, however. Breton regionalists paid for it dearly in the form of the general indifference they encountered among the Breton people whose interests they claimed to defend. Breton regionalism also foundered because its lack of analytical precision and programmatic clarity cost the sympathetic attention of many more potential supporters in Brittany. True enough, its leaders were clear about what they disliked, namely the modern industrial world that emerged out of the sweeping social changes at the end of the eighteenth and beginning of the nineteenth centuries. On the other hand, the regionalists were much less clear about what they wanted to put in the place of this modern industrial world, although in some form or other it involved reconstitution of Breton society as it had existed under the ancien régime. But above all, they knew neither how those things they disliked could be changed nor how those things they desired could be obtained.

Breton regionalists after 1919 were particularly incapacitated by their inability to realize that the post–World War I world was vastly different from the one they had known before August 1914. Members of the aristocratic, propertied, or professional upper classes in Brittany, they simply could not comprehend that the ordered society that had long given them status and security had been irreversibly undermined by war-induced democratization. With the exception of the moderate Catholics of *Buhez Breiz* (and theirs was a lonely voice), the regionalists were especially bewildered by the entry of the masses into the political arena and their predilection for extremism and violence. Hence these men of the past who put their hopes for social survival in regional reform proved intellectually and temperamentally ill-equipped to understand and deal with the postwar development of nationalist extremism within the Breton patriotic movement. Therefore, in practice Breton regionalists were powerless to combat, or even to moderate, the ever-growing influence of the integral nationalists of *Breiz Atao*, a movement that by the end of the 1930s had become synonymous in Brittany with "the Breton movement."

CHAPTER 4

ꙅ Breiz Atao
and the Development of Breton Nationalism

Ethnic minority nationalism first manifested itself in Brittany on the eve of World War I. Heralded by the almost contemporaneous appearance of the Parti Nationaliste Breton and the periodicals *Breiz Dishual*, *Brittia*, and *Brug*, it was the movement of a new generation of impatient young recruits to the cause of Breton revival. Although they differed greatly on many issues, these fledgling Breton nationalists were united in their common rejection of the regionalist approach to the so-called Breton question. Simply as a practical matter, they thought the failure of the URB to make any headway toward achieving its primary goal of administrative decentralization for Brittany reason enough to condemn regionalist efforts.[1] Even more important, they rejected the decentralizing objective of the regionalists on theoretical grounds since they considered it a reform "made in Paris" for imposition on the peninsula from without. By contrast, they insisted that the movement for Breton revival, if it were ever to succeed, must issue from and be based on the self-conscious action of the Breton people itself. Unlike their elders in the URB, who had often involved themselves in French political controversies, these new Breton patriots meant to steer clear of such enervating partisan struggles. Instead, they bent all their efforts toward identifying the essential elements of Breton national feeling and seeking means to arouse it among their compatriots on the peninsula. By so doing they hoped eventually

to spark the formation at the base of Breton society of a powerful movement that would aim at the establishment of Brittany as a self-conscious national entity.

The Parti Nationaliste Breton (PNB) was an outgrowth of
the belated decision of the Rennes city council in 1910 to
commemorate in bronze the fourth centenary (which had
already occurred in 1891) of the joining of Brittany to France.
The plan was to put a statue evoking this event in a niche in the
facade of the municipal hall. A local artist named Jean Boucher
received the commission for this project. His design—two
nubile maidens, one seated on a throne representing France,
and the other, the symbol of Brittany, obediently kneeling at
the feet of the first—angered Breton patriots. The URB circulated a petition that denounced such a "monument of national
shame," while the newspaper *Le Breton de Paris* unsuccessfully
sought funds to build an "anti-monument." But it was the
reaction of the young Breton poet Camille Le Mercier d'Erm
that had the most lasting significance. In Jaffrennou's little
publication *Ar Bobl* he called on Bretons "to bar the route to
this scandalous project and to constitute without delay a
group for resolute national action."[2] Responding to his own
appeal, Le Mercier d'Erm and a half dozen of his young
friends at Rennes in July 1911 founded the Parti Nationaliste
Breton.

The function of the new PNB, its organizers announced in
their first manifesto, was "to group all the irredentist energies
of our country in order to protest the French oppression that
we have borne for centuries."[3] Le Mercier d'Erm and his
friends invoked the treaty of 1532 as the legal basis for their
Breton nationalist action. They went on to demand the full
return of the rights and liberties that they charged had been
illegally stripped from Brittany by successive French governments since the time of François I. But even that they
regarded as no more than a temporary expedient. Brittany,
these young patriots insisted, was a nation with an independent past, and national independence was what they finally
wanted for their Breton homeland. In the concluding section
of their manifesto the founding members of the new Breton
party accordingly specified that their ultimate goal was Brittany's political separation from France. So that no one would

miss the point, they appended to the inaugural PNB document an essay by Louis-N. Le Roux called "Pour le séparatisme."

During the summer of 1911 Le Mercier d'Erm and his nationalist colleagues promoted their Breton ideas by distributing copies of the PNB manifesto throughout the peninsula. They also sought publicity for their cause by attending the official dedication of the Boucher statue on 29 October 1911. When one of the speakers at that ceremony ridiculed the activities of Breton subversives on the peninsula, Le Mercier d'Erm interrupted with several loud horn blasts. He was promptly arrested and charged with disturbing the peace, although it soon became apparent that the authorities were willing to forget the incident and release Le Mercier d'Erm without further penalty. He, on the other hand, was not about to let such an opportunity slip so easily away. Invoking a provision of the 1532 treaty, he demanded a trial before the Cour Correctionnelle. He obviously hoped to turn his case into a political trial and carry it, and the Breton question, all the way through the appellate court system to the important Cour d'Assises. Needless to say, Le Mercier d'Erm's demand was rejected and he was remanded for trial to a humiliatingly obscure police tribunal, which in January 1912 found him guilty as charged and imposed a fine of twelve francs or two days in jail. Le Mercier d'Erm paid the fine and thus brought to an end what he described years later as the trial of "the first Breton patriot to be prosecuted, judged, and condemned in the name of the French people for his fidelity to the Breton fatherland."[4]

The incident at Rennes and subsequent prosecution of Camille Le Mercier d'Erm was in itself a petty and ridiculous affair. Yet it produced for Breton nationalists publicity far in excess of what they ever could have managed on their own and gave them free access to a much larger audience of potential supporters than they otherwise could have afforded. Three separate groups hoping to exploit this opportunity to win new recruits to the cause of Breton revival founded nationalist periodicals. First in the field was the PNB, which began to publish an official organ called *Breiz Dishual* (*La Bretagne Libre*) in July 1912. Written almost entirely in French and rarely more than four pages in length, the new monthly offered its readers little of real substance in the way of Breton nationalist doctrine. The "profound study of the Breton question" that *Breiz Dishual* promised in the first issue likewise never materialized. Instead, those who wrote for the publication chose simply to repeat without much further elaboration the integral Breton nationalist ideas already laid down in the PNB manifesto and Le Roux's little essay on separatism.

No more than the regionalists did the PNB nationalists have a clear conception of how they could achieve their Breton goals. Occasionally there was vague discussion in the party organ about capturing the peninsular elite "by the pen, the word, the newspaper, and the book" so that its members might in turn guide the ignorant Breton masses to the nationalist movement. But more than anything else, such proposals showed that virtually all those who wrote for *Breiz Dishual* were intellectuals of one sort or another, men more at home with words than action. In truth the PNB had no real strategy of action except, as *Breiz Dishual* conceded in 1913, to wait passively for the turn of historical fortune to deliver Brittany from the grip of French rule. Le Roux likewise speculated that the peninsula might be liberated through foreign intervention following a war or revolution in France. Le Mercier d'Erm agreed and, adapting the celebrated Irish Sinn Fein formula to the needs of Breton nationalism, hoped that one day "France's difficulty would be Brittany's opportunity."[5] To the chagrin of the gentle and decent founder of the PNB, a later generation of Breton nationalists took this formula literally and embarked on a course that finally led them to collaborate with German Nazis.

Unable to formulate a coherent program of Breton action, the PNB nationalists filled *Breiz Dishual* by attacking the motives of other Breton patriots and criticizing the depth of their national feeling. They dismissed the regionalists, for example, as false Bretons whose ideas only thinly disguised yet another means for "the perpetuation of a foreign stranglehold on Brittany."[6] But it was with rival Breton nationalist groups that the PNB most often quarreled. Francophone writers in *Breiz Dishual* claimed that knowledge of Brittany's independent past was a surer means for stimulating Breton national feeling than the ability to speak its Celtic language. This attitude was almost certain to increase the antagonism that already existed between Bretonnant and Gallo patriots. At first PNB Gallos sought to avoid the conflict by meeting their Bretonnant brothers more than halfway on the language issue. Their original party manifesto specified that Breton was the sole national language of the peninsula and should be so taught. An anonymous writer in *Breiz Dishual* subsequently noted that "the Gallos understand that their duty is to acquire the national language, to learn *Brezonek*, to re-Celticize themselves in order to affirm better their Breton nationality."[7] Le Mercier d'Erm even lamented that he remained a prisoner of his classical French education and sorely regretted that he had not been able to learn Breton as a child.

These worthy sentiments deceived no one, for the members of the PNB obviously preferred knowledge of Breton history over possession of the ancestral tongue as a means for arousing Breton national feeling. An unsigned editorial in the eighth issue of *Breiz Dishual* openly stated this preference. Although its author recognized that both "language and history are the two constituent elements of our nationality," he left no doubt that he considered history to be by far the more important. Although he did concede that the disappearance of the Breton language would be a terrible blow to the nationalist movement, he insisted that all would not be lost, for Breton history would still remain. He even concluded that "history is the surest rampart of the language and it is thanks to Breton history that our language has survived."[8] Nothing could have been more calculated to raise the nationalist hackles of the Bretonnants who, two months after the debut of *Breiz Dishual*, had begun to publish a rival nationalist periodical called *Brittia*.

The driving force behind the creation of *Brittia* was the Breton writer Yves Le Diberder, who quickly attracted most of the leading Bretonnant intellectuals on the peninsula to its banner. Impatient with regionalism and hostile to separatism, the *Brittia* nationalists declared their ultimate objective to be the refashioning of Brittany along "national and Celtic lines." Primacy in this task of nation-building they assigned to the rescue of the Breton language, since Le Diberder and his colleagues regarded it as the fundamental element of Breton nationality. Like their Francophone rivals in the PNB, however, the Bretonnants of *Brittia* had a much clearer idea of what they wanted to achieve than of how to go about getting it. They too speculated about winning Brittany's elite to the nationalist cause but were at a loss to know how to penetrate and overcome the thoroughgoing French cultural formation its members had received since birth. Otherwise, Le Diberder urged readers to demand of Parisian authorities that they respect Breton "rights and liberties, but even the nebulous "committee for Breton national action" that he recommended for this purpose was never formed. Instead, the *Brittia* team exhausted itself defending the purity of its Bretonnant national feeling against possible French adulteration by Gallo nationalist imposters. The gathering of an impressive roster of contributors—a body that included François Vallée, J.-P. Calloc'h, Loeiz Herrieu, and Meven Mordiern—was in fact about the only real accomplishment of *Brittia* during its two-year existence.

The remaining form of pre-1914 Breton nationalism is associated with the name of Emile Masson, a Bretonnant schoolteacher from Pontivy. Although he belonged to the PNB and contributed articles to both *Breiz Dishual* and *Brittia*, Masson started a third nationalist monthly called *Brug* (*Bruyère*) in January 1913 so that he could develop more freely his own novel approach to Breton nationalism. In *Brug*, as well as in his little book *Antée*, Masson linked the cause of Breton national revival with that of socialist reform on the peninsula. His was an odd species of socialism, however, for it derived less from an economic analysis of history than from Masson's outrage at what he considered the national humiliation of Bretons trapped as they were in an alien French bourgeois culture. The cruel treatment meted out to Bretonnant children who came to French schools knowing only their maternal tongue particularly angered *Brug*'s founder. Too many times in his own youth had he heard the mean couplet:

> Les pommes de terre pour les cochons,
> Les épluchures pour les Bretons!

for him to have felt otherwise. It is hardly surprising that Masson deeply believed that for Bretons socialism was above all else "an urgent stirring of the heart toward justice."[9]

According to Masson, however, neither socialism nor Breton nationalism would have much impact on the Breton population until the enormous power and influence of the church in the Bretonnant west had been overcome. He argued that this clerical power was based on the ability of parish priests to converse easily with the local Bretonnant population in its native tongue. The members of the latter thus became unwitting captives of a black army of reactionary confessors that inclined them equally against ideas of Breton national revival and socialist reform. Masson thought the only way to combat this insidious priestly influence was for Breton socialists who were also nationalists to learn the Breton national language. Like their clerical adversaries they could then go among the masses of the peninsula and proselytize effectively for the cause of Breton revival within the framework of a generous and humane socialism. From among these "new bards" Masson was convinced another King Arthur would emerge who, as so many Bretons hoped, would deliver Brittany from its French captivity. Here the influence of Masson's favorite writer, Thomas Carlyle, became manifest. The new King Arthur he so ardently desired was none other than a pagan Celtic version of Carlyle's celebrated Hero.

Emile Masson found almost no support for his ideas in prewar Brittany. Indeed, the impact of the entire Breton nationalist movement on the inhabitants of the peninsula before 1914 was negligible. Nothing revealed this more clearly than the total lack of resistance in Brittany in 1914 to the order for general mobilization that finally sent a million Bretons, including many of the most prominent nationalists, to defend the civilization of France against German aggression. For once Le Diberder had been completely on target when he admitted in the first issue of *Brittia* that the nationalists were "an infinitely small minority" in Brittany.[10] None of the three Breton nationalist monthlies in fact ever had a press run of more than five hundred copies each and many of these remained unsold or were simply given away. Without adequate financial support from readers and unable to raise additional funds by other means, *Breiz Dishual*, *Brittia*, and *Brug* hence depended for survival on the modest personal resources of their respective founders. It is hardly any wonder that the first Breton nationalist movement collapsed so abruptly and completely at the outbreak of war in 1914.

Yet many pioneering nationalists hoped that their participation in World War I would further the cause of Breton national revival.[11] Thus Yves Le Moal marched off to war believing that the nationalities principle upon which so many in the Allied camp justified the eventual dismemberment of the Austrian Empire would also apply to Brittany. He did not think it possible that "a truth admitted on the banks of the Danube could be a monstrosity on those of the Seine."[12] J.-P. Calloc'h nourished similar ideas. In a letter from the front, he confidently expected that Paris could not fail to satisfy "the just aspirations of the Bretons after a victory to which they would have contributed so much." He accordingly urged civilian Breton militants to organize for such a postwar eventuality. In particular he recommended that they gather the signatures of returning soldiers on a massive petition calling on Paris to recognize the right of Bretons to teach the language and history of their homeland in the schools of the peninsula. "Should I die," he concluded his letter, "I hope that others will take charge of this project and do everything possible to see that it succeeds."[13] J.-P. Calloc'h was killed in action during the battle of the Somme in 1917 and his project died with him.

According to Breton nationalists, Calloc'h was only one of some 240,000 Breton soldiers killed during the war. This statistic meant, they invariably point out, that Brittany lost one out of every fourteen of its prewar population, while the corresponding fatality rate for the rest of France was one in twenty-eight. No systematic attempt has been made by the nationalists or anyone else to verify these figures, and they may be inaccurate. A recent study suggests, however, that one-sixth of all Bretons mobilized were killed, a proportion that accounts for 12 percent of all French fatal casualties.[14] Since Brittany's share of the total prewar population of France was less than 9 percent, these figures indicate that Bretons shouldered a much heavier burden of fatal war losses than did the rest of the country. Breton nationalists have consequently been quick to allege a deliberate policy laid down in Paris to account for this enormous wartime loss of life by their countrymen. At the very least they charge that the French army regarded Breton troops as mere cannon fodder and hence deployed them in the most dangerous and exposed positions along the front.[15]

Such nationalist accusations are not only exaggerated but misleading as well. Their makers do not mention, for example, that non-Breton units at the front suffered equally appalling devastation during World War I. Nor do they consider that the exceptionally heavy losses sustained by Breton troops could be attributed to their devotion to the cause of defending France against Germany. But the most plausible explanation for the high mortality rate among Breton soldiers is historical and sociological. Brittany in 1914 was still an overwhelmingly peasant society. Its young men, like those from other rural areas, were conscripted into the infantry, since they possessed no special qualifications or training that would have prepared them for more technical branches of the military or that might even have won them deferments. Trench warfare as it was practiced during World War I, moreover, meant that infantrymen were assigned to the most dangerous forward positions in combat. On the other hand, skilled workers—when they were not exempted for matériel production on the home front—were quite reasonably conserved for more specialized tasks behind the lines. Since such men typically came from the most socially and economically advanced parts of France, their losses were inevitably fewer than those suffered by peasant *poilus* in the trenches. From this perspective the so-called massacre of Breton soldiers during the war of 1914–18 emerges as but another tragic consequence of Brittany's domination by its traditional clerico-aristocratic elite that for so long had generally been able to resist the social and economic modernization of the peninsula.

As it turned out, four years of unremitting war did more to release Brittany from the grip of its entrenched ruling class and catapult its people into the twentieth century than any other event. At the same time, the war seemed to be a total disaster for the infant Breton nationalist movement, which in the process vanished without a trace. In reality the opposite was true, for World War I quickened the development of Breton nationalism. By thoroughly disrupting Breton society through mobilization of its people for war production at home and military service at the front and by causing the deaths of so many of its most vigorous young men, the war generated new resentments while it rekindled old ones. Out of them both emerged a new Breton nationalist movement with leaders far better placed to plead Brittany's case against France than Le Mercier d'Erm, Le Diberder, and Masson had ever been. They were able, after all, to point to the disaster of 1914–18 and plausibly argue that it might have been averted had Brittany been master of its own fate. Indeed, the appearance and subsequent growth of intransigent Breton nationalism under the banner of *Breiz Atao* during the two interwar decades cannot be understood apart from its background in the cataclysm of World War I.

Postwar Breton nationalism had its beginnings in the Groupe Régionaliste Breton (GRB) organized at Rennes in September 1918 even before hostilities came to an end. Its founders were two university students named Maurice Marchal and Henri Prado and a soldier still on active duty in the French army, Job de Roincé. Within eighteen months they were joined by a small group of Breton comrades who were to remain active in the nationalist movement throughout the interwar period. These included Olier Mordrel and Fanch Debauvais, the two men who at length won public recognition as the very heart and soul of Breton nationalism. Various routes brought these postwar recruits to the Breton cause into the GRB. For many young inhabitants of the peninsula the Irish struggle for independence, particularly, in the case of Fanch Debauvais, the dramatic events of Easter Week 1916, was the decisive factor in arousing their ethnic Breton feeling. Thus in 1939 a local critic of integral Breton nationalism wrote that "above all else it was Ireland that hypnotized these eighteen-year-old esthetes in 1919 and made them dream dreams of a FREE STATE OF BRITTANY just like in the good old days."[16] Others became Breton nationalists out of a highly developed sense of Francophobia, which had originally been sparked by admiration for German culture. Job de Roincé demonstrated these attitudes in the closing days of the war by crossing the front line and teaching Breton patriotic songs to the German soldiers he found on the other side. Still other early GRB members, notably Maurice Marchal and Olier Mordrel, claimed that unexpectedly seeing a Bretton grammar by François Vallée in a shop window first impelled them on their nationalist way. Vallée himself soon rallied to the GRB and brought with him many Bretonnant patriots whose primary interest lay in the defense of their ancestral Celtic language.

Whatever its original stimulus may have been, the ethnic Breton feeling of many early GRB members eventually took the form of separatist convictions. Yet in many respects the new Breton regionalist society at first seemed the model of moderation. Many of its initial members belonged to the FRB and some were even admirers of the arch-French nationalist Charles Maurras. In their inaugural manifesto Marchal, Prado, and de Roincé took care to explain, moreover, that the GRB meant to work not only for the good of Brittany but for that of France as well.[17] Their regionalist proposals thus strongly resembled those of the FRB and most could easily have been embraced by Régis de l'Estourbeillon. Certain elements of the GRB charter program clashed with this moderate regionalist image, however, and foreshadowed the subsequent development of integral Breton nationalist attitudes by those who joined its ranks. In particular, its drafters declared that Brittany "formed a Celtic nation with a distinct nationality." Proof of this they found in the distinctive language, costumes, and art of the peninsula as well as in the historical circumstance of the Celtic origin of the Breton people through emigration from the British Isles. In order to preserve and defend this Celtic heritage, the GRB manifesto demanded that courses in Breton history be required in all schools on the peninsula. It similarly demanded the obligatory teaching of the Breton language in Bretonnant areas and its optional instruction elsewhere in Brittany.

The proposals of the GRB founders concerning the teaching of Breton history and language revealed their alarm that the continued advance of French influences in Brittany would end in the complete gallicization of Breton society. Accordingly, from the outset they challenged like-minded young Bretons to oppose the further "denationalization" of the Breton people and to work for its "renationalization" by the reawakening among its members of "a powerful national sentiment." To assist in this task Maurice Marchal created a periodical organ for the GRB. Thus appeared for the first time in January 1919 *Breiz Atao* (*La Bretagne Toujours*), a name that in time became, and still remains, a code word for integral nationalism and separatism in Brittany. Few would have guessed at its inception, however, that such a future awaited the new GRB publication. Years later Marchal himself acknowledged that at first his little Breton monthly was only a "four-page rag" with fifty subscribers, ten contributors, a nineteen-year-old editor-in-chief, and an administrator four years younger.[18] Although the number of its subscribers eventually reached several hundred persons, the financial health of *Breiz Atao* remained precarious during most of its twenty-year existence. That it survived until the outbreak of war in 1939 many Breton nationalists consider the one authentic miracle of the interwar Breton movement.

During its first year the pages of *Breiz Atao* were filled with efforts to define its Breton point of view. The division of its parent society into contrasting moderate federalist and militant nationalist factions complicated this task. The first group, headed by GRB president Job de Roincé and his friend Henri Prado, considered administrative decentralization and a federal relationship between Brittany and the rest of France to be its maximum program. To achieve these goals its leaders urged a policy of participation in electoral politics and common action with other Breton groups. The de Roincé-Prado strategy in effect meant working within the existing political system and the use of pressure group tactics to win regional reforms for Brittany. It also meant support for Estourbeillon's 1919 petition as well as his overture to President Wilson, since de Roincé and Prado believed that such initiatives publicized the Breton cause and simultaneously put pressure on Paris to act on behalf of the peninsula. The immediate failure of both undertakings to produce results deepened the belief of militant nationalists in the GRB that the French government would never grant even administrative decentralization to Brittany on the supposed merits of the case. Taking their lead from Marchal and Mordrel, nationalists insisted that the GRB might better concentrate on the building of a popularly based and self-consciously Breton nationalist movement. When it had become sufficiently powerful, they argued, such a movement could force from Paris concessions even more substantial than administrative decentralization. As 1919 drew to a close the Marchal-Mordrel group began to dominate *Breiz Atao* and impose on the GRB its militant nationalist views. The shift became clear in December when this faction was able to have the name of the GRB changed to Unvaniez Yaouankiz Vreiz (UYV, Union de Jeunesse Bretonne), a less restrictive title presumably more appealing to nationalist mentalities. By the beginning of 1920, especially after Prado's sudden death from tuberculosis, de Roincé found himself isolated and soon resigned as UYV president.

From the simple reason that they remained loyal Frenchmen it was probably inevitable that federalists like de Roincé would be driven from the GRB because its more numerous nationalist members sought to define Breton nationality from a consistently anti-French perspective.[19] As a group they believed that too many differences separated Brittany from the rest of France for their union to be harmonious. Marchal wrote in March 1919, for example, that their joining together had been "a marriage of reason, not love" and claimed that if a growing number of Bretons wanted a divorce, it was the fault of Paris, which "has not respected our soil, our language, and our traditions." As the months passed this anti-French attitude hardened into extreme ideological hostility. In the process France became for GRB nationalists as much a cultural enemy as it had always been a political and administrative enemy of Brittany. Thus by October 1919 Marchal was already writing that Bretons "were confronted by a moral struggle to the death between two races and two civilizations. . . . Latins against Celts, that is the entire question." Given the evolution of this tendency, the separatist leanings of *Breiz Atao* at the end of the interwar period were implicit in its ideology virtually from the beginning. Thus the separatist accusations lodged even during its earliest years against the nationalist newspaper by opponents of Breton nationalism were not exactly groundless. Nor need one insist upon the disingenuousness of the later nationalist claim that *Breiz Atao* moved reluctantly toward separatism in the 1930s only after its leaders became convinced of Paris's unyielding resolve to make no concessions to Brittany.

Meanwhile, Maurice Marchal put himself forward as the theoretician of Breton nationalism at *Breiz Atao*. His point of departure was that twentieth-century Brittany, especially its Francophone areas, had "the aspect of a disaggregated personality; only the very old and a tiny elite know their past and feel their hearts tremble at the name of Brittany."[20] What Marchal wanted to show above all was that *Breiz Atao*'s "tiny elite" of predominantly French-speaking Gallos had a role to play in the Breton nationalist movement. Claiming that most of eastern Brittany had been Bretonophone until the ninth century, he insisted that Gallos were as much a part of the Breton nation as the Bretonnants, since both possessed the same Celtic heritage, mores, and customs. The only real difference Marchal found between Gallos and Bretonnants was linguistic. But he considered this to be no more than an accidental and unimportant consequence of the Norman invasions of the ninth to twelfth centuries that brought the Latin tongue to eastern Brittany. The true source of national feeling for both Gallos and Bretonnants, Marchal in any case believed, was their common past as an independent nation and he argued that knowledge of it made the Breton hearts of each tremble with equal emotion.

Marchal went further and suggested that Gallos were perhaps even better suited than Bretonnants to promote the cause of Breton nationalism. He considered this so because they had been historically more sensitive to Latin pressure on Breton culture, since they lived closer to Paris than their Breton-speaking brothers. Moreover, he thought the inability of Gallos to speak Breton in a paradoxical way heightened their national consciousness because without the language they felt most strongly threats to their Breton identity. Maurice Marchal was no social scientist but with this observation he adumbrated the theory of marginality that scholars like Sigmund Neumann and Daniel Lerner have proposed to explain the genesis and development of nationalist attitudes. In any event, the *Breiz Atao* founder thought Gallo nationalists erred if they made learning the Breton language their first priority. He maintained instead that their time was better spent in a careful study of Breton history and customs. Once such knowledge had been acquired, Marchal concluded, Gallos would perforce learn the indigenous language of their homeland just as Irish and Czech patriots had done after recovering their national feeling.

Olier Mordrel was one of many Gallos who followed the nationalist development outlined by Marchal. Steeped in Breton history acquired during his student days, he began to study the Breton language shortly after joining the GRB and in his later years made a considerable reputation for himself in Celtic linguistics. Mordrel made his journalistic debut at *Breiz Atao* in June 1919 and proceeded to stamp his polemical brilliance and political extremism on the Breton nationalist movement for the next twenty-five years. From the outset it was clear that deeply felt antipathy for the French people lay at the base of his Breton national feeling. They were incapable of understanding the Bretons, he insisted, and in their ignorance looked on the Armorican peninsula as some kind of "grotesque carnival." He went on to argue that the heirs of Clovis understood force alone and to declare that only it could compel them to change their behavior toward Brittany. It was through recovery of their Breton consciousness, he further contended, that inhabitants of the peninsula could find the strength to oblige the French "to respect us and listen to us." Mordrel ended his first essay on Breton national action with a warning that *Breiz Atao* would have to reconsider its moderate regionalist position should the French continue "to plunder us while they try at the same time to turn us into Frenchmen."

Three months later in a second article in *Breiz Atao* Mordrel reduced the national situation of Brittany to the extreme formula of "life or death." This time, however, he emphasized Breton weakness rather than French incomprehension. His fundamental point was that nationalists could not depend on the fortuitous appearance of a latter-day King Arthur to deliver Brittany from its national decadence. On the contrary, Bretons themselves had to accomplish the national salvation of their homeland through patient labor and unremitting patriotic action. In the process they had to recognize and overcome their faults (among others, Mordrel listed submissiveness, fatalism, apathy, and extreme individualism) that had so far frustrated the efforts of Breton patriots. To impress on his readers the seriousness of the problem Mordrel urged them to repeat every day the following mea culpa: "I am solely responsible for the misfortunes of my country since it is my failings that have led to them." He was certain that, thus chastened, they would in time become "learned and industrious, hard and persevering, united and modest, and, above all, realistic in their national action." Only then could Bretons break with "the defeatist traditions of embalmers of Brittany like Renan" and help deliver their homeland from corrupting French influences. Such, Mordrel concluded, was "the price of our revival."[21]

The doctrinal content of *Breiz Atao* during the 1920s hardly varied from the positions laid down in 1919 by Maurice Marchal and Olier Mordrel. Indeed, simply to keep the little nationalist organ afloat required most of the energy and resources of the young UYV nationalists, particularly those of Fanch Debauvais who managed the business end of the operation. Subscription revenue proved insufficient for ordinary expenses and efforts were made to secure additional funds through solicitation of voluntary contributions. Originally announced at the beginning of 1921, this "campaign for *Breiz Atao*" remained open in one form or another until the early years of World War II.[22] Still, the effort was not enough and throughout the decade the editors of the UYV organ were often forced to delay publication or to consolidate several monthly numbers into a single issue. So straitened were its circumstances that sometimes there was not enough money to pay the office rent. This and the frequency with which Debauvais changed jobs caused the editorial address of *Breiz Atao* to be changed nine times during the fifteen years after 1919.

Insufficient resources also made it impossible for the Rennes-based UYV to establish and maintain a peninsula-wide network of local sections. Many of those that were organized often had no more than a paper existence. Others with more substance, Mordrel reports in his memoirs, were typically formed in communes where an active member of the UYV made his home. Local sections thus tended to become identified with and dependent on the efforts of particular individuals. In this way the vigorous Tréguier section *was* Yann

Sohier; Guingamp *was* Louis Derrien; Plessala *was* Pol Gaïc; and Rennes *was* André Gefflot. Since such UYV branches often folded with the removal of their local animators, the stability of the entire organization could easily be adversely affected. Mordrel recalls one commune, for example, where one year *Breiz Atao* counted fifty subscribers and the next only half a dozen after the local nationalist leader had moved to another town. Given this situation, it is impossible to gauge accurately the size of the UYV. Circulation figures for *Breiz Atao* do indicate, however, that it remained small during much of the 1920s. At the end of 1921 the UYV organ could boast only five hundred regular subscribers and a monthly press run of fifteen hundred copies. According to one informed nationalist, five years later the number of subscribers had risen to only six hundred, although Debauvais maintained a mailing list of nine hundred names.[23]

The failure of the UYV to attract a large following during its early years may be attributed in part to the abuse that the editors of *Breiz Atao* rained down on Bretons whose ideas differed from their own. For the regionalists they had nothing but contempt. In May 1920 Debauvais thus disparaged both the URB and the FRB as toothless societies of old men, while an anonymous colleague four years later scornfully dismissed Estourbeillon's CDIB as "an empty organization." The Catholics of Bleun-Brug and their publication *Feiz ha Breiz* hardly fared better at the hands of the UYV nationalists. Although Marchal and Mordrel much admired Bleun-Brug's founder Abbé Perrot, they repudiated the notion that the causes of the church and Breton revival were necessarily related. On the contrary, they regarded the clergy in Brittany as "merchants of gallicization" and hence enemies to be combated. They feared, moreover, that if Breton nationalism were to become narrowly linked with the defense of ecclesiastical interests in Brittany, anticlerical central authorities in Paris would have a plausible excuse "to treat every Breton national effort as an affair of purely clerical propaganda." This, Marchal explained in 1954, would have unnecessarily exposed Breton nationalists to retaliatory measures from the French government, thereby hindering the progress of the entire Breton movement.[24]

Yet it was neither the regionalists nor the Catholics of

Bleun-Brug who bore the brunt of *Breiz Atao*'s harshest criticism. This burden was reserved for members of the peninsular middle class. Keenly aware that nationalist movements in Europe had traditionally enjoyed the support of indigenous middle-class groups, the UYV leaders were angered and humiliated by the persistent refusal of Brittany's bourgeoisie to back their movement. The problem was, *Breiz Atao* editorialized in January 1922, that repeated contact with French culture, especially in the schools, had made the Breton middle class "half French in blood, values, and conduct." This exposure in turn meant, Mordrel warned the following year, that its members served as powerful agents of gallicization in Brittany and introduced into the peninsula all that "anarchy, demoralization, debauchery, perversion, and disorder that has already undermined France." But he thought the process could be halted if the amount of French blood that flowed in Breton veins were reduced. Mordrel recognized, however, that further French immigration into Brittany could not be prevented nor could those Frenchmen already there be expelled. Thus he proposed a truly remarkable solution to the so-called problem. What had to be done in his view was to encourage immigration into Brittany from the British Isles. Mordrel was convinced that young Irish, Welsh, and Scottish stallions, by inundating the peninsula with their robust Celtic genes, would in short order "reestablish the purity of our blood and the homogeneity of our population."[25] The suggestion hardly flattered the intelligence of its author or the virility of young Breton manhood.

Isolated within Brittany and scarcely noticed without, the leaders of the UYV drifted during the mid-1920s from one meaningless project to another. In 1925 they organized a women's auxiliary and an allied student association but neither ever really got off the ground. That same year there were also abortive attempts to change the name of the UYV to the Young Breton Nationalist League and to found an International Minorities Committee. But perhaps the oddest of all these projects was the effort by Mordrel and Marchal to graft a Breton nationalist variety of pacifism onto *Breiz Atao* and the UYV.[26] Although they justified this new orientation on ethical grounds, their abrupt espousal of pacifist themes actually involved a quasi-separatist motive. Arguing that wars like that of 1914–18 originated in the military organization of modern states, Marchal called for their supercession in Europe by a new order based on a federation of all ethnic nationalities, including the Breton people. This proposal obviously implied not only Brittany's political separation from France but also the dismantling of the French state as it was then constituted. It was no wonder that government officials in Paris looked on *Breiz Atao* with such unconcealed hostility.

The creation in 1925 of a Breton-language literary supplement to *Breiz Atao* was the only undertaking of the UYV nationalists during these years to have any lasting success. Called *Gwalarn* (*Nord-Ouest*), this quarterly publication was jointly inspired by Olier Mordrel and an ascetic young professor of English named Roparz Hémon. In the inaugural manifesto for *Gwalarn* they announced that cultivation of an authentically Breton literature was the primary objective of the new venture. Such a literature they hoped would ultimately play in the movement for Breton national revival a role similar to that played by the literatures of Bohemia, Flanders, and Catalonia in their respective national revivals. In this endeavor *Gwalarn*'s promoters thought it crucially important that their literary efforts be shielded as much as possible from French influences. Mordrel and Hémon thus boasted proudly in the inaugural manifesto that it would be the first and last document published by *Gwalarn* in the French language. Mordrel even opposed bilingual education, claiming that it was an infringement on the prerogatives of Brittany's indigenous and senior national language.[27]

The columns of *Gwalarn* were open to all Breton writers regardless of their political and ideological preferences. Its manifesto specifically explained that participation in its literary tasks did not require the adoption of Breton nationalist views. Although Mordrel coauthored and signed this document, he did not subscribe in fact to *Gwalarn*'s avowed apoliticism. As he put it many years later in his memoirs, it was an "illusion" to think that the Breton language could be saved apart from politics. Brittany's national revival was, he added, "*un bloc*" and none of its parts could be pursued in isolation without thereby compromising the whole enterprise.[28] Hémon vigorously disagreed and believed that the immediate success of *Gwalarn*—it quickly enrolled three hundred subscribers—was owed precisely to its self-denying apolitical attitude. He accordingly resisted all Mordrel's maneuvers to stamp a nationalist character on the new Breton quarterly. Antagonism festered between the two men until 1928 when Hémon publicly threatened to disavow *Breiz Atao* and the UYV if Mordrel did not cease his meddling in the affairs of *Gwalarn*. Even Mordrel recognized that the struggling Breton nationalist movement might not survive the scandal of such an open quarrel. He thus acquiesced quietly in the decision of his fellow UYV leaders to allow *Gwalarn* to go its separate and apolitical way. Thereafter formally independent of *Breiz Atao*, Hémon and his colleagues continued their labor on behalf of Breton literary revival until 1944 when *Gwalarn* disappeared in the maelstrom of the liberation.

Olier Mordrel yielded so easily on the *Gwalarn* issue because he did not want to endanger an apparent upturn in the fortunes of the Breton nationalist movement. The main reason for this development was the adhesion of Maurice Duhamel to the UYV, which ended the longtime floundering of its leaders. Obviously flattered that they had been joined by a well-known music critic twenty years older than themselves, Mordrel and his friends gave Duhamel a virtually free hand in determining the policy orientation of their movement. Under his direction the UYV and *Breiz Atao* soon embarked on a course that ultimately provoked the gravest crisis in the history of interwar Breton nationalism. This crisis came about because Duhamel convinced his young comrades in the UYV that their cause would benefit greatly if they capitalized on the French government's alleged persecution of a national minority, not in Brittany but in Alsace.

A popular protest movement had recently emerged in the Rhenish province against the anticlerical policies of the government of Edouard Herriot, which had taken office in 1924. In the euphoric aftermath of World War I Alsace had been welcomed back into the bosom of the French state, together with the special autonomous statute that from 1871 to 1918 had governed its relations with Berlin. Alsace therefore did not come under the 1905 French law on the separation of church and state and its system of publicly financed confessional schools remained intact. Conservative governments in Paris during the period 1919–24 were content to live with this anomaly. After the electoral victory of the left in 1924, however, Parisian authorities moved to correct this grievously reactionary oversight, as Herriot and his ministers considered it. A protest movement called the Heimatbund immediately appeared in Alsace and demanded that not only these schools be preserved but also the province's statute of autonomy. Duhamel soon persuaded the other UYV leaders that by making the cause of the beleaguered Alsatians their own they stood to win enormous free publicity for the Breton nationalist movement. In April 1926 *Breiz Atao* thus announced editorially that it fully supported the patriotic efforts of the Heimatbund. Moreover, when the government of Raymond Poincaré disclosed in early 1927 that it would prosecute the Alsatian autonomist leaders for subversion, Duhamel and his Breton nationalist friends helped secure the services of a lawyer from Quimper to defend the accused men. When Duhamel's support became known in Brittany, its entire parliamentary delegation in a joint statement denounced the Breton nationalist movement and, in the name of 250,000 Bretons killed during the recent war, proclaimed the steadfast loyalty of their province to France. Although Maurice Marchal immediately accused the peninsular political class of "trading on the dead," he voiced gratitude that the Breton question had at last been brought squarely into the open.[29]

Even if it amounted to notoriety, the public recognition by Brittany's parliamentarians that a Breton nationalist movement did exist roused the UYV from its doldrums. Numerous new members joined its ranks and the circulation of *Breiz Atao* increased considerably.[30] The much-heartened UYV leaders made ambitious plans to reorganize their movement in order to consolidate these gains. They moved their headquarters from Rennes to Guingamp and for the first time made provision for a salaried administrative staff. In addition, they undertook to issue a regular series of propaganda pamphlets, to arrange a lecture tour of nationalist speakers, and to change *Breiz Atao* from a monthly into a biweekly. In July 1927 the nationalist organ announced that the UYV itself would be transformed into a political party at a congress in Rosporden on 10 September. Meanwhile, a campaign to raise five thousand francs was opened to fund all these projects. Within three months this sum had been collected, along with enough additional money to pay for the free distribution of several hundred copies of *Breiz Atao* during the summer. So emboldened were the UYV leaders by this positive response to their efforts that they could not wait until the Rosporden meeting to form their new Breton party. They held a special leadership meeting of the UYV on 14 August and provisionally constituted themselves into the Parti Autonomiste Breton (PAB). Thus was born the first postwar Breton nationalist political party. It would last not quite four years.

CHAPTER 5

ꙮ *The Parti Autonomiste Breton*

The leaders of the newly minted Autonomist party worked hard to make certain that a respectably large number of nationalists attended the Rosporden meeting. They saw their efforts rewarded when five hundred persons turned up on 10 September to ratify the August creation of the PAB. Those present also approved the hastily amended statutes of the old GRB as the new party constitution and elected Mordrel and Marchal its copresidents. This awkward arrangement was made necessary by the presence at the congress of two competing factions, each of which vetoed the candidate of the other as party president, an early indication of trouble to come. Mordrel's cousin Yann Bricler was named secretary-general of the new organization while Fanch Debauvais was reconfirmed in his old post as administrator of *Breiz Atao*. Together these men formed the executive committee of the PAB. Maurice Duhamel headed its other major structural component, the so-called political council, a body that included the members of the executive committee and the heads of the four largest local sections of the former GRB. Before adjourning, the Rosporden assembly directed this group to draft an official program for the PAB.

Duhamel and his colleagues immediately went to work and in November 1927 published their efforts in *Breiz Atao*. Full autonomy for Brittany within either the framework of the existing French state or that of an eventual European federation they set down as the fundamental goal of the remodeled Breton nationalist movement. To achieve it, they went on to explain, the strategy of the PAB would be to direct militant political action against the central government in Paris. But except for a vaguely expressed intention to build a peninsula-wide popular movement on behalf of Breton autonomy, their draft program did not specify the particular form such political action might take. It did make clear, however, that unlike most other parties the PAB did not regard electoral politics as its only raison d'être. Such involvement, its authors almost casually added, simply meant for the Breton Autonomist party "one occasion among several to affirm its existence and to extend its influence." With this statement Duhamel's political council erected into a matter of principle the private conviction of many nationalists that it would be a long time before the PAB could present electoral candidates who had any real hope of success on polling day. No one could know in late 1927 that within three years the new Breton party would be destroyed precisely as a consequence of the ill-timed decision of certain of its leaders to contest a parliamentary election in Brittany.

Meanwhile, the PAB turned its attention once more to Alsace when Paris, after several months of delay, in November 1927 finally moved against the autonomist movement there. Three of its publications were suppressed and their editors were held for trial on charges of subversion. Hoping to turn to their own advantage the wide publicity this trial was likely to generate, the leaders of the PAB headed for Colmar where the trial of the Alsatian autonomists was scheduled to begin on 1 May 1928. On the eve of the proceeding they distributed three thousand copies of a special edition of *Breiz Atao* that in "an open letter to the Colmar jury" called for the acquittal of the accused editors. The conspicuous presence of Mordrel, Marchal, and Duhamel at the trial itself also demonstrated the solidarity of the Breton nationalist movement with the defendants. The prosecution's case was nonetheless successful and the three convicted men were sentenced to a year in prison. The PAB responded to the verdict with "an open letter to the condemned of Colmar," published in *Breiz Atao* at the beginning of June. According to the author of the letter, Maurice Duhamel, the trial's outcome proved that in France "the air had become unhealthy for free men to breathe." Breton nationalists were prepared, he dramatically ended his letter, to join their Alsatian brothers in prison "if that is necessary to restore to the sons of our race the freedom that has been stolen from them."

Duhamel and the other nationalist leaders did not go to prison but instead to Châteaulin, a little town in Finistère where the second annual congress of the PAB was to take place in mid-August. This meeting seemed likely to produce important developments since Duhamel's rise to a position of leadership in the nationalist movement had been confirmed in July when he replaced Maurice Marchal as copresident of the PAB. His steadily growing influence had been especially evident since late 1927 when he began to write a regular column on foreign affairs for *Breiz Atao*. In these articles, and in the lead editorials that he began to publish in February 1928, Duhamel increasingly sought to align Breton nationalism with the European federalist movement. He often commented approvingly on the work of the League of Nations and other international cooperative bodies as well. But while Duhamel-inspired federalist ideas grew in importance, Breton nationalist themes received correspondingly less and less emphasis in *Breiz Atao*; articles written in the Breton language almost entirely disappeared. The Châteaulin meeting would be the first real test of whether or not a majority of the nationalist rank and file endorsed Duhamel's views.

Buoyed by the evident success of a new fund-raising effort, the PAB leadership journeyed to Finistère to reveal the important developments that at the beginning of August *Breiz Atao* had tantalizingly hinted were in the offing. The nationalist congress began with an incident straight out of *opéra bouffe*. When the party delegates arrived at Châteaulin on 17 August they found that the public buildings put at their disposal by the local mayor had been barred and locked by order of Albert Sarraut, the minister of the interior. The French police were also on the scene. After interrogating several of the arriving nationalists, they requisitioned the hotel rooms that PAB members had reserved in advance. Noting that some of the women delegates had thus been thrown onto the street, *Breiz Atao* drily observed at the beginning of September that "one must come to a new conception of French gallantry and hospitality." The anonymous writer of these words scarcely hid his pleasure, however, that French authorities deemed the Breton nationalist movement alarming enough to justify these precautionary measures.

The substantive work of the meeting came on 18 August. Mordrel and Debauvais first explained the "exclusively private reasons" for Marchal's resignation. The delegates proceeded immediately to approve Duhamel as his replacement at the head of the nationalist organization. Debauvais then reported on the state of the PAB and *Breiz Atao*. In the process he acknowledged the "legitimate grievances" of those who grumbled that local sections had too little to do and insufficient contact with the party leadership. He also noted complaints of other nationalists that for them *Breiz Atao* had recently declined in interest. This situation probably reflected the dissatisfaction of those who opposed the involvement of the Breton nationalist movement with European federalism and the Alsatian question. Debauvais in any case assured disgruntled rank and filers that he and the other party leaders were aware of their various discontents and would try to remedy them. But the major emphasis of his report was on plans to hire a professional staff for *Breiz Atao* so that the party organ could soon begin weekly publication. To carry out this expansion he proposed the creation of a financing corporation through the sale of 850 shares of stock at one hundred francs each. The total yield from such an issue added to the fifteen thousand francs already in the nationalist treasury would produce a capital base of one hundred thousand francs, the sum Debauvais thought necessary to launch the undertaking. It was the beginning of *Breiz Atao*'s involvement in a complicated and nearly disastrous tangle of financial dealings from which the nationalist movement would not soon extricate itself.

The above matters were but preliminaries to the important business of the PAB congress, which was the adoption of the so-called Declaration of Châteaulin as the party's official statement of its goals and doctrines. The first five of the seven articles contained nothing that had not appeared in *Breiz Atao* sometime since 1919 and that might not have been written by any of the veteran nationalist leaders. These articles accordingly denied that the Breton movement was separatist, denounced Parisian centralization, and demanded administrative and political autonomy for Brittany within the framework of the French state. The declaration's last two articles, however, gave the PAB a special character during the next three years and clearly revealed the great influence recently won by Maurice Duhamel inside the nationalist leadership.

Article VI committed the Autonomist party and *Breiz Atao* to a federalist point of view, explaining that modern European states did not represent definitive political forms and were fated to disappear once the historical conditions that originally shaped them had passed away. It further explained that Europe was destined sooner or later to become a single economic unit, a transition that would ultimately require the formation of a new European political structure. The best such structure and the one most likely to emerge, the document continued, was a continental federation of all the ethnic nationalities of Europe, including the Bretons. Yet Article VI pointedly made the recognition of the Breton nation inside an ethnically organized European federation the long-term objective of the PAB. In the meantime it conceded that the program outlined in the five preceding articles had to be realized within the framework of the French state "for our union is a fact and does not constitute an obstacle to the attainment of our essential goals." All that it demanded was that France remodel its internal organization according to federalist principles, "today the pattern of the most advanced peoples." The Declaration of Châteaulin thus ended with the final article asserting that it was up to France to make known "if we may have confidence in its renewing forces or if we can remain Bretons only by ceasing to be French citizens."

The Duhamel-inspired section of the Declaration of Châteaulin had two important implications for the Breton nationalist movement. First, it seemed to make the cause of Brittany dependent on French or international developments while, secondly, it substantially moderated the often hostile attitude of the Autonomist party and its organ toward France. Neither was to the private liking of intransigent nationalists like Mordrel and Debauvais. Both men knew, however, that it was hardly the time to raise objections since Châteaulin appeared to mark a decisive step forward in the development of the nationalist movement. Indeed, during the second half of 1928 the prospects of the nationalists improved significantly. Voluntary cash contributions continued to flow into the party treasury so that by the end of the year a ten-thousand-franc fund drive begun in June was fully covered. In addition, all 850 shares in *Breiz Atao*'s financing corporation were subscribed by early 1929, thereby enabling the nationalist newspaper to begin weekly publication in February.

Other indications demonstrated that the Breton nationalist movement was gaining momentum and beginning to attract the notice of the general public. One of these was the rallying to the PAB and *Breiz Atao* of hitherto reluctant veterans of pre-1914 Breton action. Camille Le Mercier d'Erm was the first and most important of these figures to embrace the efforts of the postwar nationalists. In a public speech reported by *Breiz Atao* in September 1928 he saluted the PAB and claimed to see in it "the realization of the dreams of the Breton patriots of my generation." He even wrote Régis de l'Estourbeillon and urged the URB president to merge his Breton regionalist society with the new Autonomist party, "the sole movement of the future in Brittany."[1] Estourbeillon ignored the request and Le Mercier d'Erm presumably quit the URB, as he had promised to do if his call for Breton union went unheeded. His subsequent adhesion to the PAB—like that of Louis-N. Le Roux at the end of the year—was of considerable symbolic importance since it helped bridge the gap between the pre- and postwar Breton nationalist movements.

Even more important to the PAB nationalists than the public approval of their prewar predecessors in Breton national action was the publicity their Châteaulin congress received in the French and international press. While journalists virtually ignored the Rosporden meeting, they gave the second PAB assembly widespread, if hostile, attention. No fewer than seventy-seven French papers, including all the major Parisian dailies except the Catholic *Le Croix* and the communist *Humanité*, carried stories on it. In addition, seventeen German papers, nine from Switzerland, two from Italy, and one each from Belgium, Estonia, Poland, and Scandinavia published reports of the Châteaulin proceedings. Olier Mordrel consequently observed in December 1928 that the second PAB congress would go down "as a great date in the history of national minorities in general and in the renaissance of Brittany in particular."[2] Although the nationalist leader surely exaggerated, the extensive press coverage of the PAB congress at Châteaulin nonetheless helped make Breton nationalism, perhaps for the first time, a real public and political issue in France.

The accelerating hostility French authorities directed at the PAB and *Breiz Atao* also showed that the Breton nationalist movement was becoming a matter of official concern. Even before Châteaulin the police searched the homes of leading nationalists at Rennes and Quimper in a futile effort to uncover incriminating evidence that would tie both the Breton and the Alsatian autonomist movements to German subsidies.[3] After the congress had taken place, the police in October seized a display of allegedly seditious postcards and pamphlets exhibited by the PAB at a fair-exposition then being held in Morlaix. No doubt, Mordrel wrote at the time, "France was in deadly peril and the timely action by the police at Morlaix was destined to rank in the annals of French heroism just after the lifting of the bedsheets of Châteaulin!" *Breiz Atao* regularly reported similar instances of official harassment during the next several months. In March 1929 Rennes police painted over PAB posters on the walls of the city and their Parisian counterparts arrested a young nationalist named Ronan Arot for selling the PAB organ on the streets of the French capital. By the end of April Arot had been arrested another seven times for the same offense. Agents of the central government also did their best to harass the Breton nationalists. In March 1929, for example, transportation officials forbade the sale of *Breiz Atao* in French rail terminals and military authorities in December prohibited its receipt by Breton soldiers in French army barracks.

Hoping to draw political profit from all this newfound notoriety, the PAB in 1928 committed itself to contesting the 1932 parliamentary elections, a premature announcement if ever there were one. Nationalist leaders thus brought under close scrutiny the public actions of French politicians, especially deputies and senators sent to Paris by Breton constituencies. During the two years after Châteaulin the pages of *Breiz Atao* were consequently crowded with sniping attacks on "anti-Breton" deputies from the peninsula and with menacing language about electoral reprisals to come in 1932. The forty-four representatives of Brittany in the Chamber, Duhamel typically declared in January 1929, were "only beggars after decorations, draft deferments, and tobacco shop licenses." In the following month he ridiculed Senator Jenouvrier as a victim of senility when the latter noted in parliament that he had difficulty finding a copy of *Breiz Atao* at Rennes. When Senator de Kereguézec seconded his colleague's remark, Duhamel said that the nationalists would have some surprises for him in his "electoral fief" in Trégor. Mordrel's favorite target was Joseph Cadic, a deputy who insisted that the Breton nationalist movement was "the work of a few excitable Parisians not originally from Brittany." Such a man, Mordrel sneered in February 1929, was unfit to speak for Brittany because he had "nothing in his belly, heart, or head. The man is empty. He covers his country with shame and ridicule every time its name comes up in the Chamber." The nationalist leader promised that Cadic would also be taken care of in 1932.

Much as nationalist writers liked to assail Brittany's parliamentary representatives in *Breiz Atao*, they enjoyed even more showering abuse on prominent French politicians, especially cabinet ministers. These public figures were usually attacked for their supposed neglect of Brittany's interests or their alleged persecution of Breton culture. Breton nationalists did not shrink, however, from the most grossly unfair kind of vilification. In April 1929, for example, an anonymous writer in *Breiz Atao* sought to discredit the French minister of justice Louis Barthou by making much of his brother's record as a deserter from the French army. But it was the stiffly correct premier Raymond Poincaré who drew the most consistently hostile treatment from the Breton nationalists. The campaign against Poincaré peaked in early 1929 after he charged in a January Senate speech that the PAB "was born in Alsace, if not further away in the pan-German associations on the right bank of the Rhine."[4] In a February "open letter" to the French premier Fanch Debauvais heatedly denied this accusation, arguing that Breton autonomism was the product of unrelenting French efforts to assimilate Bretons and to destroy their Celtic nationality. He went on to accuse Poincaré of making a straw man of the Breton danger in order to win support for the so-called *loi scélérate* drafted by his government to prosecute Alsatian autonomists. After referring to Barthou as an "anthropoid," Duhamel simply dismissed Poincaré's entire government as one of "immature fascism in the form of a ridiculous praetorian dictatorship."

The Breton nationalist campaign against the Poincaré administration continued for the next several months and virtually became the leitmotif of *Breiz Atao*. In March the PAB endorsed a nationwide French movement that sought legislative repeal of the *loi scélérate*. In April the nationalists refused to join the official mourning for the just-deceased Marshal Ferdinand Foch. In May Duhamel went to Strasbourg, where he accused the French premier of denying some time before that an autonomist movement existed in Brittany and then several months later spending more than an hour of public time refuting its claims. Poincaré abruptly retired from office in July 1929, however, and the Breton nationalists thus lost their favorite whipping boy. The new premier, Aristide Briand, seemed a much less suitable target for their abuse since he was a federalist of sorts and a native-born Breton in the bargain. Duhamel nevertheless rejected Briand's sudden proposal for a European federal union in 1929 because it involved only limited cooperation among the existing states of the continent and did not call for the recognition of all Europe's ethnic minorities. The leaders of the PAB in any case had more pressing things to worry about by midsummer 1929 than Aristide Briand's vague federalist ideas.

The major cause for their anxiety was that the rapid growth of the nationalist movement in recent months was beginning to outstrip its meager resources. Duhamel reported in June 1929 that the material situation of *Breiz Atao* was not encouraging. Immediate post-Châteaulin enthusiasm was flagging, proselytizing efforts were waning, and pledges to buy shares in *Breiz Atao*'s financing corporation were not being honored. Furthermore, and in part a consequence of the Poincaré devaluation, the cost of editing, printing, and distributing the nationalist organ had more than doubled. The very success of the new weekly format of *Breiz Atao*,

Duhamel lamented, had encouraged apathy among the nationalist rank and file. The sluggish response to a new twenty-thousand-franc fund drive opened in June showed how real that apathy was. After a month fewer than twenty-four hundred francs had been collected. The financial situation of the nationalist movement continued to worsen during the summer and became so critical in August that Mordrel bruited the possibility of suspending publication of *Breiz Atao*. These problems were further aggravated when dissension within the PAB surfaced in July. Although its nature was not immediately made known, it undoubtedly involved objections by those who opposed the new Duhamel-inspired emphasis on European federalism. Whatever it was, Mordrel assured the nationalist membership that the problem would be thoroughly examined at the upcoming PAB congress scheduled for Rennes during the first week of September.

The first order of business at Rennes was to deal with the deteriorating situation of the PAB and *Breiz Atao*. Mordrel did not try to hide how serious that situation had become. The twenty-thousand franc fund drive was still only three-quarters pledged. Although its weekly press run had been doubled since the first of the year, the number of *Breiz Atao* subscribers had grown by only 21 percent. Newsstand vendors willing to sell the nationalist organ had been found, moreover, in fewer than one-third of the communes where the PAB leadership considered its sale essential. Mordrel ended his doleful account by reporting that many of the local sections of the Autonomist party were languishing for lack of money and members. In accordance with his recommendations the assembled delegates took immediate measures to stave off what was clearly an impending crisis. First they issued an urgent appeal to the rank and file to put the uncompleted fund drive over the top. Then they voted to group the local sections of the PAB into federations in order to reanimate those that were nearly moribund. The most important of the measures recommended by Mordrel and endorsed by the congress was a plan to reduce expenses through the organization of the Imprimerie Commerciale de Bretagne to print *Breiz Atao* and all other nationalist publications. Put under the formal control of Debauvais, the new printworks was to be capitalized by the sale of five hundred shares of stock at five hundred francs each. The plan seemed an immediate success, for by the end of the following month the entire stock issue had been pledged, one-quarter of it by the Banque de Bretagne alone. Finally, Debauvais—already weakened by the tubercular condition that eventually killed him in 1944—had his administrative duties at *Breiz Atao* lightened by the addition of Yann Bricler and two other nationalists to his staff.

During the ideological discussions that followed, considerable resistance developed to the post-Châteaulin federalist line of the PAB. The leader of the dissent was none other than Olier Mordrel, who in his report on the "moral" situation of the party insisted that federalism was never "the motive force of our enthusiasm" but had been embraced for simple reasons of expediency. He explained that these reasons were to give the Autonomist party a broader appeal than it otherwise possessed and to shield its members from charges of "blind particularism" that, the French often used to discredit movements like their own. But, Mordrel warned, Breton nationalists would never fall into what he called "a federalist exaggeration." Nor would they wait passively on events in France or elsewhere for the winning of Breton autonomy. "With or without federalism," he concluded, "we must have autonomy and we will have it. We haven't time to wait."[5] Duhamel and those who backed him were thenceforth on notice that they threatened the internal cohesion of the PAB if they continued to insist on their federalist ideas at the expense of particular Breton nationalist interests.

For the time being Mordrel's warnings were unavailing because the federalists had a majority at Rennes and insisted over his objections that the Châteaulin line be continued. Moreover, during the months that followed, federalism all but replaced Breton nationalism as the characteristic ideological motif of the PAB and *Breiz Atao*. By the end of the year Mordrel and Debauvais had been virtually supplanted by Duhamel and a group of left-leaning federalists. They were soon joined by Maurice Marchal—by this time a fervent federalist and moving further to the left every day—who once more became a prominent figure in the PAB leadership. With the apparent triumph of the Breton federalists over the integral nationalists the stage was set for the gravest crisis since 1914 to strike the Breton movement. Politically oriented by nature, Duhamel, Marchal and their colleagues were too quick to commit the fortunes of the nationalist movement to the outcome of an electoral contest. Their decision to enter the French political arena and present a PAB candidate at the next parliamentary bye-election in Brittany indeed provoked the upcoming crisis. This decision had been overwhelmingly ratified at Rennes despite the warnings of Mordrel that the nationalists were embarking on a dangerous course. He feared, quite rightly as events soon proved, that the Breton nationalist party was still too small to win an electoral victory and too weak to sustain a crushing defeat.

The federalist leadership of the PAB had to wait until the spring of 1930 for a chance to offer their candidate. On 22 March *Breiz Atao* announced that Goulven Mazéas, associated with the nationalist movement since 1919, would contest the parliamentary bye-election scheduled for 6 April at Guingamp as a PAB republican federalist. The Autonomist party mounted a major effort on behalf of Mazéas, who stood on an electoral platform of autonomy for Brittany within a federalized French state. Its leaders spent more than ten thousand francs on his three-week campaign, most of the money going for printing and distribution of twenty thousand copies of *Breiz Atao* for each of the two weeks remaining before 6 April. On the eve of the election itself every voter in the district received an additional special issue of the PAB organ, while buildings near the polling place were heavily postered. Despite his misgivings, even Mordrel threw himself into the campaign and with the aid of Debauvais organized sixty nationalist rallies. All these efforts were to go unrewarded, however, for Mazéas obtained a scant 349 of 13,872 votes cast in the first round and only a few more, 376, in the second.

Although the nationalists showed great ingenuity in making excuses for this stunning defeat, nothing could hide the obvious fact that Breton nationalism had been crushed at the polls.[6] The decision of the federalist leadership to participate in the electoral system of France had, by an ironic turn of events, revealed the political isolation of the PAB in Brittany.

To suggest, as Mordrel subsequently did in his memoirs, that extrapolating the vote for Mazéas in 1930 to the rest of the peninsula indicated the existence of twenty thousand nationalist sympathizers at the time in Brittany hardly diminishes the sense of that isolation.[7] More to the point was his original opposition at Rennes to the involvement of the PAB in electoral politics, an attitude entirely vindicated by the verdict at Guingamp. As it turned out, Mazéas's overwhelming defeat had a decisive impact on the future direction of the Breton nationalist movement, for it immediately put PAB federalists on the defensive and thus provided the integral nationalists headed by Olier Mordrel and Fanch Debauvais with an excellent position from which to resume control of the party and its organ. Indeed, their claims to leadership had been all the more strengthened by their recent soldierly efforts on behalf of a policy they considered both strategically inappropriate and tactically inopportune.

Leading the PAB immediately after Guingamp was in any case a far-from-enviable task. The ill-fated Mazéas campaign left the nationalist movement plunged deeply into debt and with little prospect of raising enough money for even its most pressing financial obligations. At the end of April *Breiz Atao* urgently called on its readers for voluntary contributions of ten thousand francs so that electoral expenses not assumed by Mazéas himself could be paid; it took until mid-December to collect this sum. In May Mordrel openly admitted that lack of funds and the nationalists' failure to pay outstanding debts had completely paralyzed the PAB.[8] Subscriptions to *Breiz Atao* began to fall off, declining by nearly 50 percent in June 1930 alone. It was in the midst of this sense of approaching disaster that the fourth annual congress of the PAB convened at St.-Brieuc in early September. At that meeting Debauvais confirmed that the nationalist movement found itself in a gloomy situation. Advertising had produced only ninety-five hundred francs of revenue for *Breiz Atao* during the previous year, while approximately one-fifth of its press run every week went unsold. Debauvais thus concluded that not only would the price of the nationalist organ have to be raised but additional funds would have to be found by other means if *Breiz Atao* were not to revert to monthly publication or to disappear altogether.

After Debauvais's somber remarks Mordrel followed with a "moral report" on the general situation of the nationalist movement. In it he called for an end to abstract theorizing and more attention to building a truly mass party. Above all he thought it essential to rekindle in the PAB a new sense of unity while at the same time "keeping our doctrines pure." Mordrel clearly aimed his words at the federalists and told them in effect either to conform to the ideas of Breton nationalism pure and simple or to get out. Maurice Duhamel elected to get out, but not before another six months had passed. In his letter of resignation he lamented that, unlike himself, the integral nationalists who now controlled the PAB considered federalism a matter of secondary importance, and thus he had to leave. Duhamel also offered his own explanation of the PAB's poor showing in the Guingamp bye-election. The fundamental reason, he thought, was that Mazéas had tried to claim political and ideological neutrality on all matters except those that directly related to Breton national revival. But the peninsula's voters, he reasoned, however sympathetic they might be to Breton nationalism, would never give their electoral support to a PAB candidate so long as they did not know where he stood on other issues. Yet PAB candidates themselves were compelled to claim such neutrality precisely because there was so much general political and ideological disagreement within the nationalist movement.[9] It was a closed circle from which Duhamel believed there was no easy escape and which he thought spelled defeat at the polls for Breton nationalist candidates in the foreseeable future.

Mordrel and Debauvais did not address themselves directly to the issues raised by Duhamel in his explanation of the PAB failure at Guingamp. Instead they simply dismissed Duhamel and his federalist supporters as a factional group of left-wing deviationists and hoped that all those who remained in the Autonomist party would follow their leader's course of resignation. They nonetheless agreed with Duhamel that the issue separating them from the federalists was one of priorities. The reorganization of Europe was the primary aim of the latter, while for Mordrel and Debauvais the revival of a "free Brittany" came before everything else. "We have problems that are not necessarily European," they further explained, "but on whose solution our daily life depends. We are interested in international federalism, but as Bretons. We are international federalists, but we are Bretons first of all."[10] They therefore declared that Duhamel's withdrawal meant the Breton nationalist movement, though it had been "materially diminished," had for all that been "morally reinforced." The PAB and *Breiz Atao*, Mordrel and Debauvais assured their audience in conclusion, would endure and continue their historic mission.

The two nationalist leaders publicly expressed at St.-Brieuc more confidence in *Breiz Atao*'s chances for continued survival than they actually believed in privately. In fact Debauvais had already confidentially suggested to his colleagues in December 1930 that it might be "judicious" to withdraw *Breiz Atao* from general circulation while retaining it as a purely internal party organ. Publicly, he proposed to replace it with a new weekly called *Le Peuple Breton*, whose primary focus would be on the defense of Breton economic interests. Since it would by design be kept free of "compromising political ideas," Debauvais felt certain that such a Breton periodical was more likely to attract the adequate financial backing that always seemed to elude *Breiz Atao*.[11] This proposal was not acted upon and in February 1931 Debauvais had to announce that for lack of funds the publication of *Breiz Atao* would have to be temporarily suspended. He also revealed that during the previous two months several thousand francs of anticipated income from subscription renewals had been spent. Unfortunately, however, most had not been renewed and there were no new subscriptions to take their place. Moreover, some of the prospective investors in the Imprimerie Commerciale had failed to honor their pledges to buy shares of its stock. The consequence of all this was that *Breiz Atao* not only was broke but also had an outstanding debt of twenty-two thousand francs that fell due at the end of April. Debauvais recommended that an emergency congress of the PAB be convened at Rennes on 5 April to deal with this perilous situation. Meanwhile he once again appealed for voluntary contributions so that the PAB could meet its most pressing obligations. That fewer than thirty-five hundred francs had been collected by 5 April only confirmed the gravity of the crisis into which the Breton nationalist movement had fallen.

The meeting at Rennes was a tumultuous affair. Those present split into two factions. On the one side were those who shared the integral nationalist views of Mordrel and Debauvais, while on the other were those who favored the federalist doctrines of Maurice Duhamel. Most of the latter group belonged to the local Rennes section of the PAB and had Maurice Marchal and Ronan Klec'h for their leaders. They demanded that Debauvais make a full and detailed accounting of the financial situation of *Breiz Atao*. He was thus forced to reveal that nine-tenths of the one hundred thousand francs originally raised to capitalize the nationalist organ's financing corporation had been spent, while the current short-term indebtedness of the nationalist movement stood at forty thousand francs. The Marchal-Klec'h group promptly accused Debauvais of mismanagement and introduced a motion of nonconfidence in his and Mordrel's stewardship. Its quick approval shocked the two veteran leaders and brought home to them the folly of their careless decision to convene the PAB crisis meeting in the only Breton city where the local party section was dominated by federalists. Mordrel and Debauvais resigned. The unexpectedly triumphant federalists then proceeded to adopt a resolution that protested the earlier departure of Duhamel and called for a return to Declaration of Châteaulin.[12]

Mordrel and Debauvais protested this resolution and insisted that a full-scale debate be held on the proper ideological line for the PAB to take. Confident of its majority, the Marchal-Klec'h group yielded to the demand. Debauvais began by asserting that the Autonomist party must base its action on a specifically Breton point of view. Such an orientation meant above all else that the party must aim for the creation of an autonomous Breton state, an objective that could not be subordinated "to the more or less distant application of the federalist system." Federalism might well be a bewitching idea, he argued, but it was only one of several ways to gain autonomy for Brittany, not an end in itself. Debauvais concluded by advising his listeners that instead of pursuing such ideological detours, the PAB ought to confine itself to more narrowly "nationalist and educative" tasks. Marchal rejected

Debauvais's "too narrow view of Brittany and the world." He believed on the contrary that Bretons were obliged in the name of justice to associate their efforts with those of other peoples who also struggled for their national existence. He thought, moreover, that Brittany's salvation was a matter of politics and that it could be best accomplished by means of a combined Breton and federalist policy. As he put it, the federalists favored "the political over the sentimental vision of the Breton question."

Marchal had more sympathizers in the audience than did Mordrel and Debauvais and his views won the support of a large majority, which again reaffirmed the Declaration of Châteaulin. The federalists then proceeded to reorganize the nationalist movement. Five of their number were named to form a new editorial executive committee for *Breiz Atao*, which was returned to semimonthly publication.[13] Debauvais was ousted from his post as administrator of the party organ but, perhaps as a sop to the integral nationalists, he was appointed to the largely meaningless position of provisional secretary of the PAB. The Marchal-Klec'h majority chose to make no conciliatory gesture at all to Olier Mordrel and simply left him out in the cold.

The apparent victory of the federalists at Rennes blew the Breton nationalist movement wide open. The new five-man editorial board of *Breiz Atao* brought out two issues of the PAB organ and then, without consulting either Mordrel or Debauvais, on 7 June abruptly changed its name to *La Nation Bretonne*.[14] An enraged Debauvais reacted by single-handedly bringing out his own version of *Breiz Atao* the following week. He began it with number 145 in order to emphasize continuity with the past and declared that his publication was the official organ of the nationalist movement. The federalists responded by expelling Debauvais from the Rennes section of of the PAB. He was also censured in a joint resolution proposed by the Trégor-Geolo and Haute-Cornouaille party federations that had rallied to *La Nation Bretonne*. In retaliation for what he called his "exclusion from the affairs of the party" Debauvais refused to turn over to its new federalist leaders the PAB account books that he had always kept. He also prevented them from using a postal box at Rennes that had long

been the permanent mailing address of the nationalist movement. Finally, at a stockholders' meeting of the Imprimerie
Commerciale on 28 June Debauvais assured his control of the
recently purchased PAB printworks. He thus deprived his adversaries at *La Nation Bretonne* of the most valuable material
asset in the possession of the Breton nationalist movement.

Although Klec'h and his federalist colleagues were able
to publish *La Nation Bretonne* until the middle of August, they
faced increasingly serious difficulties. First there was the resignation in June of Fant Roseg-Meavenn, the only female
members of the new editorial staff, who quit amid charges
that she was incompetent and a gossip-mongerer.[15] More
important, by July there were growing complaints of deficits
at *La Nation Bretonne* and the inability of the new party leadership to raise money to cover them. The situation of the federalist organ soon became so grave that its continued existence
hung in the balance. Indeed its editors announced in early
July that the next regular congress of the PAB, scheduled to
take place the following month, would decide the fate of the
periodical. The new leaders of the nationalist movement at
the same time began to show signs that they regretted the
schism that had developed at Rennes. Ronan Klec'h himself
took the initiative in organizing a meeting of "compromise
and reconciliation" at Guingamp on 19 July to which he invited delegates from all the quarreling nationalist factions. At
that time representatives ranging from the extreme right to
the communist left signed a "statement of solidarity" affirming that *Breiz Atao* was the sole official organ of the PAB.[16] The
practical effect of this action was that *La Nation Bretonne* disappeared after the publication of its fifth issue on 16 August.
The heady April triumph of the federalists had obviously
turned sour only four months later.

While federalists and integral nationalists struggled for
control of the PAB, further splintering of the Breton nationalist movement occurred elsewhere. In the spring of 1931 dissident Catholic conservatives split away from the PAB and
founded an ephemeral Parti Nationaliste Intégral Breton
whose ideological organ was *Breiz da Zont* (*La Bretagne de De-
main*). This tiny group of Breton extremists advocated separatism pure and simple for Brittany.[17] Their political ideas

otherwise amounted to a confused jumble of notions drawn from assorted right-wing ideologies. Thus *Breiz da Zont* variously announced that members of the PNIB were anti-Semites, racists, admirers of Italian fascism and German Nazism, and proponents of all dictatorial forms of government. They were also supposed to be hearty advocates of the leadership principle though they themselves remained leaderless. After a perfectly quixotic existence that finally saw all these reactionary political ideas grafted onto enthusiasm for monarchical government, the PNIB and its organ folded in June 1934. Its members, few as they were, rejoined the *Breiz Atao* movement in the mid-1930s.[18]

Breiz da Zont had its counterpart on the extreme left of the Breton nationalist movement when the turbulent Guingamp section of the PAB founded *War Zao* (*Debout*) in July 1931. Most of this group were Bretonnants who in the tradition of Emile Masson called themselves progressive integral nationalists. Its leaders believed that a thorough housecleaning of the Breton nationalist movement was in order. They rejected federalism as the abandonment of Breton national feeling and demanded that *Breiz Atao* return to the exclusively nationalist program of its pre-Châteaulin period.[19] On the other hand, the *War Zao* leaders had little use for Mordrel and Debauvais, whose oft-expressed aversion for progressive social ideas they found repugnant. What in fact the nationalist movement had to do, a *War Zao* spokesman insisted in July, was to link militant Breton national feeling with advocacy of socialist revolution. He pledged that his group would press these views at the upcoming PAB congress to be held the following month at Guingamp.[20]

Mordrel and Debauvais meanwhile prepared carefully for the August meeting of the nationalist movement so that they would not be caught short as they had been in April at Rennes. These precautions paid off, for the two veteran leaders enjoyed a decisive majority at Guingamp. The victory was clear at the outset when André Gefflot, one of the leading federalists, presented a favorable report on the short-lived *La Nation Bretonne* and moved that it be adopted by the assembled delegates. Instead the report was almost unanimously rejected. He immediately announced from the floor the formation of the Ligue Fédéraliste de Bretagne and then with the rest of the federalists quit the PAB congress.[21] After denouncing Gefflot and his friends as a pack of troublemakers, Debauvais solemnly declared that their departure "morally strengthened" the nationalist movement. Yet he and the others who remained at Guingamp felt that the PAB had been so badly damaged in the affair that a radical reorganization was necessary. They accordingly adopted a resolution that repudiated the existing party statutes along with the Declaration of Châteaulin. They then rechristened their movement as the Parti National Breton (PNB) and charged a committee headed by Debauvais to draft a new party constitution.

Debauvais planned to offer this document at yet another meeting of the nationalist movement in December. In the meantime he resumed publication of *Breiz Atao*. The first issue of the revived nationalist organ in November 1931 devoted much space to the Mordrel-Debauvais version of the recent crisis of the PAB. It was also replete with attacks on the *War Zao* group, which stubbornly remained in existence after the August congress. This group's frank espousal of socialism was castigated as divisive. Moreover, its emphasis on an "alien ideology"—Marxism—tended, like federalism, to relegate the Breton question to a position of secondary importance. Its anticlericalism allegedly contained the germ of heresy. But worst of all from the point of view of Mordrel and Debauvais, the *War Zao* group seemed determined to provoke another rupture in the Breton nationalist movement by insisting on its separate organizational existence. This attitude, *Breiz Atao* warned, could only lead to anarchy and indiscipline. Should it persist, the exclusion of the Guingamp section of the Nationalist party would be rendered inevitable.

Mordrel and Debauvais could hardly afford the luxury of another intraparty quarrel. It was task enough to keep *Breiz Atao* alive. The last months of 1931 and the first half of 1932 indeed produced little more than frustration for the two nationalist leaders. The movement they had so laboriously nurtured since 1919 lay in ruins, shattered by conflicting ambitions, personal rivalries, and ideological disagreements. So many nationalists had been alienated by this confusion that fewer than two dozen persons attended the Landerneau congress of the PNB in December 1931. In this progressively desperate situation all that Mordrel and Debauvais could do was reprint tired old articles from earlier *Breiz Atao* issues, complain about lack of money and supporters, and hope for a sudden gift from Providence. But it seemed a losing battle. The nationalist organ declined from a pamphlet-sized monthly of thirty-two pages in April 1932 to sixteen in May and finally to eight in June. The number of its subscribers had also fallen off to three hundred by June and many of these had not renewed their subscriptions for the following year.

Even the most sanguine nationalists would have been inclined to concede at midyear 1932 that the Breton nationalist movement was in its death throes. It was no more than retrospective insight that permitted Olier Mordrel to claim forty years later in his memoirs that "the crisis through which *Breiz Atao* had just passed was in reality only a financial embarrassment complicated by a doctrinal controversy, and in no way the swan song of our movement."[22] To nationalists at the time, perhaps even to Mordrel himself, it must have seemed that only a miracle could stave off the impending final death. The miracle, less the work of Providence than that of desperate calculation, came in the form of a sensational explosion at Rennes in August 1932. With that event was initiated not just the revival of the Breton nationalist movement but also the beginning of its involvement with terror and proto-fascist extremism.

CHAPTER 6

❧ *The Parti National Breton and Separatism*

In 1932 the city of Vannes decided to commemorate the fourth centenary of the Franco-Breton treaty of union on 7 August. The newly installed government of Edouard Herriot voted a subsidy of three hundred thousand francs for the event and the premier himself announced that he would attend. Anticipating that the occasion would be used to stress the Frenchness of Brittany, all the Breton patriotic societies denounced the planned celebration and unanimously refused the invitation of the Vannes mayor to take part in its festivities. Predictably, the PNB was the most vehement in its denunciations and urged party members to be in Vannes on 7 August so that they could "express the Breton people's disapproval of this shameful commemoration of our annexation."[1] The PNB leaders would themselves be in Vannes to jeer the French premier and, as Mordrel much later explained in his memoirs, so that they would have alibis for events elsewhere. There was a hint on 6 August of what those events might be. An anonymous note in a Rennes newspaper that day warned obliquely that the notorious Boucher statue of 1911 was a possible target for attack. The author of the note went on to say that he could never understand why Breton patriots had tolerated the statue for so long as a symbolic representation of Brittany's union to France. "Brittany need kneel before no one," he added, and called on the Rennes city council to remove the insulting *"salade de bronze"* it had placed in the facade of the municipal building.[2]

Despite the 6 August warning the authorities took no exceptional measures against the possibility that someone might try to remove the "bronze salad" by force. They were thus caught completely unprepared when in the early morning hours of 7 August Boucher's so-called monument of national shame was dynamited into a tangle of twisted metal. Informed of the explosion aboard his train during a stopover at Redon, Herriot consulted with his advisers and decided to continue on to Vannes as if nothing out of the ordinary had happened. There the commemorative ceremony proceeded without further incident, although several of the participating dignitaries took the occasion to condemn what had happened at Rennes. Herriot himself called the explosion "an idiotic act."

The Vannes police meanwhile ordered the arrest of all suspected autonomists. In the ensuing roundup Debauvais, Bricler, and a score of other PNB militants as well as nationalists associated with *War Zao*, *Breiz Digabestr*, and *La Bretagne Fédérale* were seized and held overnight for questioning. Protracted interrogation yielded no information and all were released the following morning. That same day Brittany's major dailies editorially denounced the Rennes explosion. They demanded arrests and hoped that those found to have committed the foul deed would be executed.[3] The headquarters of the PNB were indeed searched on 8 August but no incriminating evidence was found. The next day Debauvais and two other nationalists once more came under interrogation but again the police learned nothing. The peninsular press and French officialdom thereafter tended to downplay the importance of the incident. Breton nationalists on the other hand reacted to news of the explosion with guarded approval and insisted on its historic significance. An unsigned *Breiz Atao* editorial of 13 August hence proclaimed it to be "the first sign, the first cry of an awakening of our people." High-mindedly observing that violence "ill-served the best of causes," Fanch Debauvais nonetheless denied that the nationalists were in any way responsible for the explosion.[4]

On 11 August a sensational new development in the case impelled the authorities to redouble their efforts to find the perpetrators of the Rennes affair. That day the Paris press published the text of a communiqué that all the major dailies of the French capital had anonymously received on 7 August.

Mysteriously signed "Gwenn-ha-Du" ("Blanc et Noir"), the popular name of the Breton nationalist flag designed some years before by Maurice Marchal, the communiqué read as follows:

> The French today celebrate the fourth centenary of their victory over and annexation of Brittany. Forever Bretons, unconquered despite four centuries of French occupation, we have decided for the greatest good of the Breton nation to put once more the destiny of their fatherland in the hands of Bretons. We open the struggle for the deliverance of our country on this anniversary of our annexation with the destruction of the symbol of our servitude that occupies the place of honor in the center of our capital.[5]

Who the authors of this document were, what influence they had in the Breton nationalist movement, when, where, and how they might strike again nobody seemed to know. But about one thing there could be little doubt. The appearance of Gwenn-ha-Du and its use of violence against France meant that the strictly legal phase of Breton action had come to an end.

The immediate impact of the audacious Gwenn-ha-Du communiqué was to throw down the gauntlet to the authorities, who called the Sûreté Nationale into the case. Thus began what one government official called "a pitiless repression" of Breton autonomism, but what Maurice Marchal instead characterized as "a reign of terror in Brittany."[6] During the three months that followed, the police questioned dozens of Bretons, including a score of the most prominent figures active in the Breton movement since prewar days. A few were actually arrested but all were released for lack of evidence. At the same time Breton nationalists also found themselves assailed from other directions. Archbishop Duparc forbade the circulation of *Breiz Atao* in his seminaries while the prefect of Finistère and the mayor of Brest jointly ordered Bleun-Brug not to hold its annual congress at Brest in August 1932. Perrot and his Catholic nationalist friends ignored this order and held their meeting as scheduled. The following month *Breiz Atao* reported that the Bleun-Brug congress was a tense affair. This was so because four hundred uninvited policemen attended and watched suspiciously as nationalist participants paraded Breton flags and instead of the "Marseillaise" pointedly sang the Breton anthem "Bro Goz Ma Zadou."

The fruitless efforts of the police continued until November when Gwenn-ha-Du struck again. After the embarrassing incident of August, Premier Herriot decided to return to Brittany in order to refurbish his tarnished image. He planned to arrive at Nantes on 20 November to dedicate in the palace where Anne of Brittany had been born a plaque commemorating the union of her province to France. Breton nationalists once more vented their indignation at this second prime ministerial foray onto the peninsula, and the authorities expected trouble. They deployed the police in force at Nantes to guard its public monuments, while at Rennes the gendarmerie was put on alert. The police might better have been at Ingrandes, a tiny village in Loire-Inférieure that straddles the historic Franco-Breton frontier. There at five o'clock in the morning on 20 November a small dynamite blast cut the tracks in front of Herriot's train. The damage was easily repaired, however, and the French premier arrived in Nantes only fifty minutes late. The dedicatory ceremony took place as scheduled, although Herriot had to endure the insulting catcalls of several PNB nationalists who defiantly waved little Breton flags. The affair was capped when the press once more received a communiqué from Gwenn-ha-Du that took credit for the Ingrandes explosion.

Embarrassed by their failure to shield Herriot from yet a second incident, the police intensified their efforts to track down the secret Breton terrorist society. They interrogated scores of nationalists and placed several of them under arrest.[7] But, as in August, the police uncovered no trace of Gwenn-ha-Du and in fact never did officially solve the case. They clearly suspected that Debauvais, Mordrel, and their friends in the PNB were not quite so ignorant of the identities and motives of the Gwenn-ha-Du terrorists as they always claimed to be. The columns of Breiz Atao were after all readily available to Gwenn-ha-Du, either to announce a forthcoming act of violence or to gloat over one recently accomplished. If the PNB leaders genuinely disapproved of the use of violent tactics, they would never have extended to the secret Breton society such open hospitality in their party organ. Yet Breiz

Atao consistently sought after 1932 to promote the idea that Gwenn-ha-Du was a mysterious organization, completely independent of and its members unknown to the leadership of the PNB.

In 1962 a pseudonymous writer named Lugan, a man surely privy to confidential information, examined closely the thesis that Gwenn-ha-Du was actually the work of nationalists connected with *Breiz Atao*. After reviewing much circumstantial evidence he concluded that the secret Breton society was the invention of Debauvais and the other leaders of the PNB.[8] Olier Mordrel cleared up the remaining mystery concerning Gwenn-ha-Du when he published his memoirs in 1973. He revealed that it had its origin in a small direct action society called Kentoc'h Mervel (Plutôt la Mort), created in 1929 by Célestin Laîné and Gwilherm Berthou, two young Breton extremists who chafed under the strict legalitarianism of the PAB. After breaking with Berthou in 1930 Laîné recruited several young Breton émigrés at Paris who shared his predilection for violence. These included Hervé Delaporte, Robert Le Helloco, Meavenn, Jacques de Quélan, Bayer du Kern, and Pierre Denis. With them Laîné late in 1930 reorganized his direct action society under its new name of Gwenn-ha-Du. The group subsequently decided to destroy the Boucher statue and Laîné himself, a chemical engineer, constructed the explosive device out of material furnished by Jeanne du Guerny, better known as the nationalist writer C. Danio. Laîné, moreover, was the person who actually placed the bomb behind the offending statue in the facade of the Rennes city hall.

Mordrel goes on to argue that there was no direct relationship between Gwenn-ha-Du and PNB. He explained that Laîné always demanded that his partners in clandestine Breton action refrain from public involvement in the legal nationalist movement, although Meavenn violated this rule with impunity. And it is indeed plausible that there was no direct link between the Nationalist party and the secret Breton society, for Mordrel and Laîné could barely tolerate each other. Yet Mordrel admits that he knew in advance that the Boucher statue would be destroyed. He had been approached at Quimper sometime before 7 August by a young woman he knew to be Laîné's mistress. Her mission was to ascertain the attitude of the PNB leadership toward the proposed operation and to secure at least the tacit approval of the Nationalist party. "I could have kissed her," Mordrel exclaims in his memoirs, a reaction that indicates the success of the young woman's mission. Mordrel and Debauvais nevertheless resolutely opposed Laîné's further intention to raise an armed rebellion in Brittany. Mordrel in particular considered it an unrealistic tactic "at least as premature as electoral pretensions." Both required workers, money, and the support of a substantial part of Breton public opinion, but the nationalist movement, whether legalitarian or terrorist, had none of these. Thus Mordrel concluded that Gwenn-ha-Du's violent exploits, like nationalist electoral candidacies, possessed no more than symbolic value. To go beyond purely symbolic acts, he knew from recent bitter experience, risked compromising the entire nationalist enterprise in the eyes of Breton public opinion.

Keeping the turbulent Célestin Laîné within the bounds of symbolic action required the creation in May 1933 of a highly secret steering committee called Kuzul Meur (Grand Conseil). Composed of two members each from the PNB and Gwenn-ha-Du and one from Bleun-Brug, this body was ostensibly designed by Mordrel to function as a coordinating mechanism for the activities of the three nationalist groups. It actually served to keep Gwenn-ha-Du in check, for each of its three constituent societies agreed to submit in advance all their individual decisions to the others for collective approval. But the five-member Kuzul Meur had a permanent legalitarian majority in the persons of Mordrel and Debauvais for the PNB and Raymond Delaporte for Bleun-Brug. Such a distribution meant that these three possessed an effective veto to restrain violent projects by the two Gwenn-ha-Du extremists on the committee, Laîné and his lawyer friend Le Helloco. How Laîné was induced to serve on the Kuzul Meur and to accept his nemesis Mordrel as its permanent secretary, the latter chose not to explain in his memoirs.[9] Given the total ruthlessness of Mordrel's character, blackmail in the form of a threatened anonymous tip to the police concerning Laîné's illegal activities cannot be excluded. The Kuzul Meur arrangement was in any case so effective that Laîné withdrew from overt Breton action for several years and Gwenn-ha-Du was not heard from again until 1936.

The significance of Gwenn-ha-Du's appearance was there-fore not that it signaled the beginning of a prolonged campaign of violence on behalf of Brittany. It lay rather in the abrupt reversal that Gwenn-ha-Du's sensational entry on the Breton scene in August 1932 provoked in the declining fortunes of the Breton nationalist movement. A week after the Rennes explosion Mordrel and Debauvais were able to bring out a special *Breiz Atao* edition of twenty-five thousand copies, a figure several times the average press run for the spring of 1931. They performed a similar feat after the Ingrandes inci-dent. There were other signs of recovery as well. The continu-ing debt of the PNB, which at the end of 1931 stood at 46,631 francs, had by the end of February 1933 been almost halved. During the same period, Mordrel recalled in 1960, the number of *Breiz Atao*'s subscribers rose 65 percent while membership in the PNB grew 40 percent.[10] Many of those who had sepa-rated themselves from the *Breiz Atao* movement in 1931 were obviously returning to the fold.

Yann Sohier, the foremost leader of the Guingamp dissi-dents, gave the signal for this return when he agreed to discon-tinue *War Zao* and fully reunite with the PNB. There was a price to be paid for Sohier's gesture, however. Mordrel and Debau-vais had to agree to his plans to publish a Breton-language review for use by Bretonnant lay school teachers who favored classroom instruction in the old Celtic language. The problem was that Sohier—like so many of his former *War Zao* colleagues —was a communist determined to promote Marxist ideas in his new publication, which he provocatively called *Ar Falz (La Faucille)*. Mordrel and Debauvais abhorred Sohier's political ideas but they liked even less the prospect that the *War Zao* leader might gather the fruits of Gwenn-ha-Du violence and outflank the PNB on the integral Breton nationalist left. They had no other choice but to support *Ar Falz* morally and mate-rially while they gave it and its independent-minded director complete freedom of expression.

Mordrel and Debauvais meanwhile convened another na-tionalist congress at Landerneau on 3 September 1932 where they sponsored a reorganization of the PNB and supervised the reformulation of its Breton program. The thrust of their new party organization was to cast it in a decidedly authoritarian mold.[11] No more would the nationalist leadership be at the mercy of a hostile rank-and-file majority as at Rennes in April 1931. Top positions in the nationalist movement would no longer be filled by election but their occupants, according to the revised party constitution, would henceforth be "recruited by co-optation." Olier Mordrel promptly recruited himself to be editor-in-chief of *Breiz Atao* and claimed sole reponsibility for determining its political orientation. Fanch Debauvais likewise made himself leader of the PNB, although he formally served as head of a three-member executive committee that stood at the top of the new party organization. His position in the PNB was really no different than Mordrel's at *Breiz Atao*, for Debauvais's two executive committee colleagues possessed neither power nor responsibility and merely served at the pleasure of their chief. Within the nationalist movement the team of Mordrel and Debauvais was all-powerful. Only they could admit new members and expel those who opposed them. Only they could accredit new PNB sections. Only they could convoke party congresses and determine the agendas. Only they had the power to interpret party rules and doctrines. There was in fact no way short of resignation that dissidents could express dissatisfaction with the Mordrel-Debauvais leadership or try to alter the direction of party policy. The leadership principle so popular on the European right during the interwar decades had clearly been grafted onto the Breton nationalist movement.[12]

In the revision of its nationalist doctrine the PNB for the first time openly declared that it aimed for the political separation of Brittany from France and the creation of an independent Breton state on the Armorican peninsula.[13] "We do not want to be French," Debauvais explained in *Breiz Atao* at the end of August 1932, for "it is not just humiliation that we suffer but also the feeling of no longer being ourselves." The only way to end such personal alienation, he continued, was to raise the Breton people to "the rank of the other free peoples of Europe" and to restore to Brittany "the plenitude of its autochtonous culture, its rights, and its liberties." But there were those within the Nationalist party who rejected the separatist solution to the so-called Breton problem. Mordrel and Debauvais feared that these persons would leave the PNB if separatism were to receive pride of place in the doctrinal structure of the nationalist movement. The two leaders were also fully aware that achievement of the PNB's separatist goal still lay so far in the future that it was unrealistic to stress the alluring prospect of an independent Breton state in the party's militant action. For these reasons Mordrel and Debauvais drafted a minimum program of immediate concessions to be extracted from Paris while they waited for the day when they could present their full separatist demands for Breton independence.

Their minimum program aimed to return Brittany to an autonomous status like that enjoyed by the peninsula from 1532 to 1789. It thus called for Brittany's political and administrative reintegration into a unified governing structure through amalgamation of its five existing departmental councils into a single all-Breton assembly. This body would be endowed with exclusive legislative authority in all those areas that concerned the particular needs and interests of the Breton people. Culturally, the Mordrel-Debauvais minimum program called for the immediate introduction of the Breton language throughout the educational system of the peninsula and for the creation of courses in Breton history and geography. It also demanded the prompt establishment of a school of Breton-Celtic fine arts in Brittany and the formation of faculties of law and medicine. The remaining points of the minimum program dealt with economic affairs and sought to introduce the principle of compensation for centuries of alleged French neglect of Brittany's vital interests. The program accordingly demanded that Brest be transformed into a modern commercial seaport, that all peninsular railroads be of the same gauge and unified under the management of a Breton company, that a network of social insurance credit banks be established, and that tariffs be imposed in order to protect Breton agricultural and maritime industries from foreign competition.[14] Consistent with the European vogue of autarky at the time, Mordrel and Debauvais confidently expected that these measures would help create a self-sufficient Breton economy able to withstand the ruinous fluctuations of the French economic system.

Financially strengthened, structurally reorganized, and doctrinally revised, the Breton nationalist movement had by the end of 1933, according to a *Breiz Atao* editorial, completely recovered from the crisis of 1931. It was not an idle boast. The PNB's outstanding debt had been amortized and in September receipts began to exceed expenditures at the party treasury. Contemporaneously, *Breiz Atao*'s regular press run passed five thousand, while the party organization counted more than sixty local chapters. Yet despite the general optimism these developments engendered, the nationalist leadership saw two threats to the recovery of their movement's fortunes. The first of these, the danger that Breton patriotism might be compromised by thoughtless acts of Gwenn-ha-Du violence, had been effectively dealt with by the creation of the Kuzul Meur. Far more dangerous, and perhaps more difficult to counter, was the threat that Charles Maurras's Action Française posed to the Breton nationalist movement.

The substance of the threat lay in the nearly identical attacks that Action Française and Breton nationalism aimed, for different motives, at the regime in Paris. Accusations of corruption, rejection of parliamentary democracy, hostility to the republic, admiration for authoritarian forms of government —all these attitudes were shared by Maurras's followers and many members of the PNB. Several nationalist leaders had as a matter of fact been attracted to Action Française before they became involved in Breton national action. But they quickly realized that membership in both was contradictory; one could hardly be an integral French and Breton nationalist simultaneously. It was not ideological consistency that concerned Mordrel and Debauvais, however, but Action Française's superior drawing power. They particularly feared that Bretons disposed to authoritarian ideologies would be drawn to Maurras's movement rather than to the PNB simply because the chances of the former for success seemed so much greater. In the spring of 1933 Action Française therefore came under relentless attack in *Breiz Atao*. The case Breton nationalists developed against Maurras's movement centered on rejection of the notion that replacing the republic with a monarchy in Paris would mean the reversal of French centralizing policies. On the contrary, *Breiz Atao* pointed out in May that "decentralization runs counter to the work of the forty kings who during a thousand years made France." As for the federalism that

Action Française purported to champion, the nationalists dismissed it as wholly spurious. Maurras's party might be federalist in principle, an anonymous *Breiz Atao* writer warned in September, but its outspoken opposition to the cause of the Alsatian autonomists showed that "it is chauvinist in action." Once installed in power at Paris, he concluded, Action Française "like all French governments would demand that we sacrifice ourselves to the so-called general interest."

The PNB nationalists were not content simply to challenge Action Française in the columns of their newspaper. They were also anxious to meet them in face-to-face public confrontation. Mordrel and Debauvais accordingly announced a counter-rally to one organized by Maurras's best-known lieutenant, Leon Daudet, at St.-Goazec in Finistère on 10 September 1933. Both rallies proceeded without incident until the president of the local Action Française chapter observed in his welcoming speech that "the union of Brittany to France was sealed in blood. . . . We regard those who want to separate them as fools or criminals." The nationalists instantly began to taunt the Maurrasian speaker. A dozen or so Camelots du Roi then set upon Debauvais, the leader of the jeering Breton nationalist chorus, with clubs and beat him severely. Felled by a blow to the skull and bleeding profusely, the PNB leader was carried off the field with his nationalist compatriot Louis-N. Le Roux, who had also been injured in the melee.[15] *Breiz Atao* writers tried strenuously for a time to cast Debauvais and Le Roux in the image of Breton nationalist martyrs, but with no success. Enemies of the regime injured in a brawl with other enemies of the regime were perhaps not the most credible candidates for heroic treatment.

PNB leaders soon concluded that journalistic denunciations of Action Française and fisticuffs with its thuglike Camelots were inadequate means for dealing with the Maurrasian threat. They decided instead, as Olier Mordrel had been arguing for some time, that the nationalist movement had to counter this threat by outflanking Action Française on the authoritarian right with the PNB's own specifically Breton variety of fascism. This tactic found expression in SAGA (Strollad ar Gelted Adsavet, Réunion des Celtes relevés), a program of Breton fascism that Mordrel had been outlining in a series of *Breiz Atao* articles since March 1933. It is difficult to analyze

SAGA's intellectual content systematically because it flowed from Mordrel's disordered and eclectic mind in a confused jumble of irreconcilable ideas. These diverse fragments included bits and pieces of fascism, snippets of revolutionary communism, a dash of Christianity, and, for good measure, healthy respect for private property and other characteristic features of the capitalistic system. The basic appeal of the SAGA program was in any case racialist, for the fundamental assumption on which all Mordrel's ideas rested was the ethical superiority of the Breton people.

Mordrel made clear his racial point of departure in his very first SAGA article when he asserted that "race is a network of profound affinities that unites Bretons to each other and attaches them to their native soil, all joined together by 2,000 years of common life. That is what makes us something other than a common horde."[16] And he said it was SAGA's central task "to preserve our race, to nurture it, and to guard closely its unique qualities." But such an undertaking could be accomplished only if Brittany were separated from its French enemies and established as an independent state. Mordrel went on to explain that the fundamental organizing principle of such a future Breton state would be racial since only persons of ethnic Breton background would enjoy full civic rights. Foreigners, especially Latins, Jews, and Negroes, would be excluded from all responsible public positions. Other "undesirable and unassimilable" foreigners were simply to be expelled. Mordrel added that Bretons who did not subscribe to this new spiritual community of race would be stripped of their civic rights and made subject to the laws on foreigners.

Clearly, an independent Breton state cast in the SAGA mold would be politically reactionary, authoritarian, and anti-libertarian. The postindependence Breton society that Mordrel sketched indeed bore striking resemblances to Nazi Germany. Thus political authority was to be hierarchically organized from the top downward. Small-scale enterprises would be encouraged and protected because they "attach men more securely to the soil and family." The working population would be organized into syndical corporations according to occupations rather than classes, since Mordrel believed that "the nation labors for the well-being of all and not for a privileged class." The educational system would be made to serve the ideology of the Breton racial state and would have as its primary goal the training of morally and physically healthy men. This objective was to be pursued in conjunction with organizations very much like the Hitler Youth. Another important function of the schools would be the integral restoration of the Breton language, which meant its imposition on the French-speaking Gallo population of eastern Brittany. But nothing more revealed Mordrel's leanings toward Nazi Germany than his SAGA pronouncements on the foreign policy of an eventual Breton state. Once independence had been achieved, Brittany should form an "alliance with any great power for economic and military protection." That Mordrel had Hitler's Germany specifically in mind became clear when he went on to urge the abolition of German reparation payments, revision of the Versailles treaty, and Reich frontier rectifications by arbitration and plebiscite. It was an omen for the future that Mordrel was already willing in 1933 to exchange French domination of his homeland for that of Hitler's Nazi dictatorship.

Mordrel assumed that *Breiz Atao*'s readers would quickly fall into line behind his ideas and rally enthusiastically to the banner of SAGA. He could not have been more mistaken. For most party members his ideas were a case of too much too soon and *Breiz Atao*, obviously reacting to rank-and-file criticism, editorially explained only a month after the first SAGA article that the PNB "reserved" its attitude toward Mordrel's program. The next month *Breiz Atao* once more affirmed this "reserved" attitude and announced that the forthcoming PNB congress would pronounce on Mordrel's ideas. Although the anonymous author of this editorial denied that the PNB leaders had already opted for the SAGA program, he scathingly dismissed its critics as defeatists and admitted that he was favorably impressed by Mordrel's efforts. The defeatist critics had the last word, however, and at the party congress held in September at Carhaix they marshaled a decisive majority against SAGA.[17] The rank and file of the Breton nationalist movement was clearly not so captivated by fascist ideas as were its intellectual and ideological mentors.

Although severely rebuffed at Carhaix, Mordrel continued to publish his SAGA articles in *Breiz Atao*. But the increasing violence and eccentricity of his ideas seemed likely to provoke a rupture in the nationalist movement if this were to go on indefinitely. Even Mordrel acknowledged forty years later in his memoirs that his controversial ideas drove the PNB to the edge of crisis in late 1933. The party leaders therefore decided to employ once again the stratagem that had been used to keep the communist Yann Sohier attached to the Breton nationalist movement while insulating *Breiz Atao* from his direct influence. Mordrel would be given his own publication, which he could run as he pleased and in which he could indulge his ideological fancies without compromising the rest of the PNB leadership in the eyes of the rank and file. *Breiz Atao* accordingly announced in December 1933 that henceforth it would devote itself exclusively to "popular action," while doctrinal matters would be explored in *Stur* (*Gouvernail*), a new publication scheduled to appear in March of the following year. Unlike the case of Sohier, however, this arrangement did not result in the removal of Mordrel's direct influence at *Breiz Atao*, for he retained his post of editor-in-chief of the PNB organ. He disingenuously explained in his memoirs that this dual responsibility enabled the nationalists to preserve the "interdependence" between *Breiz Atao* and *Stur*.[18]

For lack of subscribers Mordrel's new periodical did not appear until September 1934 and until its suppression by Paris in 1939 led a troubled existence. *Stur*'s publication was often interrupted and its format constantly diminished in size. Mordrel's little review in fact always tottered on the edge of insolvency, mainly because it was never able to attract more than 250 subscribers. To plow through its nearly impenetrable prose style is to understand why. There is almost nothing in Mordrel's articles and those contributed by others, moreover, that had not already been more effectively presented in the SAGA series. When all the cumbersome language is stripped away, *Stur* is indeed found to contain little else than lavish - praise for the Breton race in particular and for the eminent good sense of racialism in general. In its first issue Mordrel had boasted that his doctrinal organ would be "anti-literary and anti-intellectual." In view of *Stur*'s extremely limited reader appeal it seems that he succeeded only too well in achieving these objectives.

PNB leaders had another reason for confining Mordrel's controversial ideas to *Stur* besides anxiety that their continued appearance in *Breiz Atao* might provoke a rupture in the Nationalist party. This reason was simply that the domestic political situation in France counseled moderation. Nationalist leaders were especially beginning to appreciate the danger that French fascism posed to their movement. Their reaction to the rightist-provoked riots in Paris on 6 February 1934 that led to the formation of the conservative government of Gaston Doumergue evidenced that awareness. "We have everything to lose by a fascism of the fight or the left," *Breiz Atao* warned editorially in mid-February, "that would throw our militants into prison and destroy our movement, the only and last hope of the bewildered Breton nation." The editorialist added that for Breton nationalists the best French government was one both liberal and feeble. Only such a regime could "guarantee the full exercise of our democratic freedoms without which our action and propaganda would be impossible. The Breton interest demands parliamentarianism and democracy in Paris." To encourage the spread of fascist ideas in Brittany, even if tinctured with Breton nationalism, hardly squared with that interest.

Since survival of the Third Republic seemed less inimical to the continued growth of the PNB than did a fascist takeover in Paris, nationalist leaders in early 1934 began to soften their hitherto violent campaign against the existing French government. Yet they made sure that *Breiz Atao*'s readers would not construe what amounted to tactical support for the republican regime as a tacit reversal of the nationalist movement's long-standing hostility to the government of France. Whenever possible, therefore, the PNB opposed Paris in its foreign policy, which in practice meant general approval of Hitler's analysis of the European situation and support for his foreign policy initiatives. Thus *Breiz Atao* congratulated Hitler for his "enormous success" when the Saarlanders voted to return to the Reich. They also backed the German Fuhrer's plans to reoccupy and remilitarize the Rhineland. This early support for Hitlerian policy was consistent, moreover, with the nationalists' long-held belief that France's difficulty was their opportunity. In the light of later events, some PNB leaders in the mid-1930s may even have calculated that such support would be remembered in Berlin on the day when Germany found itself in a position to dictate the fortunes of France.

The PNB leadership had meanwhile decided to participate in the 1936 general parliamentary elections. Despite their disastrous electoral experience of 1930 the nationalists were too caught up in the political excitement that gripped France in the mid-1930s to do anything but regard these elections as a means to promote their cause. But there was a far more compelling reason behind their decision to reenter the French electoral arena. The leaders of the PNB had been jolted by the startling success of Yann Fouéré's Ar Brezoneg er Skol (ABES, Le Breton à l'école). This undertaking involved a campaign to persuade communal and departmental councils on the peninsula to put themselves on record in favor of the teaching of the Breton language in the schools of Bretonnant Brittany.[19] In addition, many leading economic organizations on the peninsula as well as some twenty-eight Breton scholarly and regionalist societies had thrown their support behind Fouéré's efforts. These ABES successes seemed to indicate that Breton patriots had at last found a conjoined issue and strategy capable of striking a responsive chord among the political and cultural elites of Brittany. Unfortunately for the PNB nationalists, however, the initiative had come from outside their movement and threatened even to eclipse it. They thus felt compelled to neutralize it before Fouéré and his colleagues emerged as the most popular and prestigious of the Breton militants. The leaders of the PNB were nonetheless eager to draw profit from the momentum that had been generated by Fouéré's endeavor. To achieve both objectives they cleverly decided to intervene in the 1936 elections behind a moderate Breton program that incorporated the essential features of the ABES campaign.

Once involved in the parliamentary electoral process, the Breton nationalists almost inevitably came to adopt some of the political rhetoric and style of the Popular Front coalition. Thus they voiced their opposition to the conservative governments of Doumergue and his successors. Thus they cautiously advocated measures to improve the lot of Breton industrial, maritime, and agricultural workers. Thus they were prompted finally to create a so-called Breton Front as a key element of their electoral strategy. Although *Breiz Atao* claimed in December 1935 that the objective of this Breton Front was to expel the French regime from Brittany, the moderate program that the PNB later drafted for it fell far short of demanding such expulsion. Its five points instead called only for more equitable distribution of deputies, proportional representation, regional decentralization, formation of a Breton interest group in the Chamber, and legal provision for the teaching of the Breton language in all the schools of Breton-speaking areas of the peninsula. A far cry from the Breton extremism of SAGA, these demands made the PNB appear much closer ideologically to Estourbeillon's URB than to Mordrel's *Stur*. Debauvais himself acknowledged at the beginning of March that even a French nationalist candidate in Brittany could embrace without much difficulty the tame ideas of the Breton Front. A few actually did.

The PNB ultimately chose not to present candidates of its own under the Breton Front banner. "We have neither the workers, the organization nor the financial means to do so," Debauvais lamented in March. Instead the Nationalist party and its tacit allies in ABES tried to persuade parliamentary candidates who belonged to established French political parties in Brittany to endorse the moderate demands of the Breton Front. Several such candidates accordingly received PNB form letters to sign, which would thereby commit them to help form in the new Chamber a Breton interest defense group pledged to seek legislative enactment of the Breton Front proposals. Forty-one eventually did sign this document, three-quarters coming from the right side of the French political spectrum. A scattering of communist and socialist parliamentary aspirants also gave highly qualified support to the Breton Front program.

A month before the balloting the electoral chances of the nationalist-supported Breton Front candidates were menaced by the violent reappearance of Gwenn-ha-Du after four years of silence. During the night of Easter 1936, the twentieth anniversary of the wartime rising of the Irish at Dublin, incendiary bombs exploded at the prefectures of Rennes, St.-Brieuc, Nantes, and Quimper. The Vannes prefecture had also been slated for attack, but these plans went awry when the auto carrying the man chosen to place the bomb broke down twenty miles outside the city. In a communiqué to the press Gwenn-ha-Du claimed responsibility for the attacks and promised new acts of violence until the final goal of Brittany's liberation had been achieved. Even if some might privately have approved the new Gwenn-ha-Du exploits, the leaders of the PNB nonetheless feared that Breton electors would respond adversely to such terrorist tactics by voting against the Breton Front candidates supported by the Nationalist party. Thus on behalf of the PNB Olier Mordrel at the end of April hastened to repudiate Gwenn-ha-Du's attacks on the four Breton prefectures and to deny that the Nationalist party had anything to do with them. His words have the ring of truth, for in his memoirs Mordrel indicates that the prefectural bombings were the work of stormy petrels inside the clandestine Breton society who acted without consulting either Laîné or the other members of the Kuzul Meur.[20]

Gwenn-ha-Du's promise of further violence went unkept in any case and the remainder of the 1936 parliamentary electoral campaign proceeded without incident. When the results were known in mid-May the PNB claimed an impressive victory for the Breton nationalist movement. Fifteen Breton Front candidates had been elected, polling 207,022 of 686,507 votes cast in the first round and 157,806 of 361,447 in the second. In addition, Olier Chevillotte, who stood as an independent nationalist candidate at Morlaix, garnered 2,680 votes in the first round. An almost delirious *Breiz Atao* proclaimed on 17 May that these results "marked a decisive turning point" in the history of the Breton nationalist movement. The PNB organ added that the true meaning of the 1936 electoral outcome was that for the first time in several generations "a moral divorce has been pronounced between the French and Breton peoples." That was an exaggeration, for the apparent Breton nationalist triumph in May almost certainly reflected electoral successes won on other grounds. Subsequent events, particularly the failure of the fifteen winning candidates who received PNB backing to follow up on their Breton Front commitments, showed the plausibility of the latter explanation.

Whatever the exact meaning of the electoral verdict of

1936, Breton nationalists for a time enjoyed what they took for a stunning victory. And since moderation had apparently produced that victory, moderation became the order of the day in the PNB. Above all else the new position meant continued disapproval of Gwenn-ha-Du terrorism, an approach to Breton action that Mordrel in September characterized as "the most outmoded form of romanticism." There were other signs of PNB moderation immediately following the 1936 elections as well. The most important was the creation in June of the *Bulletin des Minorités Nationales de France*, a new auxiliary publication with which party leaders hoped to bring breakaway Breton federalists back into the PNB. The new periodical accordingly sought to situate the Breton nationalist movement within the context of a wider nationalities movement in France but without reference to any particular political or social ideology, themes dear to federalist hearts. Its pages were therefore confined to reports of the activities of various ethnic minority nationalist movements in France and were conspicuously free of anything that smacked of separatism or racialism of the SAGA or *Stur* variety. The appointment of Yves Delaporte, the youngest of a three-brother team that headed the democratic and moderate Catholic faction inside the PNB, was also intended as a reassuring gesture to the federalists. All these efforts failed to move the federalists, who remained deeply skeptical that the PNB leadership had genuinely foresworn its previous advocacy of extremist Breton doctrines. That Yves Delaporte shared their skepticism became clear at the end of 1937 when he resigned as editor of the PNB nationalities review—in the meantime renamed *Peuples et Frontières* —and with his brothers founded *War-Du ar Pal (Vers le But)*. The purpose of their new Breton publication, the Delaportes explained in its first issue, was to combat the intransigent Breton attitudes that had once more come to dominate the PNB.[21]

Already by mid-1937 it was obvious that the leadership of the Nationalist party was growing impatient with its moderate policy of support for the Breton Front program. None of its five points had been enacted into law and even a limited proposal for the legal recognition of the Breton language, although supported by all forty-four Breton deputies, failed to survive the committee stage of the legislative process. It is little wonder that Mordrel and Debauvais returned to their long-standing belief that it was naive to expect solutions to Brittany's problems from the French parliament. The PNB might in fact have reverted to its characteristic hostility for France sometime before mid-1937 had Debauvais been in charge of the party and Mordrel less preoccupied with keeping *Stur* afloat. But temporarily incapacitated by tuberculosis, the former had in December 1936 provisionally turned over direction of the nationalist movement to Raymond Delaporte, his compliant deputy on the PNB executive committee since 1934. Debauvais seriously misjudged his man, however. Once in control of *Breiz Atao*'s editorial policy Delaporte, under the name of Robert Furic, opened a determined offensive against the authoritarian and racist ideology of the Mordrelian wing of the Nationalist party.

Delaporte's campaign came to a head in April 1937 when in a lengthy attack on *Stur* he referred to Mordrel's review as the exponent of "a dangerous ideology." Debauvais immediately resumed his former active role as head of the PNB and made clear that his sympathies lay with his longtime nationalist partner. He repudiated his deputy's campaign against *Stur* and gave Mordrel ample space in *Breiz Atao* to defend his views. Realizing that his effort to moderate the ideological line of the PNB had ended in total failure, Raymond Delaporte resigned from the Nationalist party. The PNB congress at Carhaix in August strongly supported Debauvais and Mordrel in their recent quarrel with Delaporte and proceeded to reinforce Debauvais's position by abolishing the three-member PNB executive committee and naming him as sole leader of the party apparatus. With Mordrel's assumption of the editorial direction of *Peuples et Frontières* in October, the last trace of Delaportian moderation was eliminated from the PNB. Debauvais and Mordrel thereafter exercised undisputed authority over the Nationalist party and *Breiz Atao*. So great was this authority that they were able to demand, and receive, of the rank-and-file party membership regular monthly salaries for their work on behalf of Breton national revival.[22]

Under the double aegis of Debauvais and Mordrel the PNB took on an increasingly militant anti-French, separatist, and pro-German orientation from mid-1937 until its suppression two years later. Like most other politicians in France and elsewhere on the continent the two nationalist leaders turned their attention almost exclusively to foreign affairs during this period. Certain that France was headed for a national catastrophe, they began to urge in July 1937 that Breton patriots should not fail to grasp the opportunity that such an eventuality might furnish. Since it was likely that a French disaster would take the form of military defeat at the hands of the Third Reich, Debauvais and Mordrel joined these urgings to ever more enthusiastic applause for German foreign policy successes. In March 1938 *Breiz Atao* editorially praised the Nazi takeover in Austria and sarcastically noted Paris's "indignation at the destruction of the rights of a small nation." In May the PNB organ argued that Germany had a clear right to Czechoslovakia's Sudetenland on the basis of "the fundamental principle of the rights of nationalities." At the end of August Debauvais again took up the Sudeten question and in a dangerously titled editorial, "Pas de guerre pour les Tchèques," reminded his readers that "the blood of Bretons belonged exclusively to Brittany." The PNB leader edged even closer to treason when he declared at the party congress at Guingamp on 28 August that "not a drop of blood must be shed for foreign causes." This disloyal campaign culminated in September when *Breiz Atao* printed an ethnological map of Czechoslovakia that carried the legend: "Ça un peuple? Une guerre pour sauver ça? JAMAIS!" To the surprise of no one the nationalist leaders applauded the subsequent Munich resolution of the Sudeten crisis and went on to charge that the only power in Europe that wanted war was "the so-called eldest daughter of the Church."[23]

Open sympathy for German aggression formed the basis of the defeatism that for different reasons the PNB shared with the French right and made of the two tacit allies against the ministry of Edouard Daladier. But no government worthy of the name could tolerate forever such frankly treasonable and subversive behavior. Even as early as April 1937 French authorities had moved against the nationalists by forbidding a PNB-sponsored pilgrimage to St.-Aubin-du-Cormier, scene of Duke François II's decisive defeat by the French in 1488. In

May Daladier's government banned *Breiz Atao* from all army barracks and military installations in metropolitan and overseas France. Under government pressure the Messageries Hachette contemporaneously refused to accept any longer the nationalist organ for distribution in the newsstands of the French rail system terminals.[24] Yet for the time being Paris took no more severe measures against the Breton nationalist movement. French officials probably reasoned that to move against it frontally would only create needless nationalist martyrs and give their cause much unnecessary free publicity. In 1938, however, the Breton nationalist movement challenged Paris on terrain that finally compelled an otherwise vacillating Daladier government to take decisive action against it.

This challenge came in the form of an armed Breton paramilitary force called the Kadervenn (Sillon de Combat). First organized by Célestin Laîné in 1936, the Kadervenn found its members among youthful Breton separatists "who had had enough of talking and now wanted to fight."[25] During spring and summer maneuvers on deserted heaths near Trévézel in Finistère Laîné accordingly instructed his eager recruits in the art of small-arms weaponry, the construction and use of explosives, and the techniques of guerrilla warfare. The most adept and fanatical of his trainees he selected for membership in an elite unit, ominously called the Service Spécial (ss), that had responsibility for intelligence gathering and the carrying out of ultraconfidential missions. But few in Brittany or anywhere else knew of the existence of either the Kadervenn or its Service Spécial until 8 May 1938. On that day the nationalists defied another prefectural order and staged a lightning march at St.-Aubin-du-Cormier. At their head strode a so-called *bagad stourm* ("storm troop") composed of Laîné and several Kadervenn members who led those present in swearing what later became known as the oath of St.-Aubin. Each participant thereby pledged himself "to lead a worthy and upright life, to dedicate a healthy body, a fearless soul, and a resolute heart to my race. . . . [and] to be a faithful soldier, to obey my leader, to be prepared always to give my life if necessary for Brittany."[26] The newly consecrated Breton nationalists then quickly dispersed, jubilant that they had outwitted their French adversaries.

Their joy was misplaced, for the authorities had been informed in advance about what was going to take place at St.-Aubin and two undercover agents were present to witness the oath-taking ceremony. When these agents reported what they had seen, Paris resolved to have done with the Breton nationalist movement once and for all. By the end of the month Laîné and several of his young followers found themselves in a French jail, while Debauvais hid out in Belgium as a fugitive from justice. This quick result came about because certain Kadervenn members had become as skillful with paintbrushes as they were proficient with firearms. Since the beginning of 1938 commando teams of such budding Breton artists had been smearing nationalist slogans on public buildings all over Brittany. One struck at St.-Brieuc on 16 May just prior to an official visit by the French president Lebrun, covering the walls of that city with signs that proclaimed "La France est foutue," "La Bretagne aux Bretons," and *"Breiz Atao* vaincra." A police patrol chanced upon the scene and attempted to place the busy nationalist exterior decorators under arrest. The commandos were able to elude their would-be captors, however, but not before the latter had gotten good descriptions of them all. Their identities became known when subsequent detective work established that the slogan painters had formed the *bagad stourm* that led the recent St.-Aubin march. The police put the painters under constant surveillance in the hope of catching them once more with their paintbrushes in flagrante delicto. Five days later a six-member team made up of Laîné's closest associates in the Kadervenn walked into the trap. All were captured and charged with defacing public property.[27] After prolonged interrogation they implicated Laîné and Debauvais, who immediately became the subjects of arrest warrants. The French police apprehended the former on 29 May although Debauvais managed to cross the border and find refuge in the home of Fred Moyse, a Breton nationalist then living in Brussels.

Laîné and his colleagues were brought to trial at the end of June. Throughout the proceeding the Kadervenn leader refused to speak French but instead read a statement to the court in the Breton language. He took full responsibility for the St.-Brieuc incident and demanded the full penalty of the law. "The more severely I am punished," he explained, "the more I can help deepen the gulf between my fatherland and France, the more I can help prepare the advent of the Breton Republic, an event that no one can any longer prevent occurring in a few years."[28] The court was not impressed by Laîné's statement and on 22 June found all defendants guilty as charged. It sentenced Debauvais in absentia to six months in prison. Laîné received three months and five others two months each, while a sixth, because of his youth, was given a one-month suspended sentence. *Breiz Atao* expressed great satisfaction over the outcome of the trial, claiming that its true meaning was that for the first time the French government had publicly recognized the existence of a Breton nationalist movement by prosecuting its leaders in a court of law. And the PNB would only be stronger and benefit in "seriousness and audacity," the nationalist organ added, "because certain of us have undergone the test of prison. We will be stronger still when certain of us will have given our lives."[29]

Paris was not going to provide the Breton nationalist movement with any dead martyrs if that could be avoided. Yet the French government was not reluctant to use the courts against the PNB leadership, particularly after Laîné immediately upon his release from prison put twenty-five members of the Kadervenn through open military drill at Lanvaux in late summer 1938. The authorities waited only for a proper opportunity, which came in the fall of the same year when *Breiz Atao* offprinted its inflammatory editorial "Pas de guerre pour les Tchèques" as a handbill. Since they were the legally responsible directors of the PNB organ, Fanch Debauvais and Olier Mordrel were indicted on charges of sedition. Hoping to draw maximum propaganda advantage from the affair, Debauvais surrendered to French authorities on 25 October for prosecution and promptly received a four-month sentence for evading the earlier verdict. The one-day sedition trial of the two PNB leaders on 14 December ended in conviction for both men. Each was fined twenty-two thousand francs and sentenced to a year in prison, although in Mordrel's case the court suspended the latter penalty. Two days later *Breiz Atao* crudely observed that these verdicts proved only that the trial judges of Mordrel and Debauvais were "drunks and thugs."

The response of Gwenn-ha-Du was more dramatic. Using explosives furnished by Mordrel, it replied to the convictions of the two nationalist leaders by blowing up at Pontivy a monument that commemorated the Franco-Breton Fédération during the French Revolution.

During the early months of 1939 the PNB, under the provisional presidency of Célestin Laîné, made much of Debauvais's "martyrdom" in a French jail.[30] Debauvais himself cooperated actively in this effort by protesting that his jailers were denying him privileges normally accorded political prisoners in France. The authorities summarily rejected his protest and on 29 January Debauvais began a hunger strike to force them to yield. He won his point later that same day when Breton and Alsatian parliamentary deputies intervened by warning Daladier's government that the PNB leader's case might become a cause célèbre. Debauvais's lawyers concurrently appealed his conviction for sedition only to have it confirmed by the Cour d'Appel on 15 February. Twelve days later Gwenn-ha-Du marked this judgment by exploding a bomb at the prefecture in Quimper. In April *Breiz Atao* asked that the imprisoned nationalist leader be amnestied on the occasion of a visit to Rennes of President Lebrun. Daladier's minister of justice ignored the request. Debauvais was not finally released from prison until the end of July, slightly more than a year after his original condemnation in 1938 for defacing public property.

Paris meanwhile grew steadily more nervous about subversive activity inside France as the prospect of war with Germany loomed larger. In this tense situation the PNB seemed deliberately to draw attention to its defeatist attitude by applauding in *Breiz Atao* every new instance of Nazi aggression. The nationalist organ indeed could hardly find praise enough at the end of March for Hitler's destruction of what remained of the truncated Czech state and the incorporation of Bohemia and Moravia into the Reich. The proclamation of a German protectorate in Slovakia particularly marked, it went on to explain, "an important date in the history of European nationalities and an important stage in the evolution of minority rights." *Breiz Atao* added that Breton nationalists looked forward to Germany's imminent creation of a new nationalities-based European system that would be "organized, disciplined, and hierarchical in spirit." This amounted to endorsement of the Hitlerian scheme for a "new order" on the continent and was bound to provoke retaliatory measures from the French government.

The first came on 22 July when Daladier's ministry suppressed *Peuples et Frontières* and confiscated its last issue. Several weeks later customs officials at Locquirec commandeered the *Gwalarn*, a yacht that belonged to the nationalist lawyer Le Helloco and accused its crew of smuggling arms and seditious literature in preparation for a separatist coup in Brittany. Although their suspicions were far from unfounded, the police could not substantiate them and all involved were released for lack of evidence.[31] The end came for *Breiz Atao* in late August 1939. After the signature of the Nazi-Soviet pact, the crisis for which many Breton nationalists had long been hoping was upon France. The leaders of the PNB became almost delirious with excitement and too bold. In what turned out to be their last issue of *Breiz Atao* they demanded in a banner headline on 27 August that Daladier resign as prime minister and called on Bretons not to die for Danzig. Realizing that no French government could disregard such an open challenge to its authority, Mordrel and Debauvais fled across the border into Belgium.[32] A few days later Paris suppressed *Breiz Atao* by administrative decree and also forbade the upcoming congress of the PNB at Pontivy. Breton nationalists had apparently become in the eyes of French justice what *Breiz Atao* charged in September 1932 they always had been: outlaws.

CHAPTER 7

ꙮ*Breton Nationalists and Nazi Occupiers: The Collaborationist Gamble*

Before crossing into Belgium, Olier Mordrel and Fanch Debauvais changed their minds and decided that it might be a good idea if a few Breton nationalists died for Danzig. They therefore advised their PNB colleagues who remained behind not to resist an order from Paris for general mobilization should France and Germany go to war. The two nationalist leaders were convinced that any such war would be brief and would end in defeat for France. "We must not give the government in Paris an excuse," they explained, "to move against those nationalists who will have their role to play once the fate of France has been decided by force of arms. Laîné remains with you. We will meet again when the moment is opportune."[1] For once Laîné agreed with Mordrel and Debauvais and ordered his Kadervenn followers to lay aside all previously discussed plans for sabotage and obediently join their French military units if so instructed by the war ministry in Paris. These decisions for nonresistance were crucial for the subsequent course of wartime Breton national action. Based on the presumption of total German victory and perhaps even the dismemberment of France, they committed the nationalist movement to a cautious "wait-and-see" attitude insofar as the war and Berlin's intentions toward Brittany were concerned. But caution became an impasse when the war unexpectedly ended in an armistice that left the French state intact. This outcome instantly made the Breton nationalist movement the hostage of German policy toward Vichy and forced its leaders to play a frustrating and seemingly endless waiting game, more acted upon by external forces and events than shaping them. After June 1940 German victory in World War II represented the only way out of this *attentiste* dilemma for Breton nationalists, and that was not to be.

In conformity with the principle of "the enemy of our enemy is our friend," Mordrel and Debauvais meanwhile continued on to Germany from Belgium and on 29 August took up temporary residence at Berlin. Their plan was to mobilize support in the German capital for the idea of an independent Breton state should France suffer military defeat and have to accept a Nazi *diktat*. Yet passage to the enemy camp of France on the eve of war looked to most Bretons, including many nationalists, like an act of dishonor if not one of outright treason. Nor did Mordrel and Debauvais have any illusions about the possible dire consequences of their action. At the very least they expected to be accused of having stabbed France in the back, a ridiculous charge, Mordrel later insisted in his memoirs, since it was simply a matter of good strategy to attack a more powerful enemy when he was in straitened circumstances.[2] Everything depended in any case on the ability of the two nationalist leaders to win the Germans to the cause of an independent Brittany. If they failed, both understood that they would surely meet the fate reserved for traitors to France. But if they succeeded, Mordrel and Debauvais were just as certain that they would return to their homeland as great Breton heroes.

Back in Brittany the outbreak of war brought an end to virtually all nationalist activity. Laîné responded to the call for general mobilization and joined his regiment on 27 August. All other able-bodied PNB militants followed his example. Those who were ineligible for military service voluntarily suspended their nationalist action. Still Paris took no chances. On 20 October Daladier's government dissolved the PNB by decree and seized all its property as "enemy goods." At the same time the French police searched the headquarters of the loyalist Union Régionaliste Bretonne and the nonpolitical Bleun-Brug as well as the homes of a hundred prominent Breton nationalists. Even such unoffending places as the summer camp for Bretonnants at Lopérec and the Breton reception center in Paris, Ker-Vreiz, were closed down.[3] From exile Mordrel and Debauvais responded to these police actions with a manifesto called *Diskleriadur* (*Déclaration*). In it they maintained that only Brittany's separation from France could end such persecution of Breton patriots. If treason and alliance with Nazi Germany were necessary to achieve that objective, they added, then Breton nationalists should unhesitatingly follow that course. Yet although they had drafted this document in Berlin, Mordrel and Debauvais still claimed in its conclusion that they were not "in the service of a foreign power."[4] Paris was not impressed by this disclaimer. In December a French court sentenced the two nationalist leaders in absentia to five years imprisonment for insubordination in time of war.

Ironically, German officials during this period only barely tolerated the presence of Mordrel and Debauvais in Berlin. Hitler hoped to end the war in the west through negotiation with Paris rather than by military action and did not want to compromise this goal by showing undue consideration for importuning Breton nationalists. The German police thus kept the two men under close surveillance, while the press ignored the Breton propaganda they disseminated in successive mimeographed bulletins called *Lizer Brezel* (*Lettre de Guerre*) and *Ouest-Information*. So hostile was the political climate in Berlin that in late 1939 Mordrel and Debauvais quit Germany for Italy and the Netherlands, respectively. Despite their lack of success in Germany, Paris still looked on the two nationalist leaders as dangerous traitors, particularly since they in frustration had begun to encourage sedition in the French army. In January 1940 they managed to get *Lizer Brezel* to Breton troops at the front, a copy even reaching Laîné although he had been in the stockade since his arrest on 28 October for defeatism. In it Mordrel and Debauvais assured their readers that the PNB still existed in clandestinity and that its leaders were actively preparing for the advent of an independent Breton state. They therefore called on all soldiers from the peninsula "to respond to the appeal of Brittany, to act and to die when the moment comes. No true Breton has the right to die for France."[5] That was subversive language and retribution swiftly followed. On

23 February a military tribunal sentenced Célestin Laîné to five years in prison. The turn of Mordrel and Debauvais came in May. Three days before the opening of the German offensive in the west a court at Rennes found the two men guilty in absentia of treason and placed them both under sentence of death.

The German attack on 10 May got both the war and the hopes of Mordrel and Debauvais off dead center. In this new situation an apparent convergence between Breton nationalist and German interests took place over the disposition of French prisoners of war from Brittany captured by the Wehrmacht. Mordrel and Debauvais, who had meanwhile returned to Berlin, saw in these men a reservoir from which they might recruit a Breton military force to give armed support to their plans to assume power in Brittany. For their part the Germans, who had decided to occupy the peninsula, thought it wise to have their troops preceded by an advance force of reliable and knowledgeable men from the area. The function of these men would be to prepare local opinion for the imminent occupation as well as to gather and relay back to the German command information concerning French troop movements in Brittany and the location of munitions depots and communications installations. Breton POWs seemed a ready source of such operatives and the two nationalist leaders a convenient means for recruiting them. Thus when Mordrel and Debauvais suggested to the OKW (Ober-Kommando der Wehrmacht, the High Command of the Armed Forces) through an intermediary that special camps be created for Breton prisoners, Berlin approved the idea with alacrity. Sixty thousand such men soon found themselves reassigned to new camps at Luckenwalde, Neu Brandenburg, Bad-Orb, Sagan, and Hoyerswerda, where German officials hinted that "autonomists" would receive preferential treatment.

Mordrel and Debauvais spent most of their time until mid-June going from camp to camp in an effort to seek out familiar nationalist sympathizers and to recruit new ones. Everywhere they made the same offer. The Germans would release those who agreed to accompany the nationalist leaders back to Brittany. Most Breton prisoners replied to this proposal with scorn or outright hostility. Mordrel might even have been lynched at Hoyerswerda had it not been for the timely intervention of a Landsturm unit.[6] For all their efforts the two men were able to persuade fewer than 150 Breton POWs to join them in their journey to Brittany. And a significant number of these, according to an informed observer, were no more than shirkers from military duty or unsophisticated peasant conscripts who wanted to return home whatever the cost. The collapse of France was in any case so sudden and the advance of the German army so rapid that Debauvais and a ragtag band of former POWs reached Brittany only after the first Wehrmacht contingents had already penetrated into the peninsula.

Debauvais's appearance at Rennes on 27 June and that of Mordrel ten days later inevitably gave rise to the impression that the two nationalist leaders had arrived in the baggage of a foreign occupation power. Less propitious circumstances for the proclamation of a popularly supported independent Breton state can hardly be imagined. The signature of a Franco-German armistice on the same day that Debauvais showed up at Rennes in any event put an end to all immediate hopes for a separate Breton state. From the outset of negotiations French plenipotentiaries had insisted that German authorities respect the territorial integrity of France. Berlin, anticipating that an armistice with France would lead to the cessation of all hostilities in the west, gave satisfaction on this point. Indeed the armistice signaled the renewal of Hitler's earlier wartime policy of conciliation toward Paris and thus dealt an apparently mortal blow to the separatist hopes nourished by Mordrel and Debauvais since September 1939. Before 1940 came to an end it would be made brutally clear to the two former PNB leaders just how much the enemy of their enemy had turned out to be even less than a fair-weather friend.

Mordrel and Debauvais meanwhile sought to reestablish contact with their old comrades in the outlawed Breton Nationalist party by urging its former members to assemble at Pontivy on 3 July. Hostile occupation officials permitted this gathering only on condition that it be kept strictly private. They need not have been so concerned, since only two hundred persons turned up for the affair, a number that included eighty of the ex-POWs who had accompanied Debauvais on his return to Brittany. The only real worry for the Germans that day in fact was to protect the arriving nationalists from the anger of local French patriots, who resented their coming to Pontivy.[7] At the meeting itself Mordrel and Debauvais secured the adoption of a declaration of nationalist principles as well as approval of an eighteen-point program that envisaged the future creation of an authoritarian, hierarchical, corporative, and anti-Semitic Breton state.[8] But the major business of the Pontivy meeting was the formation of the Conseil National Breton (CNB) whose members besides the two veteran PNB leaders included Célestin Laîné, recently released from Clairvaux prison by the Germans, and Marcel Guieysse. Although Mordrel talked grandly of the CNB one day forming the nucleus of a Breton state, the immediate function of the new four-member council was, in the absence of the PNB, to coordinate all nationalist activity in Brittany.

German occupation authorities denied formal recognition to the CNB. The Feldkommandant at Rennes even refused to accept a copy of the Pontivy declaration and its accompanying eighteen-point program. An OKW order of 17 July that enjoined local occupation authorities from giving political support to the Breton nationalists made this attitude official policy.[9] This decision greatly pleased the peninsula's new Vichyite administration as well as the Catholic hierarchy in Brittany, and both became even more disposed than before to cooperate with the German occupiers. Less pleasing was an earlier German decision to allow the CNB to create a new journalistic voice for Breton nationalism, an act that carried the implied threat of further aid to the nationalists if Pétain's officials in Brittany made difficulties for occupation forces. So that Vichy would not miss the point the Germans made cash subsidies and a delivery truck available to the CNB publishing enterprise. With this valuable assistance Mordrel and an ailing Debauvais were able to bring out the first issue of *L'Heure Bretonne* on the maliciously chosen date of 14 July 1940.

From the very beginning Mordrel impressed his militant separatist views on the new nationalist organ. This alarmed local occupation officials and caused German headquarters in Paris to send an OKW officer to Rennes on 18 July with orders to bring *L'Heure Bretonne* and its troublesome chief editor to heel. The officer forthwith ejected the nationalists from the *Ouest-Journal* printworks, which they had illegally seized some time before, imposed a Propagandastaffel censor on the CNB organ, and ordered Mordrel to eschew all Breton nationalist political action in its columns. He permitted the continued publication of *L'Heure Bretonne* only on condition that its content be confined to the diffusion of news and other useful information.[10] But Mordrel was an extremely clever editor and he soon found a way to circumvent these restrictions without exposing himself to immediate German disciplinary measures. He simply devoted great space in *L'Heure Bretonne* to news of and information about Vichy, all of it reflecting unfavorably on the regime. Since this stratagem coincided nicely with the picadorlike role that the Germans meant for Breton nationalism to play vis-à-vis Vichy, it was unlikely that Mordrel would arouse for the time being the active hostility of occupation authorities.

Mordrel's relentless campaign against Pétain's government began to conflict in the fall of 1940, however, with the developing exigencies of German policy toward Vichy France. This disagreement was especially evident after Hitler and Pétain met at Montoire on 24 October and formally endorsed a joint policy of Franco-German reconciliation and collaboration. After their meeting there could be no immediate prospect of German support for Breton separatism against French unity. At best, the nationalists could count on no more than grudging toleration of their activities by local occupation officials. In this situation many nationalist leaders, including Fanch Debauvais, began to realize that their movement had to come to terms with the post-Montoire reality of Franco-German collaboration or disappear from the Breton political scene for good. But Mordrel remained obdurate. In successive *L'Heure Bretonne* editorials in November he charged that both parties had sold out the Bretons at Montoire, ridiculed the notion of Franco-German friendship, denounced continuing French perfidy, and implied that both Berlin and Vichy lacked character. Neither government could tolerate such defiance forever, although the Germans were at first content to let Vichy act alone. It therefore instructed prefects and subprefects on the peninsula to organize a boycott against *L'Heure*

Bretonne. The prefect of Finistère went further and forbade its sale throughout his department. He also obtained an episcopal order from Archbishop Duparc condemning the Breton action of the separatists and threatening them with excommunication if they did not recant their political beliefs. Vichy officials concurrently sought German approval for a direct assault on the Parti National Breton, which Mordrel had suddenly revived on 20 October.

The way in which Mordrel reconstituted the Breton Nationalist party proved to be his undoing. He brusquely pushed aside the very ill Debauvais and claimed sole executive authority in the PNB for himself. This action angered his CNB colleagues Laîné and Guieysse, who not only wanted a share of the party leadership for themselves but also feared the evil consequences of continued Mordrelian intransigence. They decided to act in mid-November when Berlin suddenly disbanded the special Breton POW camps, a move that the two men feared signaled the imminent liquidation of the Breton nationalist movement itself. Their alarm seemed the more justified when the Germans in mid-November placed Mordrel and Debauvais under virtual house arrest at Paris where they had fled to escape arrest by the Rennes prefecture. But realizing that the situation contained opportunity as well as danger, Laîné and Guieysse contacted the Zivilburo of the Abwehr in Rennes where a deal was struck. In exchange for Mordrel's removal from the PNB leadership and reversal of *L'Heure Bretonne*'s bitter hostility toward Vichy, occupation officials promised that the nationalists would suffer no further punitive action from the French and would receive a German subsidy of one hundred thousand francs a month.[11]

After complicated maneuvering that eventually saw Debauvais range himself with Laîné and Guieysse, a meeting of the hastily revived Kuzul Meur ousted Olier Mordrel from his posts of party leader and editor-in-chief of *L'Heure Bretonne*. Occupation authorities simultaneously ordered both Mordrel and Debauvais to cease all political activity. While the latter was permitted to slip into obscurity on the peninsula, Mordrel was sent to Germany for a six-month internment at Stuttgart. Neither man would ever again resume an active political career on behalf of Breton national revival. Mordrel returned to

Paris in May 1941, but only after he pledged to stay out of the five Breton departments, to eschew all contact with former nationalist colleagues, and to register twice a month with the occupation police. The Germans did allow him to revive *Stur* although during its one-year existence Mordrel did no more than to repeat on its pages the violent Francophobe, Naziphile, and anti-Semitic themes that had characterized the prewar series. As for Debauvais, he kept busy with historical research and the drafting of a constitution for a future Breton state until he moved to Alsace in late 1943 in a vain attempt to recover his health. His long struggle with tuberculosis finally came to an end on 20 March 1944 when he died in a Colmar sanatorium.

A few days after Mordrel's elimination, the PNB unanimously followed Laîné's recommendation and chose the thirty-three-year-old lawyer Raymond Delaporte as its new leader. He was a logical choice. A man of unbending integrity, he had neither tarnished his reputation by flight to Germany in time of war as his predecessor had done nor been compromised by close past association with the proscribed nationalist leader. On the contrary, it will be recalled that Delaporte had led the internal PNB opposition to Mordrelian extremism in the mid-1930s. Moreover, as a devoted Catholic and former president of Bleun-Brug he enjoyed excellent relations with the ecclesiastical hierarchy in Brittany, a factor that seemed likely to produce a softening in Archbishop Duparc's hostile attitude toward the PNB. But most important of all the affable and pragmatic Raymond Delaporte was a reassuring figure who could credibly execute the required moderate revision of nationalist policy toward Vichy. Indeed, for Delaporte to lead the PNB on its new course of moderation vis-à-vis Pétain's regime corresponded as much with his own long-standing personal convictions as it did with the exigencies of German policy.

Delaporte virtually completed the task of reorienting PNB policy in his first *L'Heure Bretonne* editorial as party leader.[12] Acknowledging that the Breton nationalist movement had in the past been "almost entirely negative," he declared that the PNB would no longer be hostile on principle to the French state or to those Bretons who remained loyal to it. He justified this change on the ground that France under Pétain was being refashioned into a new set of procedures and institutions that would be fundamentally different from those of the highly centralized Third Republic. He and the Breton Nationalist party thus awaited from Vichy concrete indications of Pétainist good will toward Brittany. From the beginning of his rule Marshal Pétain had in fact expressed vague sentiments in favor of administrative decentralization and reconstitution of France's historic provinces. His officials at Vichy had even shown themselves disposed to make at least token gestures in the direction of Breton ethnic sensibilities. At the end of 1940, for example, Radio-Rennes-Bretagne received formal authorization to devote an hour of its programming each week to Breton subjects.[13] The consequence of all this was that a good many Bretons were led to expect that their homeland would soon enter a new era of significant regional reform.

Heartened by what he took to be a positive response to the new PNB moderate line, Delaporte kept his olive branch of hopeful expectation extended toward Vichy for three years. It was often a difficult task because an ultra faction inside the Nationalist party believed that Pétain's regime was no more capable of reforming the French state than the old Third Republic had been. The leaders of this group were none other than Laîné and Guieysse who, having originally sponsored Delaporte for PNB leader in late 1940 as an unavoidable *pis aller*, soon began to hanker after what is best described as Mordrelian extremism without Mordrel. They in any case remained firmly attached to the idea of a totally independent Breton state. Yet for a long time Laîné and Guieysse hesitated to challenge Delaporte's moderate leadership. The cashiering by the Germans of Mordrel and Debauvais and their subsequent isolation in the political wilderness showed only too well the probable consequences of such a rash act. Although neither they nor Delaporte ever fully understood it, the ultras found themselves in a situation that made their fate entirely dependent on the fortunes of German arms. So long as there was any possibility of a German victory in World War II that might prove the wisdom of Delaporte's new waiting game, his moderate line toward Vichy had to be maintained. But defeat for Germany, and with it the certain disappearance of

Pétain's regime, was worse still, for it meant the destruction of extremist and moderate hopes alike. Since the Breton nationalist who believed most passionately in the ultimate success of German arms was the ultra leader Célestin Laîné himself, Delaporte's position as leader of the PNB remained relatively secure.

Boxed in by these circumstances Laîné in early 1941 reverted to his favorite role as clandestine paramilitary chieftain. He began to lay down the organization of a secret Lu Brezon (Armée Bretonne) that he hoped one day would serve as an IRA-style Breton liberation army. Based on five-man units called *bodou* that were in turn grouped by fours into *keriou*, Laîné's little Breton force had its *pendall*, or general staff, fixed at Rennes. In addition there were recruiting and training posts in at least fifteen other Breton communes. Once a month each unit gathered for field drill and instruction in firearms use and communications techniques. Rumors about Laîné's renewed paramilitary activities soon reached occupation officials. The Feldkommandant at Rennes ordered him in early July to hand over the arms of his Lu Brezon and warned that refusal to do so would be taken "as a lack of confidence in Germany."[14] On 5 July Laîné accordingly surrendered his arsenal to the Germans with a note complaining that this action left his group helpless in the face of unnamed "powerful adversaries" and calling on the Feldkommandantur to protect his band of Breton volunteers should the need arise. In actuality he held back part of his arms cache from the Germans. With this equipment Laîné and his men, under greatly tightened security precautions, continued their secret paramilitary activities until late 1943 when the Lu Brezon began to operate openly against the *maquis*.

While Laîné and his guerilla band drilled in remote corners of the peninsula, the PNB prospered under the moderate leadership of Raymond Delaporte. After only six months at the party helm he saw the number of its members quintuple. After another six months the Nationalist party boasted sixteen times more members than when Delaporte took over as leader. At the end of 1941 the PNB had a total membership of between three and four thousand persons.[15] New sections of the party were formed and for the first time the nationalists extended their organization over the entire peninsula. As for *L'Heure Bretonne*, it appeared in weekly editions of at least twenty-five thousand copies, while the sale of its propaganda pamphlets numbered in the tens of thousands. Voluntary cash contributions flowed into the party treasury and for a time added significantly to the income produced by the nationalists' various publishing ventures.[16] The Delaportian PNB had indeed become so vigorous by the spring of 1942 that on 19 April its leaders were able to organize an impressive rally of fifteen hundred militants at the Paris Mutualité.

Reports of Laîné's clandestine paramilitary activities and the evident growth of Delaporte's PNB soon made Vichy officials fear that the Breton nationalists were a genuine political force on the peninsula. A few even thought that the PNB was already capable of disturbing public order in Brittany, especially in the event of dramatic but unforeseen international developments. Most in any case agreed that the most effective way of dealing with the Breton nationalist movement was to cut the ground from under it by eliminating the resentment-generating grievances that lay at the center of its case against France. In the spring of 1941 the Vichy regime thus embarked on a policy of concessions to Breton ethnic feeling. On 19 March the education ministry gave its approval to the teaching of the history of Brittany in primary and secondary schools on the peninsula. At the same time it lifted the official prohibition against the use of the Breton language for instructional purposes in the classrooms of Bretonnant areas. In late December Vichy authorized the creation of optional courses in the study of the Breton language itself.[17] The following May it began to pay Bretonnant teachers who took on the supplementary task of Breton-language instruction six hundred francs a year.[18] At the end of the same month Vichy named Jean Quenette, a man personally sympathetic to the policy of Breton concessions, as prefect for all of Brittany and invested him with broad discretionary authority to deal with the special problems of the peninsula.

The chance always existed that credit for winning these concessions would redound to the nationalists, the very ones whose influence Vichy wanted to undercut. What Pétain's regime needed was a competing expression of loyalist Breton opinion that it might officially patronize at the expense of the PNB and toward which it could direct these concessions. The former ABES leader Yann Fouéré was willing and possessed the means to satisfy this need. He headed an evening daily at Rennes called *La Bretagne*, which he and a group of Quimperois industrialists had founded in March 1941. Although Fouéré from the beginning made his newspaper "the vehicle for the popularization and channeling of a powerful current of opinion in favor of essential Breton reforms," he remained unswervingly loyal to Pétain.[19] His attitude enormously pleased Vichy officials and they encouraged Fouéré to expand his new publishing enterprise. Later in 1941 he accordingly extended *La Bretagne*'s influence beyond its base of several thousand readers in Rennes when he and his partners acquired the three departmental weeklies *Le Morbihan*, *Les Côtes-du-Nord*, and *L'Ille-et-Vilaine*. In April 1942 Vichy officials covertly aided Fouéré in his successful attempt to buy the second largest newspaper in Brittany, *La Dépêche de Brest*, whose daily circulation of seventy to eighty thousand was entirely concentrated in Finistère.[20] Thus at the time of Quenette's appointment in May 1942 Fouéré's loyalist Breton views daily reached an audience of at least one hundred thousand persons in Brittany.

As Fouéré had long been urging in *La Bretagne*, Quenette almost immediately announced that he would sponsor a project of regional renewal for Brittany. To assist him in this task in October 1942 he created the Comité Consultatif de Bretagne (CCB), which he expected to study and give its opinion on "cultural, linguistic, and folkloric questions as well as on all other matters involving the traditions and intellectual life of Brittany."[21] Composed of two dozen prominent Bretons appointed by Quenette from a broad range of patriotic groups, the new committee had only a limited advisory capacity and was in no way meant to function as a regional assembly for the peninsula. Although Fouéré welcomed the creation of the CCB in *La Bretagne* as "a historic event," it was never more than a negligible quantity and during its year and a half of life had few accomplishments to its credit. It may even be that Quenette's real purpose in forming the CCB was to quarantine the PNB nationalists, since he never appointed a single member of Delaporte's party to serve on it. Its creation in any event meant that a French government had at last formally recognized the existence of a separate Breton culture with its own identity distinct from the French. Thus it happened that the culturally oriented Breton movement, led by nonpolitical moderates and encouraged from the sidelines by PNB nationalists, displayed notable vigor in these Vichyite conditions of relaxed vigilance.

The prewar publications *Feiz ha Breiz*, *Gwalarn*, *Dihunamb*, *Sav* (*Sauf*), and *Studi hag Ober* (*Etudes et Travaux*) stood in the vanguard of this cultural activity. Together they reached a monthly audience of five thousand persons throughout the entire occupation period, providing readers with a wide variety of specialized articles on Breton topics. Subsequently, several new wartime periodicals appeared, with names like *Galv* (*Appel*), *Ar Vuhez Christen* (*La Vie Chrétienne*), *Sterenn* (*Etoile*), and *An Eost* (*La Récolte*).[22] But the most influential cultural periodical that appeared during the war was *Arvor*. Founded by Roparz Hémon in January 1941 and published solely in Breton after August 1942, it eventually attained a weekly circulation of three thousand copies and thus became the most widely diffused Breton-language cultural review the peninsula had ever known. *Arvor*'s founder also took the lead in the creation of the Institut Celtique de Bretagne in late 1941. Although this body was designed primarily to serve a liaison function for the various cultural activities, it had achievements of its own. The most important and longlasting was the formation of the Bodadeg ar Sonerion in May 1943, a society dedicated to the preservation and encouragement of indigenous Breton music.

The Institut Celtique de Bretagne ultimately enrolled more than three hundred persons, a membership that included virtually the entire intellectual establishment of the Breton movement. But it rigorously shunned members of Delaporte's PNB and persons formerly connected with *Breiz Atao*. Indeed, the leaders of the wartime Breton cultural movement, fearing that their efforts would be compromised by association with separatist ideologues, sought as a matter of policy to exclude PNB nationalists from all their activities. Their caution was calculated not only to mollify Vichy but also to serve as a hedge against the future. In particular they hoped, should Pétain's regime disappear, that untainted by separatism their wartime Breton achievements would remain intact under any succeeding French government. Moderate Breton regionalists like Fouéré also hoped that in such an unpredictable post-Vichy situation they would not be penalized for their Breton action during the German occupation. Events soon showed that all these hopes were misplaced. Liberation authorities in 1944 simply annulled Vichy's concessions to Breton ethnic feeling and exacted a heavy price from those who had continued their patriotic Breton action under Pétain's regime. But the highest price would be paid by the PNB nationalists, the Bretons who had played the least role in bringing about the most notable successes on behalf of Brittany during the war years.

No Breton thought of paying any kind of price until it became obvious that Germany would lose the war. Raymond Delaporte and his PNB colleagues first began to realize at the end of 1942 that the German victory they had been waiting for since late 1940 was not to be. They thus scrambled to protect themselves from resistance-inspired reprisals that were sure to follow the collapse of the Nazi occupation of the peninsula. But all that the PNB could do was to put distance between itself and the Germans and to declare its neutral attitude in the developing struggle between Breton collaborators and resisters, a position spelled out in *L'Heure Bretonne* at the beginning of 1943.[23] Such late-in-the-day neutrality impressed neither the German occupiers nor their resistance adversaries and served only to complete the isolation of the nationalists in Brittany. This position also made the nationalists the most exposed and expendable political force on the peninsula, which meant that they faced the real prospect of coming under double assault by drawing the vengeful and deadly fire of both sides in the violent partisan struggle that engulfed Brittany during the closing stages of World War II.

How dangerous the nationalists' position actually was became brutally clear in the second half of 1943 when a series of political assassinations claimed the lives of several Breton militants. The first to fall was Yann Bricler, cousin and confidant of Olier Mordrel, administrator of *Stur*, and follower of

Breiz Atao since 1920. Partisans who suspected him of being an informer for the Germans shot Bricler execution-style in his Quimper office on 4 September. A few weeks later a young nationalist farmer named Yves Kerhoas was gunned down at a wedding party near Plounévez. The murder of Abbé Perrot on 12 December as he returned from morning mass at the chapel of St.-Corentin, however, had the greatest impact on the Breton nationalist movement. Not only did the *maquisard* assassination of this longtime Bretonnant militant anger Breton patriots in general but it also drove the Laîné-Guieysse ultras within the PNB into open rebellion against the leadership of Raymond Delaporte.

Since the summer of 1943 Delaporte had encountered increasing difficulty in maintaining the new "neutralist" line of the PNB against ultra pressure. Calculating that Brittany had nothing to gain and everything to lose by a German defeat and believing that secret weapons would soon turn the tide in Germany's favor, Laîné and Guieysse insisted that the PNB should collaborate fully with the Germans against the resistance. Thus in July Laîné gave an ultimatum to the PNB leader bidding him to align nationalist policy with the ultra desire for close and active collaboration with the Nazis. As if to underline his demand with the threat of force, Laîné in August put his 150-man guerrilla contingent through a series of maneuvers in full view of the public. Delaporte was not intimidated. In September he ended the PNB subsidy that Laîné's paramilitary force had been receiving. At the same time he expelled a few of the lesser-known ultras from the PNB. In November he moved against the ultra leaders themselves, telling Laîné and Guieysse either to cease their divisive activities or to quit the Nationalist party. Delaporte also announced that membership in Lu Brezon was henceforth incompatible with membership in the PNB.

The two ultra leaders immediately chose the first of the two options given them by Delaporte and struck out on their own. While Guieysse endeavored with little success to revive *Briez Atao* and the "real" PNB, Laîné and his armed followers made vague plans "to defend Breton militants and organize their protection" from resistance reprisals.[24] But it was not until the murder of Abbé Perrot that Laîné resolved on a specific course of action. At the funeral of the assassinated priest he pledged to avenge his death by swearing that "war is declared between ourselves and the enemies of Brittany wherever they may be found. . . . We are ready. Tomorrow we will take up arms."[25] Laîné then renamed his paramilitary unit the Bezenn Perrot (Formation Perrot) and asked German occupation authorities that he and his men be allowed to wear a special Breton uniform and to carry arms freely. The Germans turned down these requests and offered instead to enroll the Bezenn Perrot in the Waffen-SS. In a decision heavy with consequences Laîné accepted this offer and with his men put on German battle dress.

Laîné was fully aware that henceforth the Bezenn Perrot had no other status than that of a local auxiliary to the German police. But he continued to tell his men, many of whom were still impressionable teenagers and easily influenced by the charismatic Laîné, that their organization remained an autonomous Breton fighting unit. He beguiled them as well with stories of other peoples who in the past had aligned themselves with the wartime adversaries of their rulers. The Bezenn Perrot was only following the trail, he thus informed his young disciples, already blazed by the Polish and Czech legions during World War I. In any case Laîné assured his men that despite everything Germany would still win the war and that they, by aiding Hitler's armies, would finally emerge as the heroic deliverers of independent Brittany. In the end the entire Breton patriotic movement, whether regionalist or nationalist, moderate or extremist in orientation, would suffer greatly because Célestin Laîné cynically deceived youthful members of the Bezenn Perrot into drawing on uniforms of the Waffen-SS. That act lent plausibility to the contention of the opponents of Breton particularism that Breton patriotic action carried to its logical conclusion ended in treason and therefore had to be rooted out and destroyed. Such a line of reasoning in fact lay behind the postwar effort of French political and judicial authorities to purge the Breton movement.

Laîné and his SS-garbed followers meanwhile spent the spring of 1944 vainly trying to track down the murderers of Abbé Perrot, who were thought to be hiding in central Brittany. During the same period they also assisted a German paratroop unit in a series of forays in the departments of Ille-et-Vilaine, Morbihan, and Côtes-du-Nord. After the allied landings in Normandy on 6 June, however, the Bezenn Perrot disintegrated and only a few of its members escaped with Laîné in the baggage trains of the fleeing German occupation forces in August. Many of them, later placed under sentence of death in France, remain today scattered about in Germany, Spain, Ireland, and South America.[26] Some of those who could not get out of Brittany were found and prosecuted by French authorities. Laîné eventually made his way to exile in Ireland and then to the United States, where he is reputed to have acquired American citizenship. A chemical engineer by profession, he has recently lived in the Netherlands, working for an American petroleum company by day and dabbling in Breton nationalist politics by night.

While the Bezenn Perrot during the spring of 1944 helped the Germans against resistance forces, Delaporte's PNB did little more than mark time, waiting desperately for those "lightning victories that are slowly being prepared in the shadows."[27] Reduced to tabloid size at the beginning of February and to two pages in May, L'Heure Bretonne finally ceased publication altogether with its number for 11 June. As for its regionalist rival La Bretagne, Yann Fouéré filled its columns during the last part of 1943 and the first five months of 1944 with bland items about various aspects of Breton life and German communiqués imposed on him by occupation authorities. He prudently ended its publication on 6 June, the day of the Allied landings in Normandy. All other Breton action periodicals had likewise disappeared by June. The CCB lingered on until 20 July when it held its last meeting and then slipped into limbo. On 10 August French officials arrested its last secretary-general, none other than Yann Fouéré, and charged him with having illegally advocated "an inadmissible political regionalism."[28] Released on bail, he escaped into exile in Ireland where he lived until 1955 when a French court acquitted him of all outstanding criminal charges.

The summer of 1944 was indeed a time of extreme confusion in Brittany. With Allied armies pressing toward the peninsula and German occupation forces preparing to leave, a situation of virtual lawlessness soon prevailed, which gave the *maquis* and other resistance groups a free hand, and the vengeance they meted out to their Breton nationalist enemies was harsh. Most of the important leaders, however, eluded their grasp. Debauvais was dead, while Mordrel, Laîné, the Delaporte brothers, Roparz Hémon, and Marcel Guieysse were able to escape and set out on the path of exile toward Germany. Although Hémon and Guieysse were caught by American officials and turned over to the French for disposition, it was nonetheless true that the vengeance of resistance forces was directed almost exclusively against secondary figures in the Breton nationalist movement.

This vengeance, known as revolutionary justice in the idiom of the time, took the form of summary executions. During the months of June, July, and August at least thirty nationalists, all members of the PNB or prewar followers of *Breiz Atao*, lost their lives in this fashion.[29] Some of these, notably Jeanne du Guerny alias C. Danio, were surely authentic collaborators, motivated by more than just their attachment to the cause of independent Brittany. But many were Breton patriots pure and simple and seem to have been eliminated for that reason alone. Yves de Cambourg and Louis Stephan were both connected with *La Bretagne*. Paul Gaïc and two brothers named Tastevin belonged to the most moderate wing of the PNB and were news agents for *L'Heure Bretonne*. Abbé Lec'hvien was a disciple of Perrot, while the teenaged Jean Philippon had imprudently made a pilgrimage to the grave of the murdered priest where he was shot as he knelt in prayer. These, rather than willful and opportunistic collaboration with the Germans, were their crimes. One who understood this and promised to act accordingly was Charles de Gaulle. In a statement to the press at Vannes in early 1945 he remarked that "if the Breton autonomists have committed treason, they will be punished for it; if they have only been autonomists without having betrayed France, that is another matter."[30] In the dramatic and chaos-filled days of summer 1944, however, the opponents of Breton national feeling had neither the time, the grace, nor the inclination to make those elementary distinctions that might have spared the lives of otherwise innocent Breton patriots like Jean Philippon.

With the withdrawal of the Germans in August and the subsequent establishment of liberation authorities in Brittany, the repression of Breton nationalism began in earnest. Although juridically nonexistent since October 1939, the PNB was formally dissolved on 18 August 1944. *L'Heure Bretonne*, *Arvor*, *La Bretagne*, and *La Dépêche de Brest* were also legally suppressed and their property seized by the state. Liberation officials then turned their attention to individual Breton nationalists. They made only sporadic arrests, however, until 20 November when Dr. Victor Le Gorgeu, the newly installed special *commissaire* for the four departments of Ille-et-Vilaine, Côtes-du-Nord, Morbihan, and Finistère, ordered a general roundup of all known nationalists.[31] Perhaps as many as a thousand suspects were thus apprehended and confined in internment centers at Rennes, Langueux, Sarzeau, Quimper, Châteaubriant, and Pont-de-Buis.[32] Many of the arrests were indiscriminantly made. One report even had it that in Trégor some children were taken into custody for wearing shoes with Celtic decorations. Several hundred of the detainees were eventually released without further penalty. But several hundred more remained in internment centers in early 1945 awaiting disposition of their cases. Although few important nationalists besides Roparz Hémon and Marcel Guieysse figured in this group, French authorities decided in the spring to proceed with the judicial purge of Breton nationalism.

Two special courts, *cours de justice* and *chambres civiques*, were used to try Bretons charged with collaboration with the Germans or membership in collaborationist parties. The *cours de justice* had jurisdiction in cases dealing with offenses defined as crimes and could impose severe penalties, including death. The *chambres civiques* were designed to try lesser offenders and could levy punishments of civic degradation, banishment, and confiscation of property. Civic degradation (*indignité nationale*) was a new and extremely harsh penalty that meant the loss of civic rights, cancellation of civil and military decorations, reduction to the ranks, cessation of pensions, even for disabled persons and widows, and prohibition of employment in many professions, particularly the civil service, teaching, publishing, and journalism. A person sentenced to civil degradation could even lose his driver's license.

These penalties inflicted great suffering on many Bretons, since after sentencing they lost their positions and thus often their only means of earning a livelihood. Banishment from Brittany, usually imposed along with civic degradation, added to the burden. Scores of Bretons so judged had to expatriate themselves to other regions of France, losing in the process their jobs, their homes, and contact with their relatives. As late as 1950 Bretons under sentence of banishment were still being arrested in Paris as they furtively boarded trains at Montparnasse station to return to Brittany for a few hours in order to visit dying parents and other relatives and friends.[33]

The cases of several hundred Breton nationalists, many in absentia, finally passed before the *cours de justice* and the *chambres civiques*. At least a score of them ended in condemnation to death (although only a fraction of these sentences was ever actually carried out), while some seventy other defendants received terms of forced labor ranging from five years to life. All the others who were found guilty suffered civic degradation and in most cases banishment from the five Breton departments. The trial of the leadership of the PNB and *L'Heure Bretonne* took place in June 1946 at the *cour de justice* in Rennes. But only Marcel Guieysse, a blind and bent old man of sixty-five, appeared in the dock. His original codefendants— Olier Mordrel, Raymond and Yves Delaporte, Célestin Laîné, and the lesser figures Charles Goanac'h, Yann Goulet, and René Bourdon—remained in hiding and French authorities decided to defer action on their cases until a later date. During his trial Laîné's former ultra colleague sought to sacrifice himself for the others and even claimed full responsibility for the Naziphile attitude of the Bezenn Perrot. Affirming from the stand his unshakeable belief in the eventual victory of Breton nationalism, Guieysse proclaimed his readiness to die in the name of independent Brittany. His forthright manner impressed the court, which had in any case failed to impute to him a specific act of collaboration. He received the unexpectedly light sentence of five years in prison.

Those originally charged with Guieysse were tried in absentia at the Rennes *cour de justice* in March 1947 and found guilty. Mordrel, Laîné, and Goulet were sentenced to death and confiscation of all their property. Raymond Delaporte, who addressed a letter to the court from exile claiming that he had always been a federalist and never a separatist and that he had opposed the creation of the Bezenn Perrot, was sentenced to twenty years at hard labor, banishment from Brittany for another twenty years, and seizure of all his property. The remaining three defendants received identical sentences of ten years at hard labor, ten more years of banishment, and confiscation of all their goods. A few years later, however, a military tribunal at Paris overturned the convictions of these last three and acquitted them. The others have since come under the terms of various French amnesty laws. Mordrel elected to avail himself of such clemency and after more than twenty years of South American exile returned to Brittany at the end of the 1960s.

Besides Laîné at least twenty-five members of the Bezenn Perrot stood trial at the Rennes *cour de justice*. Only one of these gained acquittal while nine, four in absentia, were condemned to death. Five others were sentenced to hard labor for life and six more to lesser terms of such confinement combined with varying degrees of civic degradation, banishment, and confiscation of property. One of the defendants received a simple prison term of eight years, while the cases of the remaining three were never completed. Extenuating circumstances rarely mitigated the severity of sentences imposed. Joseph Malgieux, for example, was sentenced to hard labor for life, although at the time of his trial he was certifiably insane.[34] Those who suffered execution met their deaths with almost arrogant pride. Guy Vissault de Coëtlogen, shot at Paris in 1945, refused to seek clemency because he did not want to be indebted to the French chief of state for his life. He even thanked the members of his tribunal for the honor they conferred on him by placing him under sentence of death. Hervé Botros and Corentin Kergoat were shot at Quimper in September and October 1945, respectively. As Botros fell he shouted "Breiz Atao!" while Kergoat died with "Vive la Bretagne!" on his lips. After his condemnation Léon Jasson proudly declared that he regretted nothing and wrote to his mother that he faced death calmly, his heart full of hope that a new nationalist generation would emerge to finish the work he and his comrades had begun. He and André Geffroy were executed by firing squad at Rennes in July 1946 while they sang the Breton national anthem "Bro Goz ma Zadou."[35]

No one has yet studied in detail the purge of the Breton movement in the immediate postwar period. Indeed such a study cannot be made until official French archives are opened. In recent years Breton writers have nevertheless sought to portray the prosecution of Breton militants during the period 1944–47 as part of a vast French conspiracy to destroy the Breton nationalist movement. Individual Bretons who suffered in the process have accordingly been viewed as the innocent victims of this plot, guiltless of any crime of treason or collaboration during the war.[36] And in fact it is easy to find a number of cases in which injustice was clearly done to Breton patriots after 1944. For example, the grand druid Fanch Jaffrennou was sentenced to five years in prison, civic degradation, and confiscation of one-fourth of his property, even though he had engaged in no political activity during the occupation and had been an outspoken opponent of *Breiz Atao* and the PNB throughout the entire interwar period. Similarly, Fanch Vallée was arrested for collaboration (the charges later being dropped) despite the fact that he was more than eighty years old and had been bedridden for years. The arrests of Goulven Mazéas, Yves Le Diberder, Keravel, Marguerite Gourlaouen, and the widow and daughter of Theodore Botrel were surely unjust as well. Mazéas's arrest seems particularly inexcusable. Long opposed to separatism, he had stayed clear of politics during the war and eventually saw his Jewish wife and daughter deported to Germany by the Nazis.

It is one thing to point out these obvious cases of injustice but quite another to assert that they prove the existence of a palpable anti-Breton conspiracy on the part of the French government. It may even be that they resulted simply from errors committed by careless and overzealous French purgers determined to punish all collaborators in Brittany regardless of whether or not they had ever been Breton militants. Such mistakes, regrettable as they may be, were probably inevitable in the confused and passion-filled atmosphere that prevailed in Brittany after the beginning of 1944.[37] Generalizations based on obvious miscarriages of justice—whether arising from conspiracy, vendetta, or simple error—in any event hardly excuse the conduct of men like Olier Mordrel, Fanch Debauvais, Célestin Laîné, and to a lesser extent Marcel Guieysse and Raymond Delaporte. Until the very end these men either collaborated directly with the Germans or at least favored such a policy. Many cooperated, moreover, with the carrying out of the most obnoxious German policies, particularly the application in Brittany of the Service du Travail Obligatoire (STO) with far more enthusiasm than the occasion demanded.[38] Others spied, informed, and served as *francs-tireurs* for the Germans against resistance forces. A few, notably Célestin Laîné, exploited the Breton idealism of their followers and slyly tricked them into choosing the path of treason and dishonor. From the point of view of French justice, these men were notorious traitors and deserved to be treated as such. What their latter-day Breton apologists are in fact unwilling to admit is that Mordrel and many other Breton nationalists in 1939 gambled on a German victory in World War II and lost. But it is always dangerous to lose such political wagers, for the stakes are usually total and the winners invariably in a position to eliminate, in the name of justice and history, their luckless opponents. From this perspective the reprisals subsequently taken against these Breton nationalists by the French government were in the logic of the situation, to be expected and perhaps not even unreasonable.

At the end of World War II it appeared to most Bretons that the nationalist movement begun amid such youthful enthusiasm in 1919 at *Breiz Atao* had ended a quarter of a century later in ignominious failure with the Bezenn Perrot. All its organizations and periodicals had been destroyed during the liberation. The nationalists themselves had been either killed, imprisoned, or driven into exile, hiding, or prudent silence. No progress had been made toward revision of the unitary relationship of Brittany to France as it had been established in 1789; the peninsula remained an integral part of the French state in 1945. Demands for lesser reforms—administrative decentralization, protection of Breton agricultural, maritime and industrial interests, and the defense of the Breton language—had fared no better. All met first the indifference and then the hostility of the French government. Certain minimal and short-lived concessions, it is true, had been won from Marshal Pétain's regime after 1941. But these were attributable less to the efforts of the nationalists than to those of Vichyite loyalists like Yann Fouéré. Concessions won from such a morally bankrupt, politically inept, and externally dependent regime as Vichy hardly counted as glittering accomplishments anyway.

Reasons for the apparent failure of Breton nationalism are not hard to find. There was first of all the problem of its incompetent and reactionary leadership, which erred by resting its case against France on the alleged unlawful abolition of Breton autonomy in 1789. Narrow legalism of that sort was in itself archaic and implausible. More important, it made the nationalists appear determined to restore a social and economic system in Brittany dominated by wealthy clerical and aristocratic classes. Since this was a prospect with little appeal for the masses of Breton peasants, workers, and sailors, the legal point of departure of the nationalist movement effectively denied it a substantial mass basis. True, socially progressive elements existed among the nationalists who might have been able to attract much-needed mass support. But it will be remembered from earlier chapters they lacked influence in the policymaking councils of the movement and were never able to mount an effective challenge to its reactionary leadership.

Interwar Breton nationalism was also weakened by the pull of the French political system on the oft-expressed argument of its leaders that theirs was a movement of the vanguard. The essential function of *Breiz Atao* and the PNB, they said, was to work for the reawakening of national consciousness in Brittany. The necessary first step was to win Breton professional and intellectual elites to nationalism. Only when that had been accomplished could nationalists realistically think of building a mass-based movement that aimed at the liberation of the peninsula by political means. The first of these objectives was far from attained in 1939; efforts toward the second had not even really begun. But throughout the interwar period the allure of electoral politics was too strong for the nationalists to maintain their single-minded pursuit of peninsular elites. Instead they were drawn almost magnetically to mass political action long before their movement was ready for so decisive a step. The results were predictably disastrous. Nothing in fact more clearly revealed how much the leaders of Breton nationalism had been socialized into and shared typical French political mentalities than their head long eagerness to run nationalist candidates in French elections. The fondest dream of every interest group in France, no matter how small its constituency or how ridiculous its cause, has long been to elect a deputy to parliament.

Even considered narrowly in terms of its vanguard role, the interwar Breton nationalist movement fell far short of the ideal. A vanguard ought first of all to possess doctrinal coherence. It was just the reverse with *Breiz Atao*, which counted among its sympathizers persons who held the most contradictory and mutually exclusive views. There were those who thought Breton national consciousness was best awakened through possession of the ancestral language, while others looked to the study of the history of Brittany for the same purpose. There were those who hoped for the restoration of Brittany as it had existed before 1789, while others looked to the political, social, and economic liberation of the Breton people by means of revolutionary socialism. There were those who hated France above all else, while others were willing to pledge at least civic loyalty to the French state. Thus if the leadership of *Breiz Atao* after 1919 constituted a vanguard, it was one that charged off in several directions at once. That sort of vanguard was the same thing as being no vanguard at all.

Yet failure is too harsh a verdict for the interwar Breton nationalist movement. Those who belonged to it could claim a sense of genuine accomplishment. To have survived as an organized movement for so long in the face of the hostility of the French government was itself no mean achievement. Moreover, the nationalists after 1932 began to attract a substantial following in Brittany. By 1935 *Breiz Atao* was being printed at the rate of ten thousand copies every two weeks and penetrated into all 218 Breton cantons. It flourished as well among the large emigrant Breton populations in Paris, Le Havre, and Angers. A recent estimate placed the number of PNB militants at five thousand on the eve of World War II.[39]

The consequence of this growth was that peninsular opinion became increasingly aware of the so-called Breton question. Electoral campaigns thus took on a notably Breton tone during the 1930s. In 1936 the incumbent Morlaix deputy Trémintin even found it advisable to circulate a special manifesto denouncing his nationalist opponent Olier Chevillotte as a stalking-horse for *Breiz Atao* and an apologist for the "stupid and odious" violence of Gwenn-ha-Du.[40] There were accomplishments in the cultural field as well. The nationalists worked tirelessly to organize Cercles Celtiques in Brittany. Although none of these Breton folklore societies existed in 1930, more than a hundred were active in the 1940s. The nationalists also assisted the campaign to save the traditional flute-like Breton musical instrument called the *biniou* from extinction. In 1930 there were only two dozen known *biniou* players in all of Brittany, while twenty years later nearly two thousand of the instruments had been sold on the peninsula.[41]

Surely the most significant achievement of the interwar Breton nationalists, however, was that they established a tradition of militant Breton action. This was important not so much for the results it produced at the time but rather for the aid it would give to future efforts on behalf of Breton national revival. In particular this tradition would allow postwar nationalists to connect their militant action with efforts that existed before the *attentiste* disaster of 1940–44. For it is true that after 1945 it became an accepted part of World War II historiography in France that the Breton nationalist movement had been fabricated in 1940 by German occupation authorities virtually out of nothing.[42] But knowledge of the continuous existence of *Breiz Atao* after 1919 makes it impossible to maintain that historiographical fiction. Present-day Breton nationalists can thus refute with facts the charge that they represent nothing more than vestigial holdovers from the wartime occupation period. So it happened in September 1968 that a writer for the influential *Le Monde* described the authors of a series of nationalist political bombings in Brittany the year before as "the heirs of Breiz Atao." He made no attempt to blacken their reputations with the tarbrush of collaboration.

Historiographical legends die hard in France, particularly as they relate to World War II, Vichy, and the resistance. What

Le Monde did after all was to admit tacitly that Breton nationalism is an enduring reality in Brittany rather than simply a war-related German invention. That admission only confirmed twenty years after the fact what Joseph Martray, the eminently loyal Breton patriot and political confidant of the soon-to-be French prime minister René Pleven, had already argued in 1948. By virtue of its very thoroughness, he observed in March of that year, the postwar purge of Breton nationalism revealed how deeply Breton national feeling had penetrated on the peninsula. It also showed, he added, that "it would be henceforth difficult to speak of a 'handful of agitators' since the police themselves ended up by making lists containing the names of thousands of persons from all walks of life: doctors, priests, professors, industrialists, businessmen, farmers. It would finally have been necessary to transform all of Brittany into a concentration camp if all those touched by nationalist and regionalist ideas since 1932 were to be arrested. The effort was abandoned."[43]

Martray wrote the above words in valedictory tribute to the Breton nationalist movement begun in 1919 under the aegis of *Breiz Atao*. These words equally presage the reappearance of ethnic minority nationalism in postwar Brittany.

CHAPTER 8

❧ *The Failure*
of Breton Regionalism
after 1945

Those who hoped that the purge of Breton nationalism after 1944 had for the foreseeable future put an end to all patriotic action on behalf of Brittany and its Celtic culture soon were disappointed. Hostilities had hardly ended before Breton patriots embarked on a new course of action in favor of their homeland. Despite the recent crimes of its ardent champions and the destructive vengeance of its equally determined adversaries, ethnic Breton feeling had become too deeply rooted in the Armorica peninsula for Breton action to be abandoned. At first Breton patriots narrowly confined themselves to questions of language and culture. In the second half of the 1940s several new Breton-language periodicals appeared in which a postwar generation of Bretonnant writers continued the work of literary and linguistic revival undertaken for the previous twenty years in *Gwalarn*.[1] Others worked for the legal recognition of the Breton language in peninsular classrooms. Even the conservative members of the venerable Association Bretonne at their first postwar congress defended the rights of the Breton language with unaccustomed vigor and called for an end to its official proscription in Brittany's schools.[2]

Since so many of its members had proven their loyalty to France during the resistance, the left seemed best placed after the war to win concessions in favor of the Breton language. Thus in May 1947 the communist deputy from Finistère Pierre

Hervé introduced in parliament a draft-law authorizing Breton-language instruction in the schools of the three Bretonnant departments. It carried the signatures of 189 other communist and fellow-traveling deputies. Since the non-communist legislative majority at Paris considered Hervé's proposal a transparent maneuver to increase the electoral support of the extreme left in western Brittany, there was no chance that it would be enacted into law. Four years later this majority itself passed the Deixonne law of January 1951, which sanctioned optional instruction of regional languages in French schools. But hampered by restrictive application, insufficient funding, and ill-disguised hostility on the part of officials in the education ministry, the new law left the status of the Breton language hardly changed in the schools of western Brittany.

Catholic patriots also renewed their Breton action after the war and in 1948 revived Bleun-Brug. However, when its new leaders sought to rehabilitate the memory of Abbé Perrot, still thought by many on the peninsula to have been a German collaborator, they ran into the combined opposition of local Catholic notables and episcopal authorities. Before long Bleun-Brug lost even the slightest trace of combative Breton spirit. Finally, on the occasion of the fiftieth anniversary of its founding, the cardinal-archbishop of Rennes formally put Bleun-Brug on a path of exclusive Catholic action. Since 1955 the lay society Kendalc'h (Je maintiendrai) has become the leading Catholic-oriented Breton patriotic movement on the peninsula. Founded by the longtime Breton activist Pierre Mocaër in 1950 and relatively free of episcopal control, the society found particular favor among Catholic university students who joined in considerable numbers. Although centered in the Brest-Quimper region of south Finistère, the Kendalc'h organization at the end of the 1960s extended over the entire peninsula and enrolled more than ten thousand members. Its attractively designed and well-financed organ *Breiz* in the process became an important voice for the defense of Breton language and culture and the advocacy of regional autonomy for Brittany.

The Catholic regionalism of Kendalc'h was only a small part of a much larger Breton regionalist movement that grew up after 1945. The Breton most responsible for launching it was Joseph Martray. A man of extremely nimble political instincts, he had led an active life during the Vichy years. He was a close friend and associate of Yann Fouéré, who sponsored his membership on the Comité Consultatif de Bretagne. Although Fouéré was aware that Martray had joined the underground resistance network Défense de la France in the Landivisiau region of Brittany a few months before, he nonetheless appointed him editor-in-chief of *La Dépêche de Brest* on 1 December 1943. In this new post Martray made clear his anti-German attitude whenever possible. At the end of 1943, for example, he published a front-page story on the withdrawal of the Wehrmacht from the eastern front that carried the ironic headline "German Troops Advance toward the West." He voluntarily shut down *La Dépêche* early in August and joined the *maquis* near Lamballe as an active participant. Because of this record and his resistance-forged association with René Pleven, Martray was one of the few CCB members not prosecuted after the war and the only editor-in-chief of an occupation newspaper in Brittany not jailed during the liberation. For these reasons he seemed uniquely placed to extend postwar Breton action beyond the narrowly cultural framework in which it had initially been confined.

Martray first expressed his ideas on the political, social, and economic aspects of the Breton question in *Le Peuple Breton*, a new monthly he founded in October 1947. A few months later he created an allied organization called Renaissance du Peuple Breton, which he hoped would become the basis of a genuinely popular and democratic movement in favor of Breton regional reform. Both projects quickly foundered, however, when in the March 1948 issue of *Le Peuple Breton* Martray came to the defense of Breton nationalists he thought to have been too harshly treated by French authorities after August 1944.[3] He called on Paris to amnesty former PNB members who had not yet been prosecuted for acts of collaboration and to revise punishments already meted out to those who had not actually compromised themselves with the Germans. He even implied that members of the Bezenn Perrot duped by Laîné into wearing Nazi uniforms ought to be dealt with less severely than so far had been the case.

Martray's readers apparently did not want to be associated with so controversial a cause and a large number chose not to renew their subscriptions to *Le Peuple Breton* after the appearance of the article defending nationalist purge victims. His little monthly soon fell into financial difficulties and ceased publication in February 1949 after only sixteen issues.

Joseph Martray did not withdraw from Breton patriotic action in disappointment but only altered his approach to it. He resolved henceforth to avoid all divisive political questions and to abandon his earlier intention of organizing a popular democratic movement behind Breton regional reform. Instead he would concentrate solely on exposing the economic and social problems of Brittany and direct proposals for dealing with them exclusively to appropriate local elites. But he needed a vehicle for the coordination of these efforts. In 1950 Martray thus arranged a conference at Paris to which he invited several Bretons prominent in commercial, industrial, agricultural, maritime, and public service sectors of peninsular life. Out of this meeting came the Comité d'études et de liaison des intérêts bretons (CELIB) and its monthly organ *La Vie Bretonne*. Under the leadership of René Pleven and Joseph Martray, respectively its longtime president and secretary-general, the CELIB from the beginning rigorously eschewed any form of Breton national action. Indeed, so that Paris would not suspect the new committee of hidden political motives, Pleven and Martray limited the scope of its activities to the four Breton departments included in the VIᵉ economic region established by French law in 1938. Thus, to the intense dismay of many Breton patriots CELIB Brittany did not include the department of Loire-Inférieure and its chief city Nantes, the historic ducal capital of the peninsula.

The CELIB began immediately the related tasks of studying the socioeconomic problems of the peninsula, drafting a plan for Brittany's economic development in the future, and lobbying for its adoption by the central government in Paris. Many other persons who held important managerial and official posts in Breton public life received invitations to join the work of the new committee. Those who ultimately accepted included the entire Breton parliamentary delegation (except for communist deputies and senators who refused to participate), general councillors, economists, bankers, entrepreneurs, high civil servants, labor leaders, chamber of commerce officials, and peasant organizers. This prestigious membership in turn received the formal backing and assistance of a broad range of public and private Breton organizations. By the 1960s approximately nine hundred municipal councils and two hundred other bodies—from the four departmental councils that provided the bulk of its financing to factory unions and specialized interest groups—were involved in various CELIB activities.[4] Even as early as February 1952 *La Vie Bretonne* boasted that "there is hardly a single economic, occupational or cultural group that has not contacted [the CELIB] asking it to champion its particular cause." During the decade that followed its formation Martray's committee was unquestionably the premier Breton action society.

True to its diverse composition, the CELIB involved itself in a wide spectrum of activities relating to Breton life. Its industrial promotion commission publicized Brittany as an attractive place for the location of new factories and commercial enterprises. Its sales promotion committee sponsored the adoption and use of a special regional label for Breton agricultural, maritime, and industrial products. Its cultural commission sought, with scant success, to win official recognition for the Breton language in the schools of predominantly Bretonnant areas. But by far the most important work of the CELIB was accomplished by its regional economic expansion committee. After a rapid survey of the peninsular economy, this body drafted a Breton economic development plan based on specified investment target quotas for strategic sectors in Brittany's manufacturing, maritime, and agricultural industries. Approved by the full CELIB in March 1953 as "the first Breton plan," Martray and his colleagues hoped that Jean Monnet's national planning commissariat in Paris would incorporate it into the second French three-year plan. Although Monnet's planners did note the existence of the CELIB proposal in July, they would not commit themselves to its formal inclusion in the national scheme. To secure such a commitment the CELIB looked to its parliamentary commission of deputies and senators who represented Breton constituencies at Paris.

The ultimate success of the CELIB in fact depended on the

willingness of Brittany's elected national representatives to put the interests of their local region before their loyalty to party or legislative majority. Thus the general role assigned to the CELIB parliamentary commission was to act as a pressure group on behalf of Breton interests in the French legislature. "Since everything is decided in Paris," *La Vie Bretonne* observed in 1955, "Brittany must count on its members of parliament to defend its interests."[5] In this way French centralization, which so many Bretons considered responsible for their homeland's depressed social and economic conditions, would be turned to the advantage of Brittany's regional development. During the Fourth Republic when governments in Paris depended for survival on narrow majorities in the National Assembly that invariably included the parties that captured most of Brittany's legislative seats, this tactic seemed to produce results. It was largely in response to pressure exerted through its parliamentary commission that the government with a decree of 11 December 1954 conferred official consultative status on the CELIB's regional economic expansion committee. A year and a half of further lobbying resulted in an executive decree of 13 July 1956 that established a regional action plan for Brittany. Although CELIB leaders justly claimed major credit for this formal approval of the first such regional plan anywhere in France, it was in reality a much-watered-down version of the so-called first Breton plan of 1953. In particular the plan as adopted lacked the investment target quotas that served as the central planning technique in the original CELIB proposal. The 1956 regional action plan for Brittany was destined in any case to have only desultory application during its brief existence. Within two years it had disappeared in the political shuffle that saw the Fourth Republic in France give way to the Fifth Republic in 1958.

The need for regional action in Brittany was meanwhile taking on new urgency at the end of the 1950s when the peninsula became the scene of widespread and often violent disorders on the part of Breton farmers. The local agricultural economy faced imminent collapse as the prices of leading farm commodities dropped precipitously, with no sign of governmental intervention to halt the process. It was against this background of gathering rural crisis that angry farmers dumped thousands of gallons of milk along Breton roads, burned tons of worthless potatoes in municipal squares, and blocked major transportation arteries with their tractors and harvesting machines. Distracted by the war in Algeria and the growing threat of civil insurrection over attempts to end it, the government in Paris had little choice but to try to placate the rebellious Breton agricultural population. Thus Prime Minister Debré went to Rennes in March 1960 where, in a tumultuous appearance before a mass of shouting Breton peasants, he promised relief through early government action. The disturbances continued, however, and reached a climax in June 1961 when, in an action reminiscent of an old regime *jacquerie*, hundreds of furious Breton peasants converged on the subprefecture at Morlaix and occupied it for a few hours.

The CELIB responded to these events with a massive publicity campaign linking current farmer discontent to the long-standing local resentment at Brittany's underdevelopment that *La Vie Bretonne* had been reporting for years. Sensing that Debré's speech meant that the central government was for the moment vulnerable to pressure from the periphery, Pleven and Martray hoped with this campaign to mobilize mass support behind a new plan for Breton regional action. Such a plan, or *loi-programme* as such proposals are styled in the Fifth Republic, had been under discussion at the CELIB since 1959 and was formally launched in the conclusion of a book published by Pleven in 1961.[6] A short time later the full CELIB unanimously adopted a revised version of the Pleven document that had been drafted by its regional economic expansion committee. Its parliamentary commission was then instructed to introduce it as a proposed *loi-programme* in the forthcoming Chamber debate on the fourth French three-year plan. During this debate, held in the wake of renewed peasant agitation on the peninsula and the announcement of the entire Breton Chamber delegation that its members would put their loyalty to Brittany first in the vote on the national French plan, the government appeared to yield. On 21 June 1962 it seemed to commit itself to sponsoring a *loi-programme* based on the CELIB model for application throughout the whole of underdeveloped western France.

The CELIB moved to consolidate its apparent triumph by securing pledges from eighty-four candidates for Breton Chamber seats in the upcoming 1962 parliamentary elections that they would put the interests of Brittany before those of party. They even committed themselves to voting a motion of censure against their own parties, should they join a governing coalition, if the Breton interest so demanded. Candidates who gave these assurances overwhelmingly represented the political formations of the Fourth Republic, all seemingly still entrenched in Breton constituencies. By contrast, Gaullist UNR candidates refused to make any such commitments. Unfortunately for the CELIB, it was the latter group that won three-quarters of the peninsula's seats and thus deprived the Breton regionalist society of its capacity to exert direct legislative pressure on the new Gaullist ruling majority. By 1964 the CELIB's parliamentary commission had become completely inactive. The end of the Algerian war was meanwhile returning a measure of balance to the French economy and this had the effect of stabilizing agricultural prices in Brittany. Thus the CELIB not only lost its ability to influence government economic policy at the center but also saw its opportunity to mobilize pressure at the periphery by means of a Breton peasant *force de frappe* melt away as well.[7]

Although Martray would not acknowledge it, the CELIB was powerless and soon began to lose the internal cohesion that for more than a decade had made it the most promising regionalist organization in Breton history. The governmental decision of late 1963 to create regional economic development commissions called CODERs for Brittany and the other twenty economic regions in France precipitated the actual disintegration of the CELIB.[8] Far from being the popularly elected regional assemblies to supervise regional economic development long advocated by Martray and his colleagues, the new commissions had a predominantly appointive membership, no funds of their own, and strictly advisory functions. Instead of being mechanisms for broadening local participation in regional affairs by tipping the decision-making balance from Paris to the provinces, the CODERs were really no more than regional devices for more efficient centralized administration. Because of this Michel Phlipponneau, the chairman of the

CELIB regional economic expansion committee since 1962, urged a boycott of the new Breton CODER by the regionalist movement. He also recommended that the CELIB cast its lot with the left-wing opposition candidacy of Gaston Defferre for the French presidency in 1965. But Joseph Martray successfully blocked Phlipponneau's proposed strategy by convincing a majority of his colleagues that the CELIB's pressure-group role precluded partisan political activity. He further argued that the Breton CODER should be accepted for the fait accompli it was and be infiltrated and used by the CELIB for its own ends.

For three years Phlipponneau tried to persuade Martray that the only way the CELIB could recover its lost vigor was to contest the Gaullist CODER on political terrain. At last recognizing that he struggled for possession of a lifeless body, he gave up the effort and resigned from the Breton regionalist society in May 1967.[9] Martray's adamant refusal to boycott the Breton CODER in the name of the CELIB in fact dealt a mortal blow to the whole Breton postwar regionalist movement of which he had originally been the driving force. He soon realized the bankruptcy of his policy and quit his post of secretary-general a month after Phlipponneau's resignation. The sorry state into which the CELIB had fallen became painfully evident in 1969 when it could no longer keep afloat the financially straitened *La Vie Bretonne*. René Pleven, whose position as CELIB president had meantime become largely honorific, himself abandoned the moribund regionalist society in September 1972.

The failure of the CELIB strikingly resembles that of the Union Régionaliste Bretonne a half century before. Both depended for success on the goodwill of central authorities in Paris to cooperate in a common effort to improve the conditions of Breton life. But both found that they confronted a regime determined not to yield any of its decision-making power to the provinces. There were other complications as well. The most important was the existence of a primordial ambiguity within both the URB and the CELIB between a strong desire to serve as an ideologically neutral Breton union for the defense of widely divergent interests and the often contradictory need to play what amounted to a role as a political pressure group. And behind this crippling ambiguity lay an unvoiced but nonetheless powerful desire to shield established peninsular interests from thoroughgoing social reform that might come through the emergence of a mass-based movement of the left. Indeed both the URB and the CELIB, though they claimed to speak on behalf of all Bretons, organized themselves as cadre societies apart from the masses of the peninsula. Thus each inevitably found itself isolated from the vital social, economic, and political forces that were re-shaping Breton society, unable either to influence events or even to understand them. In the final analysis, then, the failure of CELIB regionalism cleared the way, just as that of the URB had done decades earlier, for the rapid growth of more militant Breton action in the form of ethnic minority nationalism.

Survivors of the pre-1945 Breton nationalist movement were never enthusiastic about and expected little from the CELIB. But recognizing that Breton nationalism still suffered from the burden of its wartime reputation, they were hardly in a position to challenge the approach of Martray and the CELIB to the Breton problem. A few nationalists even thought it essential that the regionalist card be loyally played. If in so doing the CELIB scored important gains for Brittany, that was all to the good. If it did not, the justice of their reservations concerning its program and strategy would appear confirmed. The nationalists would then be in a position to take their case to the Breton people against the immediate background of the failure of the regionalists to improve the lot of Brittany rather than that of accusations of wartime collaboration with the Germans.[10] During most of the 1950s, therefore, Breton nationalists generally chose to remain on the sidelines as the CELIB pursued its regionalist objectives.

Yet it should not be thought that Breton nationalists were entirely inactive during the years of CELIB ascendancy. Even before Martray organized his regionalist committee, Raymond Delaporte's brother Hervé had tried without success in 1949 to revive what was left of the old prewar nationalist movement. In 1953 he joined forces with Marcel Guieysse to undertake an equally futile effort to circulate a clandestine version of *Breiz Atao*. The two veteran nationalists then decided to support the initiative of a group of young patriots headed by Jacques Quatreboeufs to create a cautiously named Breton nationalist movement called Réveil Armoricain. The backbone of this new project was the periodical *La Bretagne Réelle*, which appeared for the first time in March 1954 in a modest format of four mimeographed pages. Its entry on the Breton scene, Quatreboeufs explained in the inaugural issue, meant that Breton political nationalists had at last emerged from the semiclandestinity in which they had been living for ten years and henceforth could struggle for Brittany in the open.

La Bretagne Réelle completely failed to spearhead the emergence of an important postwar Breton nationalist movement. During more than twenty years of uninterrupted existence it has been unable to forge the comprehensive doctrine of Breton national action that Quatreboeufs promised from the outset. Instead it has functioned primarily as a forum for the promotion of the rather bizarre ideas of its founder, which have included since 1954 admiration for Celtic pagan Christianity, paramilitary fascism, authoritarian government, militant anti-Communism, racist ideology, anti-Semitism, and white supremacy.[11] Much was also made at first of *La Bretagne Réelle*'s commitment to "authentically federalist principles." But since Quatreboeufs called for the breakup of the French state into constituent parts like Alsace, Burgundy, and Provence, which with Brittany would then enter a new European federation as autonomous ethnic units, its federalism actually masked a separatist motive. In fact the only theme that has consistently appeared in *La Bretagne Réelle* during the past two decades is its emphatic rejection of the notion that Brittany's ancient Celtic language is the fundamental bulwark of Breton national feeling.

Jacques Quatreboeufs's intransigent Gallo point of view was probably enough to ensure that *La Bretagne Réelle* would not become the focus of a postwar ethnic minority nationalist movement in Brittany. He had in any case gravely compromised the prospects of his new publication by allowing it to become the vehicle through which discredited former members of the PNB sought to make a comeback in Breton nationalist action. Even as early as September 1954 Olier Mordrel wrote in its columns. It was not long before he was joined by Marcel Guieysse, Hervé Delaporte, and Célestin Laîné. Given this lineup, it was hardly an exaggeration when one of Quatreboeufs's closest associates boasted in 1964 that *La Bretagne Réelle* had kept alive "the spirit of *Breiz Atao* that so many people thought dead."[12] But it was precisely that aspect of the little mimeographed nationalist publication that earned for it the contempt of the overwhelming majority of postwar Breton nationalists. In their view the past record of the Breton nationalist movement was one to be overcome, not embraced. Quatreboeufs's original partner, the left-leaning Yann Poupinot, had made that clear even before *La Bretagne Réelle* published its first issue. When he discovered that money had been accepted from Hervé Delaporte and Marcel Guieysse to help launch the new periodical, he declared in a January 1954 letter to Quatreboeufs that either those two "ill-starred jokers" or himself would have to go.[13] Quatreboeufs's refusal to disavow the two former PNB members meant that Yann Poupinot would have to look elsewhere for a way to affirm his Breton national feeling.

After withdrawing from *La Bretagne Réelle* Poupinot continued to teach the course in Breton history he had begun several years before at Ker-Vreiz, the Breton cultural center in Paris.[14] In these classes he urged the formation of a new nationalist movement that aimed at the social and economic liberation of the Breton people rather than at the defense of the Breton language or the recovery of Brittany's putative historic rights. He therefore counseled a clean break with the Breton nationalist traditions established by *Breiz Atao* and the PNB, whose leaders he thought had relied too heavily on outmoded linguistic and historical arguments when placing their case before Breton public opinion. Poupinot's background as a prisoner in the Service du Travail Obligatoire and then as a member of the resistance only reinforced his otherwise principled opposition to the pre-1945 nationalist movement. He did share with his nationalist predecessors, however, their emphasis on the need for political action in the struggle on behalf of Breton national revival. Without it, he thought, strictly economic and cultural action of the CELIB variety was doomed in advance to failure. In his view it was simply a matter of power. So long as the Breton people lacked the leverage offered by autonomous political institutions with real decision-making power, central authorities in Paris would never accede to Breton economic and cultural demands.

In 1956 Poupinot and a group of like-minded colleagues at Ker-Vreiz drafted a document called "Projet d'Organisation de la Bretagne" (POB), which they hoped might provide the doctrinal basis for a new Breton nationalist political movement.[15] It called for the decentralization of French political and administrative institutions, the granting of a special statute for the amalgamated five Breton departments, and the creation of an elected regional assembly with original legislative authority in all areas that directly affected the social, economic, and cultural interests of the Breton people. The POB program also envisaged the formation of a specially trained civil administration for the region. Its functions would include implementation of economic development plans voted by the regional assembly and the remodeling of the peninsular educational system so that it might better respond to the particular needs and interests of young Bretons. These were long-term goals, however, and until their achievement Poupinot and his friends suggested a number of immediate measures that could be accomplished within the existing machinery of government. Thus they called for the creation of a regional executive commission composed of delegates from the five Breton departmental councils and the formation of an embryonic regional administration drawn from high-ranking civil servants already posted in Brittany by Paris. The principal functions of these bodies were to be the approval and application of existing economic development schemes such as the CELIB's first Breton plan of 1953. These new administrative divisions would also be responsible for the equitable and rational distribution of investment credits and public loans approved in Paris for the five Breton departments. Finally, the POB immediate program urged the training of a corps of Breton-language teachers for all levels of the peninsular educational system and the addition of courses in the history of Brittany to its curriculum.

Yann Fouéré, only recently cleared of all outstanding charges against him for his Breton activity during the Vichy years, quickly rallied to the POB proposals. Many of them were almost identical with ideas he had been expressing before meetings of Breton students from May through November 1956.[16] Thus he joined with Poupinot to help organize local committees to promote the POB program and to gather the signatures of individual Bretons who supported it. By the spring of 1957 more than 6,200 such signatures had been obtained, a number that included many Breton mayors, municipal and departmental councillors, and even a few senators and deputies. Encouraged by this success, Fouéré and Poupinot arranged a meeting at Lorient on 10 November 1957 in order to launch a new Breton political movement called the "Mouvement pour l'Organisation de la Bretagne" (MOB). The three hundred Bretons who assembled at Lorient adopted the POB document as the new organization's fundamental charter and founded a publication called *L'Avenir* to serve as its journalistic voice. The meeting ended with the adoption of a series of resolutions that deplored the social and economic underdevelopment of the peninsula, regretted Paris's delay in fully endorsing the CELIB Breton plan, and denied that the formation of the MOB was in any way prompted by ulterior secessionist motives.

L'Avenir appeared for the first time in January 1958. In its first editorial Yann Fouéré emphasized that the MOB was a nonpartisan movement independent of all existing political formations. He added that the new Breton organization was meant to be an ideologically neutral meeting-ground for all Breton patriots who put their devotion to Brittany ahead of any commitment to particular social and economic theories. As had been true of so many of its predecessors in Breton action, the MOB's avowed neutrality on social and economic questions was dictated by the wide and often conflicting ideological points of view represented within its membership. Even its most prominent personalities, despite their relatively homogeneous social background in Brittany's business and professional middle classes (three-fourths of the nearly two-score members who served on the MOB executive committee from 1958 to 1965 belonged to these strata), included men of remarkably diverse views, ranging from extreme right-wingers such as the Comte du Halgouët to communist sympathizers like J.-C. Veillard. In general, however, the MOB membership divided into two groups, each reflecting the views of one or the other of its original promoters. Its left wing was composed of progressives who hoped with Yann Poupinot that the MOB would become the political instrument for the social and economic liberation of the Breton people through reform of the peninsula's capitalistic institutions. By contrast, its right-wing nationalist conservatives followed Fouéré's lead and looked on the MOB as a vehicle for the national liberation of the Breton people without basically altering the established pattern of social and economic relations in Brittany. Many of them indeed hoped that the creation of regional institutions would raise a barrier against the automatic extension to the peninsula of radical reforms by means of otherwise centralized French political and administrative structures should the left take power in Paris.

MOB progressives and conservatives were united, however, on a "colonialist" interpretation of modern Breton history. First advanced by Fouéré and subsequently elaborated by the socialist-inclined Ned Urvoas, this view maintained that since the French Revolution Brittany had existed as an internal colony of the centralized state administration in Paris.[17] For two centuries it had been allegedly governed by foreign rulers who, in tandem with an entirely gallicized local elite, treated the indigenous Breton population as socially, culturally, and morally inferior stock. The only value of the Bretons was to supply cheap, unskilled labor and docile conscripts to the factories and armed forces of the ruling country. During these centuries, the argument added, Brittany had also been systematically stripped of its natural resources, kept in a deliberately retarded state of economic development, and compelled to serve as a captive market for the consumption of artificially high-priced French-manufactured goods.

Because it posited the existence of a common experience of oppression for the entire Breton population, the colonial interpretation had an inherently powerful appeal for the nationalists of the MOB. At the same time it represented a decisive step beyond the long-standing nationalist argument that persecution of the Breton language was the hallmark of French rule in Brittany. The latter view, responding as it did to the experience of only half of the Breton people, had too often in the past divided and weakened the nationalist movement.[18] The all-embracing colonial interpretation of modern Breton historical experience by contrast promised to be a source of union and strength. It also had another potentially important advantage. Since MOB leaders portrayed Brittany's relationship to Paris as analogous to that of France's overseas possessions, they obviously hoped that Gaullist-supervised decolonization would have favorable repercussions on the Armorican peninsula. Indeed, only six months after Algerians won their right to national self-determination, *L'Avenir* advised Breton nationalists that they must look to North Africa for an example; "what its poeple have done in ten years we must do."[19]

The MOB's initial impact on Breton opinion meanwhile seemed to indicate that its future prospects were bright. In the parliamentary elections of November 1958, the first held under the Fifth Republic, fourteen peninsular candidates publicly endorsed the POB charter and went on to collect almost 23 percent of the total vote case in their constituencies. Among them were three MOB activists who together captured more than sixteen thousand votes, nearly 12 percent of all the votes cast in their districts. The following month MOB candidates were elected to three municipal councils in Brittany while two members, one of whom was Fouéré's close associate Jean Fichoux, were named to the French Senate. Unfortunately for the MOB's promoters, however, it never fulfilled these early signs of promise, instead collapsing only a few short years after its foundation amid the bitter antagonism of its progressive and conservative wings. The problem was that in the politically charged formative years of the Fifth Republic the MOB was unable to maintain its original stance of nonpartisan ideological neutrality. There were local issues in Brittany and divisive controversies in France at large on which it simply could not avoid taking sides. In practice this meant that the MOB had to define its attitude toward the peasant unrest that troubled Brittany during the early 1960s and toward the war in Algeria, which was contemporaneously distorting French political life. In the process it lost the fragile balance within its divided membership.

There was no doubt that the MOB would support Breton

farmers in their protest against falling agricultural prices. Not to have done so would have violated the rule of Breton solidarity while it simultaneously provoked progressive leaders who viewed the plight of the farmers with great sympathy. Yet since peasant spokesmen like Alex Gourvennec made land reform and other structural changes in Brittany's agricultural economy an essential part of their protest program, the MOB dared not offer its support too vigorously for fear of alienating its conservative members. They were men who not only shunned social change of such magnitude on principle but who were also closely tied to the traditional Breton landed class, which was the main target of these peasant-sponsored reforms. MOB leaders finally tried to finesse the issue by supporting the CELIB *loi-programme*. This solution seemed to satisfy everybody since the CELIB proposals, although drafted and endorsed by men who in terms of their social background and political ideas closely resembled MOB conservatives, had the strong support of Gourvennec and other progressive favorites in the peasant movement. The MOB may in any case have had no real choice in the matter, for by mid-1962 the CELIB initiative seemed to have acquired irreversible momentum, even winning apparent government endorsement at the end of June.

On the face of it, leaders of the MOB appeared to have no more choice concerning the stand they would take on the issue of the Algerian war. Since the arguments they used to back their claims for self-government in Brittany had equally logical application in North Africa, automatic support for the cause of Algerian self-determination seemed inevitable. From the beginning, in fact, MOB progressives had shown considerable sympathy in *L'Avenir* for the Algerian nationalist movement. However, their conservative rivals—by instinct, tradition, and interest tied to those elements on the French right that most wanted to keep Algeria French—resisted an outright declaration of MOB support for the Algerian rebels. The influence of the latter was indeed so great that *L'Avenir* lamely advised its readers to abstain on the Gaullist referendum in favor of Algerian self-determination held on 8 January 1961. But when Breton voters overwhelmingly backed de Gaulle on this issue even conservative Breton nationalists realized that they must fall into line behind Algerian independence or face isolation in Brittany. The MOB thereafter gave unvarying support to de Gaulle on the Algerian question, advising Bretons in April 1962 to vote for the referendum on the Evian accords, which finally brought the war to an end.

The MOB's backing of Gaullist policy in Algeria became intertwined with its support for the CELIB *loi-programme* in the fall of 1962 when parliamentary elections were held in France. Unlike the CELIB, which relied for success on the return of a solid bloc of deputies belonging to the old parties of the Fourth Republic, the MOB gambled on a Gaullist victory. And it will be recalled that candidates of the regime swept three-quarters of Brittany's constituencies in November. Realizing that Martray's group had fatally miscalculated, the leaders of the MOB pushed themselves forward as the willing recipients of any official favors that might be forthcoming upon enactment of the *loi-programme* for Brittany by the new Gaullist majority. It was in order to reassure that majority concerning the moderate and loyalist character of the MOB that the conservative spokesman Yann Poilvet at the beginning of 1963 condemned in *L'Avenir* the idea of a separate Breton state independent of France. Combat on behalf of such a goal he thought "useless, desperate, and illogical" and added that whether Breton nationalists liked it or not they were irrevocably citizens of France. Poilvet even seemed to imply that the MOB could be persuaded to accept the loss of Nantes and Loire-Atlantique.[20]

Poilvet's remarks immediately drew the anger of the MOB's young left-wing radicals, who formed an ad hoc student anticolonialist committee. In the next issue of *L'Avenir* one of their leaders, Ronan Le Prohon, accused Poilvet of sowing "verbal confusionism" and warned that the MOB was playing it too cozy with the inherently anti-Breton Gaullist regime.[21] For several months the antagonism between the MOB conservatives and their radical critics simmered on the front page of *L'Avenir*, a front page that was shared almost equally by the leading spokesmen for each faction. The developing crisis came to a head in November 1963 when the MOB held its annual national congress at Brest. The radicals came to this meeting determined to make fundamental changes in the MOB charter. They wanted above all to discard its avowed nonpartisan character and end its policy of welcoming into the MOB all Breton patriots regardless of their political and ideological beliefs. Such an apolitical union of Bretons who privately expressed widely divergent views, one of them later explained, finally harmed the political effectiveness of all its members while making it impossible for its leaders to generate a coherent body of doctrine.[22] The young dissidents instead wanted the MOB to recast itself into a frankly left-wing and anti-Gaullist opposition movement. The election of a new executive committee for the MOB showed, however, that the conservatives enjoyed a decisive majority among the delegates at Brest. Even the token candidacy of Pierre Le Padellec, one of the most outspoken student leaders, was turned aside.

Frustrated in their efforts to remodel the MOB, the members of its dissident student anticolonialist committee bolted and organized a new Breton society that they called the Union Démocratique Bretonne (UDB). Since most of its progressive wing soon rallied to the banner of the new organization, the MOB virtually collapsed and increasingly slipped into a merely nominal existence. After the departure of its progressives all that really remained of the MOB was *L'Avenir* and it only expressed the views of a general staff that no longer had any nationalist troops to deploy on behalf of Brittany. It is true that the MOB's conservative remnant sought to rally new sympathizers to its side by appealing to former members of the PNB for their support. Thus by the end of 1964 Olier Mordrel had already become a regular contributor to *L'Avenir*. Although the addition of such discredited revenants from the past no doubt accentuated the Breton nationalist character of the MOB, their presence hardly strengthened the virtually moribund organization. Instead the MOB fell deeper and deeper into that same eccentricity and isolation in which *La Bretagne Réelle* had been so pointlessly floundering for more than a decade.

By contrast, the fledgling UDB prospered as its leaders established for it an explicitly democratic, socialist, and Breton nationalist identity in its monthly organ *Le Peuple Breton*. Like the MOB it recognized the "national vocation" of Brittany

and aimed to defend and develop a uniquely Breton personality in its various political, social, and cultural aspects. It
insisted as well on the territorial integrity of the five Breton
departments into which the peninsula had long been divided.
In one respect the nationalist character of the UDB was even
more pronounced than that of the MOB. Whereas defense of
Brittany's ancestral Celtic language had never loomed large
in the program of the senior Breton organization, the young
founders of the UDB meant to give the language issue a prominent place in their Breton action. Many of them in fact were
Bretonnants born in Finistère and had great affection for and
pride in their maternal tongue. But following in the tradition
of their spiritual fathers Emile Masson and Yann Sohier, UDB
leaders insisted that the language first had to be stripped of
its long-standing clerical and reactionary associations. Only
thus did they think it could become the vehicle they needed
for the involvement of the Bretonnant population in the building of an authentically popular, lay, and socialist Breton culture on the peninsula.

It was the UDB's commitment to the task of thoroughgoing social reform in Brittany that in any case most differen-
tiated it from the MOB. Its own internal structure based on
principles of rank-and-file participation, collective decision
making, and a rotating elected membership, the UDB in its
founding charter called for the establishment of an "absolutely
democratic regime" in Brittany.[23] The charter went on to explain that this objective necessarily presupposed the disappearance of capitalist economic liberalism and its replacement
by a new system of planned economic and social democracy.
In this process the founders of the UDB envisaged "primordial
roles" for existing Breton syndicalist and professional organizations. They believed in fact that construction of a just and
truly modern society in Brittany ultimately depended on the
full participation of the Breton laboring masses so long vic-
timized by the peninsula's "colonialist" social order. As the
inaugural issue of Le Peuple Breton explained it, inclusion in
the moral community called "the Breton people" in the final
analysis was a function of its members' common experience
of economic exploitation and social disadvantage.

During the years after 1964 the socialist aspect of the UDB

deepened as its leaders increasingly concerted their action with that of other left-wing opposition forces in Brittany, especially the communists and the PSU (Parti Socialiste Unifié) socialists. The most striking example of this process came in the tumultuous days of May–June 1968 when at the side of its leftist allies the UDB enthusiastically plunged into the general strike movement that nearly toppled the Gaullist regime. The Socialist and Communist parties reciprocated this gesture when their candidates in Breton constituencies for the parliamentary elections of June 1968 publicly endorsed a "minimum democratic regional program" drafted by the UDB. Among other things this program called for the suppression of departments and prefects in Brittany, the reorganization of the Breton CODER into a truly regional and democratic economic council with majority representation for workers, the creation of an elected regional parliament with real legislative authority, and the encouragement of a genuinely popular culture in Brittany based on the defense of the Breton language. For the first time the entire French left in Brittany thus threw its support behind a program of regional reform for the peninsula and in the process acquired a distinctly Breton flavor.

The UDB meanwhile carved out a reputation for itself as the champion of various local causes in Brittany. Its members marched with protesting unemployed stevedores at St.-Nazaire in early 1964. Later in the year they joined Breton peasant demonstrations against the agricultural policies of the Gaullist regime. The UDB also led the peninsular opposition to the development of atomic weapons in France. Its leaders argued that such a project absorbed vast amounts of money that might better be spent to develop the backward economies of regions like Brittany. The UDB likewise protested the Gaullist policy of concentrating French defense installations and military training schools on the Breton peninsula. Not only did its leaders look on this as an act of official intimidation but they also considered it a possible deadening influence on the future expansion of the entire Breton economy. They feared as well that the existence of a huge state-run military complex in Brittany would greatly diminish the likelihood of increasing local participation in decision-making processes insofar as they affected Breton interests. By the very nature of things, such powers of decision would remain concentrated in the central defense ministries at Paris. For similar reasons the UDB opposed the Gaullist policy of tax incentives for industrial concerns that agreed to locate new factories on the peninsula. This scheme, according to a *Le Peuple Breton* editorial assailing the construction of a Citroën automobile assembly plant at Rennes, amounted to a new form of colonization in Brittany carried out by giant French corporations based in Paris.[24] The inevitable consequence for Breton workers would be, the editorial concluded, to perpetuate into the distant future their dependence on and continued exploitation by outside economic interests.

The UDB's record of militant support for Brittany's laboring population was accompanied by steady growth in both its size and the field of its influence. After five years its expanding membership was large enough to sustain vigorous local UDB sections at Brest, Rennes, Quimper, Pont-l'Abbé, St. Malo, Vannes, Lorient, Paris-Nord, and Paris-Sud. This membership was extremely young. *Le Peuple Breton* reported at the end of 1967 that the average age of its members stood at approximately twenty-five years. The UDB rank-and-file became more socially representative with the passage of time. Although its founding members had almost all been university students, by the end of 1967 nearly a fifth of its total membership belonged to the Breton working class. It was also a membership that supported the UDB with generous donations of time and money, which meant that the organization was able to avoid the chronic financial crises that so often in the past had paralyzed the action of its predecessors in the Breton nationalist movement. This relative material stability at the same time allowed *Le Peuple Breton* to prosper. By 1969 the number of its pages had doubled from four to eight, while its monthly press run rose from fifteen hundred in 1964 to four thousand five years later, a momentum that continued unbroken into the 1970s. Thus even so hostile a critic as Olier Mordrel grudgingly admitted in 1973 that the UDB was the most vigorous and active Breton political formation in all of Brittany.[25]

The emergence of the militantly left-wing Union Démocratique Bretonne was but one aspect, however, of what may be called the hardening of Breton nationalist attitudes after the collapse of the CELIB and the MOB in the early 1960s. The Breton scholarly review *Ar Vro*, for example, that when founded in 1959 exhibited ideologically conservative and vaguely regionalist sympathies had by 1963 developed socially progressive and frankly nationalist points of view. It denounced the *loi-programme* as "an illusion and a dupery," adopted the Brittany-as-colony theme, and encouraged the notion that the Breton people constituted an oppressed "proletarian nation."[26] The conservative and Catholic Kendalc'h organization passed through an internal ideological crisis during 1962–63 that ended in the adoption of mildly nationalist views. Even the increasingly Mordrelian tone of both *La Bretagne Réelle* and *L'Avenir* in the mid-1960s may be seen as part of the growing rigidity of Breton nationalist attitudes after the disintegration of the postwar regionalist movement in Brittany. In the long run, however, the most significant example of this hardening process came in the area of Breton cultural action.

For many years Breton nationalists had been deploring the crucial role of state-run secondary schools in socializing young men and women from the peninsula into the system of French national values. They particularly understood that the central place given to French language and literature in the *lycée* curriculum established in the minds of Breton students the alleged superiority of French culture. So long as Paris enjoyed a monopoly over this vital educational experience, Breton nationalists were convinced that Brittany's native educated elite would for the most part be lost to their movement. It was in order to break this monopoly that Dr. Guy Etienne, an intransigently nationalist physician from Châteaulin, in 1963 created SADED, the so-called Association for Secondary Education in the Breton Language.[27]

Organized as an integrated system of correspondence courses pitched at the level of the final year of *lycée* and supervised by a volunteer staff of professional teachers, SADED's exclusively Breton-language curriculum featured as its core instruction in the language, literature, history, and geography of Brittany. Although they subsequently added courses in more technical subjects like chemistry, physics, and mathe-

matics, SADED's organizers were less interested in the inculca-
tion of pure knowledge than in the preparation of young
Bretons for tasks in the nationalist movement. From the beginning, in fact, they never concealed the underlying political
motivation of their endeavor, admitting openly in their first
annual report that by so acting they had put themselves "on
the road that leads to the Breton state."[28] As a practical matter
they wanted to recruit not a cross-section of the Breton student population but rather a cohesive knot of young patriots
fanatically devoted to the cause of national independence for
their homeland. The stern and exacting discipline of SADED
could appeal only the most nationalistic of Breton youth anyway and the total number of students who have completed
its program during the past decade is small, perhaps not
even exceeding a hundred.[29]

The militant attitudes that SADED teachers have labored
to instill in their students are evident in the teachers' explanation of how they handled "the question of individual freedom." Those who enrolled in SADED were simply obliged to
give it up and commit "all their time to the requirements of
the group." But in relinquishing their personal freedom, a
SADED report of spring 1965 explained, its students "gained
another kind of freedom, closer by its nature to the freedom
that we want for the restored national community of Brittany."[30] Such language is strongly reminiscent of interwar
fascist discussions of freedom, order, and authority. It is in
any case true that SADED instilled powerful notions of duty,
obedience, and self-sacrifice in the young Bretons who passed
through its rigors. The result has been the formation of a pool
of intransigent Breton terrorists determined at all costs to end
Brittany's alleged colonial status as a subject nation. It hardly
came as a surprise, therefore, that several members of the
Front de Libération de la Bretagne (FLB)—the most sensational manifestation of the hardening of Breton nationalist
attitudes in the mid-1960s—had once been students in the
SADED program. The sudden appearance of this new wave of
Breton terrorism inaugurated the most recent and perhaps
most significant phase in the history of ethnic minority nationalism in twentieth-century Brittany.

❧ The Breton Liberation Front

No one had ever heard of a Front de Libération de la Bretagne until 11 June 1966 when the press in Brittany received a communiqué purporting to come from such a source. Its anonymous authors claimed responsibility for the abortive bombing of a St.-Brieuc municipal tax office the day before. They went on to explain that the FLB had acted in order to protest the recent arrests of three Breton youths at St.-Nazaire for desecrating French flags and tossing ineffectual Molotov cocktails into the local subprefecture. These gestures, the communiqué continued, had been purely symbolic acts intended solely to draw attention to the colonial situation of Brittany in general and to the unemployment crisis at St.-Nazaire in particular. But in arresting their perpetrators and handing them over to the courts for prosecution, French officials seemed to indicate their determination to respond to Breton patriotic action with force rather than understanding. The mysterious FLB note thus announced that Breton terrorists were taking up the cause of their imprisoned compatriots and would carry out a campaign of violence against French administrative structures on the peninsula, "the symbols of the occupying power in Brittany." The note ended with the warning that "we will strike at times and places chosen by us. Our struggle will end only in victory."[1]

For several months, however, nothing further was heard from the FLB. Then in the fall of 1966 the three youths arrested at St.-Nazaire were brought to trial, convicted, and sentenced to two months in prison and a fine of one thousand francs each.[2] The FLB once more surfaced and protested these verdicts by placing incendiary bombs at a tax office in Lorient.

But the campaign against French government installatioɪ promised in June 1966 did not really materialize until the second half of 1967. During that period half a dozen FLB bombing incidents were reported at various locations on the peninsula. Five more took place in the first month of 1968, including simultaneous attempts against the prefectures at Quimper and St.-Brieuc during the night of 11–12 January. At both of the latter sites the police found notes that urged Bretons to join the FLB in its struggle against "French bureaucrats in Brittany." In the course of 1968 FLB terrorists struck on at least twenty more occasions. Most of these attacks occurred in southern Brittany in the region that stretches from Nantes in the east to Quimper in the west. Tax offices were the preferred targets, although FLB strikes were sometimes made at police barracks and electrical installations. In no case did physical injury to persons result and destruction of property was generally slight. The only exception came with the bombing of a CRS (Compagnies Républicaines de Sécurité, the French riot police) garage at St.-Brieuc during the night of 27–28 April that caused damages of more than one million francs.[3]

Bewildered French police officials seemed unable either to expose the FLB or to check the activity of its members. All they knew for certain was that a red Citroën D.S. had been seen in the vicinity of several FLB targets and that the elusive secret society funneled its communiqués through a Dublin-based Comité National pour une Bretagne Libre (CNBL). Presided over by an exiled former PNB youth corps leader named Yann Goulet, this shadowy committee had first appeared in late 1967 in the wake of Charles de Gaulle's celebrated foray into Quebec politics. Some even thought that Goulet was the real leader of the FLB and orchestrated its movements from the Irish capital, a proposition vigorously refuted by the usually well-informed Breton nationalist Marie-Anne Kerhuel.[4] Moreover, although CNBL-issued messages claimed to speak for the FLB as a whole, discipline within the terrorist organization was far from perfect. For example, a communiqué from Dublin dated 25 August 1968 announced that the FLB was suspending all activity until de Gaulle made public a widely anticipated Breton reform program during his forthcoming trip to the peninsula. Within two weeks, however, nine new bombing incidents took place in southern Brittany and all bore the characteristic FLB monogram. In the face of these apparently independent actions by local FLB commandos, a new communiqué from Dublin on 16 September simply rescinded the earlier truce.

There were in fact indications that the FLB actually consisted of competing "hard" and "soft" factions. Alain Murcier, a journalist for *Le Monde* who published a long article on the FLB in the fall of 1968, received an anonymous letter that suggested the existence of such a split. His informant went on to explain that the ideologically conservative "softs" operated out of Ireland and rejected on principle anything other than symbolic acts of violence. The Marxist-oriented and Paris-based "hards," on the other hand, were prepared not only to adopt methods of guerrilla warfare but also to combat what they called "the neo-Fascism of traditional Breton autonomism and its schlerotic leaders."[5] But there was really no way to tell which faction was responsible for particular acts of terrorism, since both used the initials "FLB-ARB." Only after 1969 did it become known that for the "softs" "ARB" stood for "Armée Républicaine Bretonne" while for the "hards" it meant "Armée Révolutionnaire Bretonne." There was in any case no doubt that the former was the larger of the two groups and responsible for the overwhelming majority of FLB strikes. The "softs" were also the first to explain, in a manifesto dated 28 December 1968, the FLB analysis of the situation in Brittany and what Breton terrorists hoped to accomplish with their mounting campaign of violence.

Brittany's domination by a foreign power and its alleged status as a domestic colony of France were the doctrinal points of departure of the FLB's Breton national action. Indeed its members saw the emergence of their clandestine national liberation front within the context of the worldwide movement toward decolonization after 1945. They had thus done no more than "to join themselves to all men of every race and color who struggle, suffer, and die for justice and liberty from one end of the world to the other."[6] But if decolonization had been achieved throughout much of the nonwestern world by the mid-1960s, in the view of the FLB manifesto it still had to be accomplished in the "reactionary" states on the European continent. That Europe should be the last arena for the working out of this process was only to be expected, the manifesto explained, since it was there that "structures of colonial domination were most ancient and deeply rooted." Insisting that theirs would be a worthy example for others to follow, the authors added that Bretons could be proud to be among the first of Europe's oppressed peoples to regain their national identity and take up the anticolonialist struggle on its behalf.

Since they believed that Brittany was but a particular case of the colonial situation in general, the FLB "softs" disclosed that they would "borrow the schemes and methods that have proven their worth in anticolonialist struggles elsewhere in the world." This statement meant in part that they placed their Breton action within the framework of the "generous principles of socialism." The "softs" were quick to explain, however, that their socialism had nothing in common with the bureaucratic, authoritarian, and imperialist socialism practiced by states that had done no more than to replace private capitalism with an equally oppressive state capitalism. By contrast, theirs would be an anticollectivist, humanist, cooperative, federalist, and communitarian socialism. In short the FLB "softs" wanted nothing to do with Soviet-style communism and strenuously sought to put distance between themselves and the peninsular arm of the French Communist party, which had lately taken up the cause of Breton regional reform. So that no one would miss the point, the FLB manifesto plainly stated that realization of its brand of socialism depended on the political liberation of the peninsula and the creation of a new Breton society entirely independent of any external hegemony whatever. It even labeled those communists and socialists in Brittany who accepted the so-called foreign tutelage of Paris-based political parties as "hypocrites, ignoramuses, and traitors."

FLB "softs" also tried to put distance between themselves and peninsular leftists over the issue of the role of violence in Breton national action. To put revolutionary violence at the core of Breton patriotic militancy as so many left-wingers in the UDB were wont to do the "softs" considered nothing more than an updated form of anarchic political romanticism. Instead, they looked on violence primarily as a means of self-defense and a dramatic way to express the anger and frustration of Bretons at having been denied the benefits of twentieth-century civilization. Yet they made it clear that they were prepared to use violence in equal measure with that utilized by the regime in Paris "to prevent the free expression of the Breton people." Since French officials appeared willing to employ any means to repress the gathering momentum of Breton nationalism and since Paris had never peacefully accepted the loss of its colonies, the authors of the FLB manifesto warned that accelerating measures of violence were needed in order to "decolonize" Brittany. At the end of their lengthy doctrinal exposition they accordingly revealed that the FLB had resolved "to intensify its acts of liberation" against the French occupation of Brittany.

After the appearance of the December 1968 FLB manifesto it was a reasonable expectation that a new wave of terrorist strikes would soon be reported on the peninsula. The document instead seemed more likely to be remembered as the swan song of the Breton liberation front. Two days before its publication police officers at Nantes had been sent to intervene in a noisy domestic quarrel at the home of a watchmaker named Jacques Nédélec. Through the door they overheard Mme. Nédélec tell her husband that he would be better off minding his own business instead of dragging their son around in a red D.S. on bombing expeditions. The officers duly noted this remark in their report to the Angers prefecture, which exercised civil jurisdiction over Nantes. There it caused a sensation because the prefectural dossier on the FLB contained a reference to the earlier-mentioned red Citroën that had been seen in the area of several terrorist bombings. Back at the Nédélec residence the authorities quickly learned that the actual owner of the car was a certain Jean-Jacques Sénart. Picked up for questioning, he admitted that he had carried out the FLB strikes in the Nantes region. Fortunately for the police, he was also currently at odds with his clandestine comrades. He thus implicated his superior in the FLB, a man named Lucien Divart, as well as several other terrorists active in the department of Loire-Atlantique. The police were consequently able to apprehend ten suspected members of the FLB at Nantes alone from 29 December 1968 to 1 January 1969.

Searches conducted at the domiciles of the arrested men turned up further valuable evidence, with which the authorties identified more FLB members. Thus they discovered that the prominent nationalist personality Jean Ollivier served as FLB chief for the St.-Brieuc area and that his principal aide was Abbé Antoine Le Bars. The latter's brother, also an abbé, coordinated FLB activity at Callac while two other priests named Le Cam and Lec'hvien exercised similar functions at Ploumagoar and Plésidy. It was also discovered that the architect Pierre Lemoine, a former leader of the MOB and currently a municipal councillor at Quimper, was directing clandestine FLB action in the Cornouaille region of south Finistère. In all, the police found FLB bands at St.-Brieuc, Quimper, Nantes, Rennes, Lorient, and Paris. Only in the northwestern part of the peninsula and in the interior of eastern Brittany did there appear to be no FLB activity. Lists of suspects were prepared and in a synchronized police action on 18 January 1969 an initial group of thirty-nine alleged FLB members were arrested on various charges of disturbing the peace. By the end of the month the number of suspects in custody had risen to fifty-three. In addition, the police uncovered several caches of explosives and confiscated numerous bundles of printed Breton nationalist propaganda material. Among the latter they found a nineteen-point charter for a Breton government-in-exile.

All those arrested were remanded to the Sûreté de l'Etat in Paris for further interrogation. As a result of this questioning the police were able to piece together the organizational structure of the FLB. In general its lines followed those of a state military system. At the top was a leader bearing the title of minister of war. The occupant of this post was never apprehended nor even identified, although many thought him to be Ned Urvoas.[7] Next came majors who headed regional FLB divisions called *kevrennou*. Although Brittany's territory had been divided into eight such units, only four were ever actually found by the police: Quimper (I), Lorient (II), St.-Brieuc (IV) and Nantes (VIII). Whether or not the other four *kevrennou* (III, V, VI, and VII) had any more than a paper existence no one knew. There was in any case a ninth *kevren* at Paris but it seems to have acted almost independently of those on the peninsula.[8] Each *kevren* was in turn divided into several *bagadou*, which were commanded by sergeants. The *bagadou* themselves were composed of groups of three to five men called *strolladou*, headed by corporals. In addition, commando units were sometimes formed on an ad hoc basis outside the formal structure of the FLB for special assignments.

The arrest of so many Breton terrorists and the uncovering of so extensive an FLB organization in the words of one observer "defolklorized" the Breton movement.[9] He added that no longer could Breton nationalism be dismissed as it had been so often in the past as the mad ravings of a few isolated eccentrics. The presence of many reputable Breton citizens among the accused ensured that. Abbé Le Cam was widely respected in ecclesiastical circles for his intelligence and good judgment. Pierre Lemoine and Jacques Ollivier had long enjoyed reputations as moderate Breton nationalists and both were well connected in those Breton circles where the CELIB had found much of its support. But it was the arrest of the ultrarespectable and establishment-oriented Jean Bothorel that caused the greatest stir. A member of an old Breton family and formerly an assistant to the Gaullist cabinet minister Yvon Bourges, he had been publisher of a glossy periodical called *Bretagne-Magazine* until its disappearance early in 1968. Although nationalists had originally viewed Bothorel as a Gaullist stalking-horse on the peninsula and his magazine a particularly odious vehicle for anti-Breton propaganda, by the mid-1960s he had begun to win their grudging respect as a champion of regional reform for Brittany. A May 1968 editorial in *L'Avenir* expressed the prevailing belief that because Bothorel had rallied to the Breton cause, his financial backers, under pressure from Paris, abandoned *Bretagne-Magazine* and forced him to end its publication.

The diverse backgrounds of the arrested FLB suspects indicated that Breton nationalist views had penetrated into most areas of the peninsula's social structure. Men and women, Bretonnants and non-Bretonnants, rich and poor, radicals and conservatives—all figured among the factory workers, farmers, university intellectuals, military officers, businessmen, and priests accused of clandestine terrorist action. One attribute most had in common, however, was their youthfulness. Of the thirty-six alleged FLB members whose ages were reported in *Le Monde* in January 1969, two-thirds were less than twenty-nine years old, while all but four of the remaining third were in their thirties. Thus, most had not been born in 1940 and fewer than half of a dozen had been more than ten years old at the beginning of World War II. The lie was therefore given to the frequent charge that the postwar Breton nationalist movement and its FLB vanguard were primarily staffed by former Breton nationalist collaborators during the wartime German occupation of Brittany. Only one of those arrested had in fact been active in the PNB during the war and nationalist sources denied that he actually belonged to the FLB. Instead they insisted that his arrest was a clumsy attempt by the government to discredit Breton nationalism by falsely associating the FLB in the public mind with the Nazis.

The response on the peninsula to the roundup of FLB members was one of widespread sympathy for those arrested. Virtually the entire organized Breton movement, whether nationalist in tendency or not, expressed solidarity with the imprisoned Breton militants and helped form *comités de soutien* for their families. Even Joseph Martray and René Pleven, although they repudiated the violent tactics of the FLB, warned that the very existence of the clandestine terrorist organization made it imperative that Paris enact a program of Breton regional reform. Only the UDB stood apart from this general wave of sympathy. In fact, it disavowed one of its members who had been jailed as an alleged FLB terrorist. Dr. Le Scouézec, a prominent UDB leader, resigned in disgust and took the lead in forming Skoazhell Vreizh (Secours Breton), the most ambitious *comité de soutien* for the FLB suspects. Few could doubt any longer the deep sympathy that flowed from many Bretons to the FLB prisoners when Pierre Vallérie, a retired French general and president of the ultraconservative and loyalist Association Bretonne, agreed to serve as chairman of Skoazhell Vreizh.

Without citing its source *L'Avenir* reported in February 1969 that a public opinion poll conducted in Brittany by *Figaro* had found that 25 percent of the peninsula's population felt solidarity with the accused terrorists. Because of this "shocking result" *L'Avenir* added that the conservative Parisian daily had chosen not to reveal the contents of this poll. A writer for the *New York Times* at the beginning of February in any case reported that the FLB arrests had had a greater political impact in Brittany than had the acts of which the men were accused. Traveling throughout the interior of the peninsula he therefore encountered a growing tide of admiration for the imprisoned Bretons. "They are devoted, selfless men," a small-town merchant told him in a typical statement. "They have done no physical harm to any one and have done more to focus attention on the economic and cultural needs of Brittany than any of the legal movements in the past."[10] The jailing of the four priests on suspicion of FLB activity generated particularly strong sympathy, especially among their ecclesiastical brethren. In less than a month nearly three hundred Breton priests had put their signatures on a petition demanding the release of their imprisoned colleagues.

In view of the aroused state of Breton opinion at the beginning of 1969 the government delayed the trial of the FLB suspects until after de Gaulle's trip to Brittany late in January when he was expected to reveal new proposals for regional reform. Some Bretons even wondered if the roundup had not originally been motivated by a wish to make sure that the presidential sojourn on the peninsula would not be marred by FLB-provoked incidents.[11] And except for some spirited jeering he encountered at Rennes on 31 January, de Gaulle's three-day Breton tour in fact went undisturbed by any such untoward episodes. As anticipated, he announced at Quimper on 2 February that the French people would soon be called upon to approve a referendum on a government-sponsored regionalizing scheme for the entire country. Shortly thereafter Paris officials fixed 27 April as the date for this vote, de Gaulle underscoring its importance by pledging to resign from office if his proposals were rejected. In a gesture of goodwill toward Breton voters in particular, he then ordered on 10 February that several of the imprisoned FLB suspects, including the four priests, be released. As it turned out, all their remaining Breton comrades were out of prison and amnestied by the end of June, a collateral result of the French electorate's unexpected rejection of the 27 April referendum on regional reform.

Most elements of the Breton movement had as a matter of fact greeted the French president's rather limited regionalist program with distinct coolness. It actually amounted to no more than a "recycled C.O.D.E.R.," Yann Fouéré typically explained, since it left Loire-Atlantique outside the proposed Breton region, provided for no elected regional assembly with real legislative authority, and served to reinforce the centralizing functions of the regional prefects.[12] With the startling exception of Olier Mordrel, therefore, no prominent Breton nationalist publicly recommended an affirmative vote on 27 April.[13] On the other hand, no nationalist group besides the UDB advised peninsular voters to cast their ballots against the Gaullist referendum either. Fouéré claimed that to do so would mean "mixing our votes with those of our worst enemies, the Jacobin centralizers of the right and left."[14] Thus the MOB and most other nationalist organizations urged Breton voters to abstain on 27 April. Although a plurality of the peninsular electorate subsequently approved the referendum, the combined abstentionist and negative vote in Brittany actually constituted a majority of all valid ballots cast.[15] Since in any event the referendum was defeated in France at large, de Gaulle immediately resigned and thereby precipitated a presidential election.

Most Breton nationalists backed the improvised candidacy of Alain Poher, the interim chief executive and a native of the peninsula. He won this support by freeing on their own recognizance all FLB suspects still in custody and promising to amnesty them if he won election as president of France. Neither of these gestures involved much risk. Poher knew as well as anyone that the accused Breton terrorists were not likely to evade prosecution and thus forsake the enormous propaganda opportunity that a criminal trial was certain to offer. His promise of an eventual amnesty was no less cheaply made; all incoming French presidents traditionally proclaim such a general pardon as their first official act. An amnesty for the FLB prisoners was probably in the offing anyway, since it provided an easy way for the government to avoid what the defendants would surely try to turn into an embarrassing trial of Breton nationalism. All those accused of FLB crimes thus were amnestied by the new French president on 20 June 1969. But in an ironic twist of fate it was Georges Pompidou, the political heir of Charles de Gaulle, who issued the legally cleansing decree a dozen days after defeating Alain Poher in the second round of the presidential election.

Apparently chastened by their brief experience with French prison life, nearly all of the amnestied FLB suspects withdrew from militant Breton nationalist action. This abandonment did not mean, however, the end of either the Breton liberation front or the clandestine terrorism on the peninsula. On the contrary, it marked the beginning of a new, more ominous, and still incomplete phase in the development of both. The FLB in fact resurfaced after only a few months, but this time as a legal organization. In September 1969 a small group of Paris-based left-wing Breton nationalists associated with a periodical called *Bretagne-Révolutionnaire* decided to appropriate the name of the Breton liberation front for their own political purposes. In accordance with the 1901 French law on associations they registered the name and statutes of a legal FLB with Rennes prefectural authorities in October. The new organization had been formed, one of its founders explained at an FLB sponsored rally in the Paris Mutualité a few weeks later, "to put the struggle of the Breton people within the framework of the international struggle for liberation." He added that the original Breton liberation front had acted clandestinely in order to draw attention most effectively to Brittany's situation of colonial oppression. But since that goal had been accomplished by the imprisonment and subsequent amnestying of several dozen FLB terrorists during the first half of 1969, legal action "in broad daylight" was henceforth the order of the day.[16]

From the beginning the leaders of the so-called FLB-II emphasized its left-wing character. A press release early in the autumn of 1969 accordingly expressed solidarity with anti-imperialist movements all over the world, especially those directed against oppression by privileged classes. Thus FLB-II members pledged to combat the alleged imperialism of the French bourgeoisie and its political instrument, the centralized French state system. In Brittany such resistance meant a relentless struggle against powerful bourgeois interests and their allies in French political parties and the state administrative apparatus who opposed the development of Breton national consciousness.[17] As Dr. Guy Caro expressed it in April 1970, the FLB-II operated on the premise that there was a "convergence" between the economic struggles of the peninsula's workers, farmers, and shopkeepers and the resistance of Breton nationalists to French cultural oppression in Brittany. He thus saw his own membership in the FLB-II as a means to affirm both his socialist convictions and his Breton national feeling.[18]

The most important reason for the creation of the legal FLB, however, was the desire of non-UDB Breton leftists to block the attempt of conservative nationalists to attract a popular following with the colonial interpretation of the Breton problem. Most such persons had recently coalesced around the banner of Sav Breizh, a political party organized in June 1968 by veteran members of the MOB who made the proposition "Brittany is a colony of French imperialism" the central plank of their otherwise vague doctrinal platform.[19] When two of its founders won more than two thousand votes in new parliamentary elections at the end of June without even conducting a formal campaign, it seemed that Sav Breizh was a Breton political party with a future. But in reality it soon proved to be the "ephemeral apparition on the political chessboard" that *Ouest-France* had said it would be at the outset; the party had become virtually moribund by the beginning of 1971. Its putative FLB-II rival suffered a similar and contemporaneous fate. Never able to attract a significant following on the peninsula, its leaders even failed to win to their banner more than two or three of the amnestied former FLB prisoners.[20] Their only success came with Guy Caro's election to the municipal council of Plouguesnast in March 1970, an electoral contest that saw three other FLB-II candidates go down to defeat elsewhere in Brittany. Even then Caro had run as a designated candidate of the PSU and managed to secure election only on the second ballot. Thereafter the legal FLB disintegrated so rapidly that by the fall of 1970 it existed only in the registry of associations at the Rennes prefecture.

Most of its erstwhile members then joined with a recently expelled Maoist faction of the UDB to form in January 1971 a miniscule Parti Communiste Breton (PCB), which has since failed to generate noticeable interest among Breton voters and exists today mainly so that its organ *Bretagne-Révolution-naire* can claim to speak on behalf of a leftwing Breton political movement.

The response on the peninsula to the collapse of Sav Breizh and the FLB-II was the recrudescence of clandestine Breton terrorism in 1971. A communiqué forwarded to *Ouest-France* by Yann Goulet announced the renewed campaign of direct action. As with the earlier wave of FLB bombings, Breton terrorists struck once more at reputed symbols of the French occupation of Brittany. A customs office at St.-Malo thus was the target of an abortive arson attempt in April, while during the second half of the year the prefecture at St.-Brieuc, the subprefecture at Dinan, and tax collection agencies at Vitré and Redon were damaged by incendiary bombs. It appeared that these operations had been carried out by veterans of the original FLB, since communiqués purporting to come from such a source claimed responsibility for the St.-Brieuc and Dinan attacks. The baffled police picked up several Breton nationalists on suspicion of FLB activity in April and then again in December but were unable to develop strong cases against any of them. All were released without being formally charged.

Even more mystifying was a parallel series of terrorist bombings aimed not so much at the symbols of Brittany's alleged colonial occupation as at the "instruments and symbols of the capitalist exploitation" of its people.[21] Four bulldozers used in the Gaullist program of forced amalgamation of small peasant holdings into large, industrial-sized agricultural units by means of specially authorized condemnation proceedings were dynamited at Pleuguenec in April. Almost simultaneously, a hydraulic crane was bombed some distance away at Lieuron. Two months later milk transport trucks operated by a Paris-based dairy trust were damaged by Molotov cocktails near Rennes. On 22 June a plastic bomb struck the home of a Fougères lawyer who had aided in the seizure of peasant properties. That same day another explosion resulted in minor destruction at a large industrial concern in Rennes. An attempt in late November to destroy two bulldozers at Saulnières aborted when the explosive device failed to function. Two weeks later, however, heavy earth-moving equipment was damaged in a second terrorist strike at the same location.

The police had meanwhile solved the case of the April 1971 attack on the St.-Malo customs house. In January 1972 they charged Gildas Durand, a nineteen-year-old *lycée* student specializing in Celtic languages, and a twenty-eight-year-old nationalist compatriot named Robert Guénard with that crime. At their trial on 3 March both admitted their membership in the FLB, Durand adding that he had undertaken the St.-Malo assignment in order to test his readiness for combat.[22] They then moved to have their cases dismissed, arguing that according to the terms of the Franco-Breton treaty of union in 1532 the French tribunal at St.-Malo in which they were being tried lacked jurisdiction in Brittany. The court rejected their argument and went on to find Durand and Guénard guilty as charged. A week later it sentenced the former to a year in prison and the latter to a term of eight months. Lawyers for the two convicted FLB members immediately appealed these verdicts. Not only did the appellate court in Rennes sustain the decisions on 29 May but, to the amazement of a large group of Breton nationalists in the courtroom, the court actually increased the sentences of both men to fifteen months.[23] Loud booing greeted this decision. The judges angrily ordered the court security police to arrest at random one of the demonstrating spectators, who was sentenced on the spot to a month and a day in jail.

While French authorities pursued Durand and Guénard through judicial channels, clandestine FLB commandos stepped up their campaign of terrorist violence. They dynamited a bulldozer at Pierric on 13 January and struck an agricultural credit bank at Rennes three days later. At the end of the month Redon was the scene of two forays directed against tax offices, one of which did not succeed because of a defective triggering mechanism on the explosive device. Bombing attempts against a government office in Auray and an agricultural credit bank in Vannes on 9 February failed for the same reason. The string of successful FLB strikes resumed on 20 February when another bulldozer was hit at Pierric. The following day Breton terrorists bombed the offices of the Côtes-du-Nord educational authority at St.Brieuc. Two days after that they attacked a statue at Quiberon of General Hoche, the French military commander who had intercepted and executed a party of several hundred fleeing Breton émigrés in 1795. FLB activity also reached into Paris when the homes of a supposed enemy of Brittany's maritime canning industry and an official active in the land amalgamation operation on the peninsula were bombed. After a month-long respite during March the FLB took up its campaign of violence again on 8 April and dynamited a bulldozer at Landon. That same day the newly constructed villa of a wealthy Parisian business-man who was said to have violated local zoning laws fell victim to an FLB bomb at Rotheneuf. The infuriated owner contacted a close friend then serving as a minister in the Chaban-Delmas government and demanded that those responsible for the destruction be found and punished.

The police moved quickly into action and the day after the incident at Rotheneuf arrested eleven FLB suspects. Most were residents of Ille-et-Vilaine in their twenties and thirties who came from working-class backgrounds and belonged to the socialist left. All were apparently part of a hitherto unknown *kevren* commanded by a thirty-two-year-old Rennes salesman named Jean Charpentier, whose political views, like those of one other member of the group, tended toward the right. More than 150 other suspects were interrogated as well. In the course of this investigation the police uncovered yet two more FLB *kevrennou*—one based at St.-Brieuc and the other operating out of Paris. Charpentier and the other ten suspects were meanwhile formally indicted on charges of subversion and transferred to Santé prison in Paris to await their trial at the Cour de Sûreté de l'Etat.

The trial of the accused FLB terrorists began on 3 October and lasted eight days.[24] As Durand and Guénard had vainly done in January at St.-Malo, Jean Charpentier and his like-minded fellow defendant Joseph Souvestre rested their defense on the claim that the treaty of 1532 denied French courts jurisdiction in Brittany. By contrast, lawyers for their nine

socialist compatriots emphasized the theme of the Breton people's status as an economically and culturally oppressed proletarian nation. Whenever possible they accordingly sought
to link the cause of Breton national liberation to the freeing of
Brittany's laboring masses from capitalist domination. They
devoted particular attention to the problem of the Breton language and its culture, arguing that since Brittany's union
with France in 1532 linguistic and cultural oppression on the
peninsula went hand in hand with the social and economic
exploitation of its inhabitants. Each reinforced the other, the
lawyers added, and the national subjection of the Breton people was the consequence of both. To underscore the point
Yves Gourvès, one of the defendants, refused to speak French
and began to address the court in Breton. When he would not
obey the judges' order to stop, he was forcibly removed from
the witness stand. The booing of the courtroom audience
turned to cheers when the other ten defendants leaped to
Gourvès's defense and tried to wrench him from the grasp of
the court police.

From the point of view of the defense, the attempt by
Gourvès to speak Breton was an adroitly conceived maneuver from which several important consequences flowed. In
the first place the incident created concrete circumstances
in which French judicial authorities unthinkingly cast themselves in roles as the persecutors of the Breton language.
Their action in turn helped forge a common attitude of Breton
solidarity among all eleven defendants toward the prosecution. Thus the formerly wary Charpentier and Souvestre increasingly came to associate themselves with the left-oriented
defense arguments of their nine fellow defendants. In much
the same manner conservative Breton nationalists at large
came under pressure to extend their sympathetic support to
Yves Gourvès, an extreme left-winger that many would otherwise have been most reluctant to defend. Not a few found the
experience far less distasteful than they hitherto might have
feared. In due course this discovery enabled many Breton
nationalists on the ideological right to coalesce around the
banner of a new and progressively oriented political party
called Strollad or Vro (sav, Parti Patriotique).

The championing of the Breton language by the lawyers

for the left-wing FLB defendants also undercut any prosecution attempt to portray ethnic minority nationalism in Brittany as no more than the backward-looking defense of a folkloric patois. Moreover, their general strategy of tying the cause of Breton nationalism to that of radical social reform on the peninsula prevented government attorneys from linking the defendants' Breton action with the right-wing extremism of discredited old-line nationalists such as Olier Modrel. And neither the court nor the prosecuting attorney in fact had recourse at any time to such defamatory tactics. The presence among the accused of Ferdinand Cormier, a much-decorated veteran of the anti-Nazi resistance in Brittany, would in any case have made that a difficult undertaking. The sworn testimony of widely respected defense witnesses like the regionalist leaders Michel Phlipponneau and Joseph Martray, the French army generals Pierre Vallérie and Paris de Bollardière, the mayor of Brest and the newly installed CELIB president Georges Lombard, and the mayor of St.-Brieuc and former PSU deputy Yves Le Foll made it all but impossible.

The court announced its verdicts on 10 October. Cormier and two other defendants were acquitted outright. The remaining eight were convicted, given sentences ranging from two to five years, and ordered to pay all trial costs. But then the panel of judges revealed that because of "extenuating circumstances" they were suspending all the prison terms just meted out.[25] Although it was never disclosed exactly what these circumstances were, they must have included the concern of French authorities that if the convicted terrorists remained in prison Breton nationalism would thereby acquire its first real martyrs. A new militancy on the part of Breton nationalists as well as a quickening of popular sympathy on the peninsula for their cause could reasonably be expected to follow. By tempering the relatively harsh penalties imposed on the FLB members with suspension of their actual prison terms, the court obviously hoped to forestall such an evolution in Breton opinion. French officials must also have hoped that the eight convicted men would slip into obscurity, that the Breton people would lose interest in clandestine nationalist action, and that, starved by such popular neglect, the FLB would soon wither away and die.

The formation of many Breton action committees immediately after the trial indicated, however, that the FLB and its terrorist action would not be so easily forgotten.[26] During the fall of 1972 and into the following year members of these committees organized a major propaganda effort to explain to the public the significance of the recent FLB trial and its place in the conjoined struggles of the Breton people for social and national liberation. The FLB itself resurfaced in the spring of 1973 when it issued a communiqué to the press in Brittany commenting on the outcome of the March parliamentary elections in France. These elections had been a sharp setback for the "reactionary majority" in power at Paris, this document explained, and a clear success for the French opposition parties of the left. Conditions henceforth obtained in both Brittany and France for a rapid development of mass struggles and a concomitant increase in the number of opportunities for intervention and rupture. Every militant Breton nationalist was therefore obliged, the FLB communiqué concluded, to make his presence felt in all mass political struggles on the peninsula so that they might be turned toward social revolution and the national liberation of the Breton people.[27]

Members of the FLB themselves resumed their clandestine action on behalf of Brittany at the end of August 1973 when three shots were fired into a military installation near Dinan. At the place where the gunman must have stood investigators found the familiar scrawled monogram of the Breton liberation front. During the last weeks of the year a series of plastic bombings occurred at various locations on the peninsula. A military barracks near Quimper was hit on 27 November. Ten days later FLB terrorists struck simultaneously at a tax records office in St.-Brieuc and a revenue collection agency at Guingamp. A destructive foray against a CRS summer camp near Tréveneuc marked the first day of 1974. Then on 4 January an exhibition hall constructed with government assistance against the wishes of the local population was bombed at Port-la-Forêt. A week later an FLB bomb damaged a villa at Fouesnant often used by Georges Pompidou when he visited Brittany. But the most daring operation in the entire eight-year history of the FLB came during the night of 13–14 February when terrorist commandos destroyed the ORTF radio tower at Roc-Trédudon that transmitted television signals to most of western Brittany.

The Roc-Trédudon explosion was by far the most serious act of FLB sabotage committed on the peninsula, since it caused damage worth five million francs that would require a year to repair. Even a temporary transmitting facility would take at least two years to install. In the meantime all television viewers in Finistère and nearly half of those in Côtes-du-Nord, as well as a large number in Morbihan, would be without their favorite programs. *Le Monde* thus considered the FLB exploit, spectacular as it was, to have been a "psychological error" more likely to provoke indignation than to generate sympathy for the Breton nationalist movement.[28] And residents of small towns in western Brittany, especially older people who had no easily available alternate form of entertainment, would doubtlessly have agreed with *Humanité* that the bombing was an act of "fascist barbarism" or with *Aurore*'s description of it as "an imbecility." On the other hand, the Paris newspaper *Libération* reported that indignation over the incident was not nearly so widespread in Brittany as French officials maintained.[29] Two months later a journalist for the *New York Times* expressed the same view after an extensive tour of the peninsula. Although he found few adult Bretons who openly manifested sympathy for the FLB, he rarely heard it condemned either. He discovered, moreover, that outright enthusiasm for the terrorist Breton action of the FLB was fast increasing among the most youthful elements of the peninsula's population.[30]

There is indeed little question that the FLB had carefully chosen the ORTF facility for destruction in order to tap and crystallize the rapid expansion of Breton national consciousness among peninsular youth in recent years. Nothing revealed this growth more than the sharply higher number of *lycée* students at Rennes who in accordance with the restrictive Deixonne law of 1951 requested an optional examination in the Breton language for their *baccalauréat*. In 1971 some 767 *bac* candidates made this request; in 1972 and 1973 the number rose to 886 and 946, respectively. The last figure meant that nearly one of every 13 *lycée* graduates in French-speaking Rennes had studied the Breton language. In addition, 3,662 secondary-school children in Brittany were enrolled in optional Breton-language courses in 1973 while 3,000 others had been denied such instruction for lack of qualified teachers.[31] These figures show not only that sympathy for the Breton language is already widespread among large numbers of Breton parents but also that the number of *bac* candidates who in the future will ask to be examined in Breton is likely to increase dramatically. Since many Breton nationalists now regard the ORTF as an even more ominous threat to the Breton language than the French educational system, the logic behind the decision of the FLB to bomb the Roc-Trédudon transmitter stands clearly revealed.

After February 1974 French authorities in Paris could hardly doubt any longer that the Breton liberation front constitutes a genuine threat to public order on the peninsula. It seems equally apparent that ethnic minority nationalism in contemporary Brittany is a force with which they will have to reckon in the not-too-far-distant future. But in this emerging confrontation Paris has lost much of the leverage it once possessed. There was a time when French officials could have slowed considerably the development of Breton nationalism if they had been more forbearing toward what at first was little more than benign particularistic sentiment on the peninsula. Nationalism might even have been stopped altogether had the authorities concurrently adopted social and economic policies for Brittany designed to raise the standard of living of its people. Most nationalists in fact concede that until very recently Paris could have effectively undercut their efforts simply by acceding to the minimum demands of moderate Breton leaders on either the language issue or that of regional reform.

The consistent failure of the French government to yield in the past on either question may now mean that concessions in both areas will not be enough to still increasingly disaffected Breton feeling on the peninsula. Token gestures like the mild regional proposals offered by de Gaulle in 1969, the addition of a few more hours of optional Breton-language instruction each week in French schools, or the daily transmission of several more minutes of Breton-language broadcasting over ORTF airwaves would surely be insufficient.[32] There is in any case little evidence that even after the Roc-

Trédudon explosion Paris is yet prepared either to reverse its long-standing hostility to Breton culture or to devise regional programs to treat the social and economic causes of popular discontent on the peninsula. The consequence of this double refusal, particularly if it is accompanied by harsh repressive action against the FLB, is certain to be a sharp increase in the resentment and exasperation that underpin much of ethnic minority nationalism in contemporary Brittany.[33] This heightened discontent in turn would likely create even more serious problems in the future for French authorities, since in SAV Breton nationalists for the first time possess an instrument that seems capable of turning such disaffection to their own political advantage.

Formed in mid-1972 out of the remains of the MOB and various other Breton nationalist groups, SAV grew rapidly to its current size of one thousand members grouped in eighteen local federations. In the process it moved steadily leftward under the leadership of its founder Jean Le Calvez and ultimately established close relations with the peninsular arm of François Mitterand's socialist movement. It also began to absorb the Parti Communiste Breton and the left-wing Breton action committees formed in the fall of 1972. The presence of the longtime UDB leader Dr. Guy Caro at SAV's second annual congress in June 1974 pointed toward the eventual absorption of that Breton organization as well. Such a merger seemed all the more likely when the congress formally declared SAV to be "on the left and in the opposition" and adopted as its official motto "Fédéralisme et Autogestion"—words dear to the hearts of UDB members. The SAV delegates then demanded, just as *Le Peuple Breton* had been doing since 1964, the formation of "an assembly of the Breton nation" and "self-government at all levels and on all issues that grow out of the class struggle."[34]

The leftward evolution of SAV acquires added significance when it is realized that this movement has taken place without the loss of its original right-wing nationalist elements. Perhaps, then, the divisiveness that has paralyzed the Breton movement so often during the past half century has finally come to an end and the united front for nationalist political action long desired by its leaders has at last been achieved. In any event, the first test of SAV's prospects as a Breton political party came in March 1973 when parliamentary elections were held in France. For this electoral contest Le Calvez and his colleagues raised a campaign fund of two hundred thousand francs and fielded SAV candidates in twenty-six of the peninsula's thirty-two constituencies. When the ballots were counted SAV was found to have captured more than thirty thousand votes, or about 2.3 percent of all those cast. This result may seem derisory until the recent history of the remarkably similar Scottish National party is remembered. After polling only 2.43 percent of the vote in the 1964 British parliamentary elections, the party increased its share to more than 30 percent ten years later and sent eleven of its candidates to the House of Commons in October 1974. Central authorities in France who have so doggedly opposed regional diversity and ethnic cultural pride in twentieth-century Brittany would be wise to heed the warning contained in the experience of this nearby Celtic parallel.

One thing seems clear enough. Buoyed by the oft-expressed solidarity of other minority peoples and heartened by the recent striking gains made by many of them in their struggles for national self-assertion, Breton nationalists will not reduce their pressure on the French state. This determination was made clear in mid-August 1975 when FLB partisans bombed a nuclear power station in Brittany and followed up that act at the end of the month with the incendiary bombing of the homes of two parliamentary deputies in Rennes. Paris authorities reacted to these incidents with a police sweep through the peninsula that netted sixty suspected Breton terrorists, including several Roman Catholic priests. But, combining the carrot with the stick, the French government for the first time indicated that it was prepared to meet at least some of the cultural demands of Breton nationalists. Thus in November 1975 the minister of education, René Haby, announced that Paris would end its long hostility to the teaching of the Breton language and would even begin a program of official state subsidies for such instruction, a promise confirmed by French President Valéry Giscard d'Estaing at Ploermel during a two-day tour of Brittany in February 1977. At this late date, however, it is unlikely that the remarkable about-face in French policy on the Breton-language issue will alone stem the swelling tide of Breton national feeling and terrorist violence on the Armorican peninsula. For that to happen, Paris must also move quickly to end the long-standing social and economic inequalities that condemn the Breton population to lower standards of living and sharply reduced opportunities for social advancement in relation to the rest of the French people. Failure to act in these areas will surely make of the Breton nationalist movement—increasingly fueled by widespread popular resentment in Brittany at social and economic discrimination perceived in ethnic terms—a genuine threat to the integrity of the French state as it now exists.

CHAPTER 10

❧ *Perspectives*
on the Present and Future
of Breton National Action

⌈The sudden reversal by Paris in late 1975 on the Breton-language issue is only the last of a series of concessions made by European central governments to ethnic minority nationalist movements during the past decade.⌉At the end of 1969 Rome granted a statute of autonomy to the South Tyrol, thus giving to the German-speaking majority in that region broad powers of local self-government. ⌊After an extended political crisis that saw the fall of a Belgian government, the dissolution of parliament, and elections for a new Chamber Brussels yielded in mid-1971 to the demands of Fleming nationalists and disbanded the French-language faculties of the University of Louvain.⌋The protracted terrorist campaign in favor of home rule that ended in the Basque-engineered assassination of the Spanish prime minister in December 1973 produced assurances in Madrid that the government would relax its rigid system of centralized control. The enormous gathering of several tens of thousands of Catalans chanting home-rule slogans in Barcelona in February 1976, the largest such political demonstration by opponents of the regime since the Spanish civil war, drew from the young government of King Juan Carlos new promises that Madrid would speed its plans for regional reform. Meanwhile, Paris in September 1975 hastily replaced the incumbent French mainland prefect with a native-born Corsican and promised that a measure of local autonomy would be granted to that island after a summer of

Corsican nationalist agitation ended in the deaths of several French policemen and a crippling twenty-four-hour general strike. And, finally, the strong showing made by Scottish and Welsh nationalist candidates in recent British parliamentary elections led the Labour government of Harold Wilson in the fall of 1975 to commit itself to the creation of a system of local home rule in both Scotland and Wales.[1]

The above examples make clear that many of Europe's long quiescent ethnic minorities are now stirring with such vigor that the centralized governments under whose authority they live find it increasingly expedient to yield before certain of their nationalist demands. The days are obviously long since past when members of such ethnic minorities respond to majority discrimination and inferior status with behavioral patterns that emphasize passivity, nonresistance, and resignation to the world as it is and perhaps ever will be. For several good reasons, ethnic minorities in the contemporary world are far less likely to respond as inertly to oppression by a majority culture as they did only a few decades ago. Wars, revolutions, and advances in mass communications have so shrunken the world that modern notions of equality, national self-determination, and democracy have penetrated to those isolated corners of European society where ethnic minorities are so often found. Thus members of one minority group after another have collectively begun to see their situation as one of unjust subordination; refusing to accept such inferior status, the hardier among them seek to improve their lot by demanding equality, recognition of their rights, and, finally, emancipation of their entire group. When such demands combine with widespread feeling within a minority that its members possess a distinct ethnic identity, then ethnic minority nationalism becomes a political force with which the dominant majority must ultimately reckon.

The foregoing chapters on the Breton nationalist movement reveal the important part that intellectuals have in the process by which an ethnic minority develops a conscious sense of its distinctive self. Such individuals, especially philologists and historians, play crucial roles as they bend their efforts toward the recovery and presentation of the linguistic, historical, and cultural heritage of their ethnic group. Unable because of majority discrimination to exercise satisfactorily their particular intellectual abilities or to participate fully in the affairs of the larger society, such frustrated persons overcome these disappointments by immersing themselves in the life of the smaller, but far more hospitable world of their ethnic community. At the same time they acquire, through elaboration of a new or rediscovered national identity for their people, a new and more worthy sense of themselves. It even happens that those ethnic traits they formerly regarded as marks of inferiority—a rustic folk dialect, mysterious religious practices, picturesque costumes, and an obscure folklore—become objects of "national" pride. Before long the newly nationalist intellectuals have transformed all these traits into positive group values on which the ethnic nationalist depends. And it is the promotion and defense of these values that in fact serve as the basis on which intellectuals assume leading positions in the emerging ethnic minority nationalist movement.

The study of twentieth-century Breton nationalism indicates that the intellectuals who provide the leadership of such movements are characteristically split into moderate and radical factions. The members of the initially more numerous moderate group have relatively unambitious objectives and usually seek from the central government the concession of administrative decentralization and regional autonomy for their homeland. With these devices they hope to establish the principle of local control in cultural affairs and to find the means by which the long-entrenched local elite to which they belong can preserve its ascendancy in the face of threatening processes of social, economic, and political change. By contrast, more militant nationalist intellectuals reject the limited goals of the moderates as unworthy of the national integrity of their people. By invoking the doctrine of national self-determination and alleging the possession by their people of sovereign statehood in some hoary past, these leaders instead demand outright political independence. This demand has generally restricted appeal within the ethnically conscious minority population at large, however, so long as moderate leaders can hope to wrest concessions from the dominant majority. But should the latter refuse to accommodate the moderates or reverse a previous policy of concessions, intransigents invariably come to assume commanding roles in the leadership of ethnic minority nationalist movements. The failure of Breton regionalists before 1914 and after 1945 to achieve their goals was thus followed in each case by the appearance of an explicitly nationalist movement.

In any event, the oft-repeated grievance of Breton nationalist intellectuals that they and their compatriots are the victims of cultural persecution at the hands of the French is an insufficient basis on which to build a powerful ethnic minority nationalist movement enjoying the support of a large segment of the peninsular population. Such a movement in fact has an extremely limited appeal and its leaders, as Breton separatists bitterly learned in the 1930s, find themselves isolated within their own people and thus condemned to lead lives of endless frustration. The goal of national liberation pursued by a so narrowly based movement necessarily depends, therefore, on the play of external factors and situationally unique circumstances. So it happened that most Breton separatists dared hope when France suddenly collapsed in 1940 that Brittany's hour had miraculously come. And for the same reason some among them were willing to gamble the card of collaboration with the Germans if that were the price of Breton national independence.

Nevertheless, the fact of cultural discrimination experienced by members of an ethnic minority is enough to make of ethnic minority feeling an enduring reality and nationalist agitation arising from it a recurrent phenomenon. But the important point is that such agitation acquires a mass basis, and hence takes on genuine significance, only when minority persons come to realize that the cultural persecution they suffer is accompanied by far more damaging discriminatory treatment in matters of economic opportunity, educational attainment, and social advancement. Thus it was only after 1945 when Breton nationalists began to emphasize the theme of Brittany's social, economic, and political exploitation by the French that their movement started to draw mass support on the peninsula and hence for the first time seriously to alarm central authorities in Paris.

Contemporary Breton nationalists have had the greatest

success in mobilizing popular support behind their ideas by picturing Brittany as the "colony" of an imperialistic French state. The leaders of most other present-day ethnic minority movements, particularly those in Scotland, Wales, Corsica, Sicily, and Flanders, have employed the same tactic with similar results. Michael Hechter has in fact argued that the homelands of most ethnic minorities in Europe may be best described as internal colonies of the larger majority states in which they are located. Exploitation rather than the development of the minority economy, he goes on to explain, is always the aim. The economic life of these regions is therefore entirely dependent on the play of external market forces and is organized above all else for the export of a single primary agricultural or mineral product to the majority society. This economic dependence is reinforced through discriminatory legal, administrative, and political practices that in turn produce among the minority population lower standards of living, retarded development of social services, and higher levels of frustration as expressed in unusually high rates of alcoholism, criminal behavior, and prostitution. Such behavioral patterns, moreover, typically serve as the basis for the construction of unflattering minority stereotypes by the majority in order to lend apparent credence to its dogmatically asserted claims of racial, ethnic, and cultural superiority. From the point of view of the majority, fecund minority populations are in fact valuable only insofar as they serve as a constant source of cheap, unskilled labor for the larger national economic system. It is hardly surprising, Hechter therefore concludes, that such internal colonies invariably have a declining population, an overabundance of the very young and the very old, and a disproportionately large number of females—all factors that not only reflect long-standing economic exploitation by the majority but also promote further social and economic deterioration in the future.[2]

The above discussion makes it obvious why leaders of most ethnic minority nationalist movements in contemporary Europe use the alleged colonial exploitation of their homeland and its people as the central argument in their cases against the majority societies in which they are subordinate and disadvantaged parts. This argument simply squares with what appears to be the objective reality of the situation. But there is another and far more compelling reason for Breton nationalists and most other ethnic minority spokesmen to emphasize the colonial theme. They want to associate their efforts with the post–World War II struggles of overseas colonial populations for national liberation. By insisting that their struggle is the "unfinished business" of the post-1945 decolonization movement Breton, Scottish, Fleming, and Corsican nationalists alike seek to gain for their cause the enormous international prestige and local popular support that enabled so many Asian, African, and Latin American peoples to win for themselves the right to national self-determination and sovereign independence.

Other reasons may be advanced to help explain why the dismantling of Europe's great overseas empires after World War II should have stimulated ethnic national feeling among minority populations at home. Vast amounts of national will, bureaucratic energy, and trained personnel were occupied in the acquisition, maintenance, and development of these empires. With their disappearance there occurred everywhere a refocusing of national will from the outside world to the metropolitan homeland. This transition was not an easy one for anyone, least of all for those who had formerly served in overseas posts but who now found themselves with no useful roles to play. Officials in former European imperial capitals soon concluded that it was politically unwise to pension off and forget the superfluous civil servants and military officers who had once staffed their empires. Most were therefore absorbed into the fast-swelling administrative bureaucracies of the home countries and thus was accelerated the growth of bureaucratic authority at the center, a process already speeded by postwar efforts toward national economic planning and welfare reform, themselves important signs of the indrawing of national will in most European countries.

Vastly increased public expenditures at home were the inevitable consequence of all these changes. So great were the sums disbursed that the savings many hoped would be forthcoming once imperial responsibilities were relinquished simply failed to materialize. On the contrary, domestic expenditures for welfare services almost immediately outstripped any economies in the form of defense budget cuts made possible by policies of imperial retrenchment. Costly new welfare obligations in turn provoked tremendous growth in the size of rapidly proliferating central administrative bureaus in all countries. Now the expansion of governmental activity and bureaucratic authority has everywhere meant—perhaps for the most generous and idealistic of reasons—interference with the affairs of local officials and private individuals through taxing, planning, authorizing, and reviewing procedures. Resistance to such accelerating central pressures might reasonably be expected to appear in time throughout an entire polity where they are present. It makes good historical sense, therefore, that resistance should first have emerged not at the solid hearts of long-established European states, but at their sensitive peripheries where most ethnic minorities are found and where centralizing pressures have always been least intense.

In ethnically distinct regions like Brittany, Scotland, Wales, and the Basque country such resistance almost naturally assumes the form of nationalist resentment and cultural disaffection when central government policies are seen to work to the social and economic disadvantage of local populations. Postwar planning schemes with the accompanying increased governmental control over national incomes in all countries have had this effect, since industrial and commercial entrepreneurs with capital to invest find it in their interest to be as near to the locus of national economic decision making as possible. In practice this has meant that the administrative cores of most European states have drawn far more investment and developmental capital than have faraway regions like Sicily, Brittany, and Corsica. For reasons of efficiency and more effective oversight procedures central governments have facilitated the concentration of new economic activity at the center by means of appropriately designed taxation, public investment, planning, and equipment policies. These policies in turn have encouraged the flow of the most vigorous and productive members of peripheral populations toward the dynamic center and its relatively greater opportunities for economic and social advancement. The distant regions from whence such hopeful immigrants come are in consequence rendered even less attractive for the investment of new venture capital.

The postwar history of national planning in Europe demonstrates that central policymakers typically view regions at the periphery mainly as zones for the supply of cheap labor, for the investment of public funds on such relatively non-remunerative projects as military bases, hospitals, and educational facilities, and for the development of strictly seasonal industries like tourism. In each case the long-term consequence is to condemn the inhabitants of such regions to chronically lower incomes and standards of living than those enjoyed by citizens nearer the center. So it happens that national economic planning schemes that are often justified on the ground that they will one day eliminate regional social and economic disparities wind up by making these problems structurally permanent. So it happens that the so-called colonial situation of many ethnic minority populations is further accentuated. No wonder that Breton and most other ethnic minority nationalists interpret these local consequences of the concentration of bureaucratic authority and economic vitality at the center as discriminatory acts of domestic imperialism. Thus they bolster the case against their majority rulers by pointing not only to long-established historical tradition but also to present-day central planning policy to show that they and their compatriots are the defenseless victims of colonial exploitation.

Perhaps the real significance of the emergence of ethnic nationalism among the minority populations of twentieth-century Europe is that it reflects the loosening hold of existing nation-states on the imaginations of contemporary Europeans. It may simply be a case of what the Italians call *distensione*, the easing of tensions through the removal of external dangers that formerly justified strong central governments. In any event it seems likely that Europe's increasingly outmoded nation-states, the characteristic political units of a socioeconomic order that is rapidly passing away, will one day disappear from the scene as well. Only time will tell whether they will be replaced by a congeries of smaller-scale ethnic communities or by a single unified political organization. It could even be that the disaggregation of existing state formations into smaller ethnic units might turn out to be the first step in the reorganization of Europe into a continental federation of so-called little peoples.[3] From diversity, after all, often springs the notion of unity. The centuries-long dream of European unity might even be achieved without reference to the historic rivalries of English and French, French and German that so often in the past have frustrated this grand design. From this perspective, then, the emergence and triumph of ethnic minority nationalism in Brittany and elsewhere in Europe would appear more directed toward the living future than to the irretrievably dead past as its adversaries so often charge.

 *Notes*

Introduction

1. See, for example, Boyd C. Shafer, *Faces of Nationalism*, p. 229.

2. Herbert Marcuse, *One-Dimensional Man*, p. 256.

3. Hobsbawm's comment and Berger's elaboration of it are found in Suzanne Berger, "Bretons, Basques, Scots, and Other European Nations," p. 175.

4. See especially the brief articles by Ronan Roudaut, Yann-Ber Piriou, Pierre Doridan, and Michel Phlipponneau in the August–September 1973 issue of *Les Temps Modernes*.

5. Shafer, *Faces of Nationalism*, p. 157. For a survey of Marxian ideas on nationalism see Horace Davis, *Nationalism and Socialism: Marxist Theories of Nationalism to 1917*.

6. The relatively well-known ethnic minority nationalist movements in Wales, Scotland, Catalonia, and the Basque country have in fact become the subject of serious scholarly inquiry only during the last decade. For a summary of the most recent work on these movements see the articles by Stanley Payne, H. M. Begg and J. A. Stewart, and Kenneth O. Morgan in a special 1971 issue on nationalism and separatism of the *Journal of Contemporary History*.

7. Cynthia H. Enloe, *Ethnic Conflict and Political Development*, p. 263.

8. See ibid., p. 267.

9. All the quoted material in this paragraph is from ibid., pp. 268, 274.

10. Walter B. Simon, "Occupational Structure, Multilingualism, and Social Change," p. 98.

11. Ibid.

12. See Michael Hechter, "The Political Economy of Ethnic Change," pp. 1165, 1173, 1176–77.

13. See the conclusion of Michael Hechter, "Towards a Theory of Ethnic Change," p. 45.

14. Hugh Seton-Watson, "Unsatisfied Nationalisms," p. 12.

15. See Berger, "Bretons, Basques," pp. 168–69, and Martin O. Heisler, ed., *Politics in Europe*, pp. 178–220.

16. See Heisler, *Politics in Europe*, pp. 185–98, and Berger, "Bretons, Basques," p. 169. On this point see also Claes Lode, "The Process of Federalization in Belgium," p. 49.

17. Berger, "Bretons, Basques," p. 168.

18. Ibid., p. 174.

19. Ibid., p. 168.

Chapter 1

1. Ernest Barker, *National Character and the Factors in Its Formation*, p. 16.

2. Cited in Boyd C. Shafer, *Faces of Nationalism*, p. 336.

3. In particular see Pitré-Chevalier's *La Bretagne ancienne et moderne* and Arthur de La Borderie, *La Bretagne aux temps modernes, 1491–1789* and *Histoire de Bretagne*. The concluding two volumes of the latter six-volume work, covering the period 1515–1789, were written by Barthélémy Pocquet on the basis of La Borderie's posthumous notes.

4. According to his successor on the history faculty at Rennes University, La

Borderie "had a passionate cult for Brittany" and hoped his exhaustive six-volume work on its history "would be worthy of its glorious past and enduring enough to come to the attention of later generations." See the note by Barthélémy Pocquet in La Borderie, *Histoire de Bretagne*, 4:i.

5. Pitré-Chevalier, *La Bretagne*, pp. 651–52.

6. La Borderie, *Histoire de Bretagne*, 1:53.

7. Jeanne du Guerny was a member of the Coroller family, which had long been associated with militant Breton action. A fervent Catholic, devoted admirer of the nationalist priest Jean-Marie Perrot, and eventually the mother of seven children, it is said that Mme. du Guerny was a woman of uncertain morals, a reputation apparently not improved by various relationships she established with German occupation officials after 1940. Almost certainly an informer for the Gestapo, she was clubbed to death by *maquisards* during the summer of 1944. Olier Mordrel has written that she "was of that race of chatelaines who hid Chouans and refractory priests and who, as they did, fell like a soldier." Jean La Bénelais [Olier Mordrel], *Galerie bretonne*, p. 20.

8. The phrase belongs to R. Pennek, *Petite histoire de la Bretagne nationale*, p. 6.

9. La Borderie pioneered this view concerning Nominoè's historical significance, according to Pierre Riché and Guy Devailly, "De l'Armorique à la Bretagne," p. 130.

10. Landevennec Abbey has in recent years been fully restored and today houses the largest collection of original documents and printed works on Brittany.

11. This is the finding of a recent study of royal charters by J.-Fr. Lemarignier, who showed that none concerned Brittany between the years 898 and 1108. Cited by Riché and Devailly, "De l'Armorique à la Bretagne," p. 143.

12. Armand Rébillon, *Histoire de Bretagne*, p. 47.

13. Ironically, the nationalist movement itself has exhibited the same alleged faults. Later chapters will show it also to be largely Francophone, located in eastern Brittany, and split into rival factions at Rennes and Nantes.

14. Joseph Chardronnet, *Histoire de notre Bretagne*, p. 96.

15. Pennek, *Petite histoire*, p. 6.

16. C. Danio [Jeanne du Guerny], *Histoire de notre Bretagne*, p. 96.

17. Cited originally in Danio, *Histoire de notre Bretagne*, pp. 117–18. See also Chardronnet, *Histoire de Bretagne*, p. 95.

18. Henri Touchard, "Le moyen-âge breton," p. 211.

19. Reprinted in Académie des Sciences Morales et Politiques, *Catalogue des actes de François Ier*, 2:198.

20. See, for example, Pennek, *Petite histoire*, p. 8.

21. This argument was first advanced by La Borderie in *La Bretagne aux temps modernes*, pp. 277–78. The most elaborate version is in Yann Poupinot, *La Bretagne contemporaine*, 1:31–35. See also Chardronnet, *Histoire de Bretagne*, pp. 152–53, and Danio, *Histoire de notre Bretagne*, pp. 175–76.

22. See Jean Egret,"Les origines de la Révolution en Bretagne (1788-1789)," pp. 189–215.

23. See Jean Meyer, "Une mutation manquée: De la révolution politique aux débuts du monde industriel," p. 386. Of the Chouans Balzac once wrote that they "remain a notable example of the danger of stirring up the barely civilized masses of a country." See the 1972 Penguin translation of his classic *Les Chouans*, p. 54.

24. Chardronnet, *Histoire de Bretagne*, p. 175.

25. Ibid., p. 178.

26. Poupinot, *La Bretagne contemporaine*, 1:44. For a recent scholarly treatment of the incident, see Daniel L. Rader, "The Breton Association and the Press: Propaganda for a 'Legal Resistance' before the July Revolution," pp. 64–82.

27. Chardronnet, *Histoire de Bretagne,* p. 191.

28. France, Assemblée Nationale, *Annales*, Vol. 21, *Enquête sur les actes du gouvernement de la défense nationale*, "Rapport de M. A. de La Borderie: Le camp de Conlie et l'armée de Bretagne," pp. 585–936.

29. *Bulletin* de l'Association Bretonne, 1897, p. 147.

Chapter 2

1. The pioneering work in the task of Breton language restoration was done by Jean-François Le Gonidec, who published his important *Dictionnaire de la langue celto-bretonne* in 1821. The subsequent Breton linguistic studies of Amable Troudee, François Vallée, and Roparz Hémon have this dictionary as their lexicographical point of departure.

2. On this point see Michael Hechter, "Towards a Theory of Ethnic Change," p. 42.

3. Hans Kohn, *The Idea of Nationalism*, p. 16.

4. C. Danio [Jeanne du Guerny], *Histoire de Bretagne*, p. 35.

5. Olier Mordrel, *Breiz Atao, ou histoire et actualité du nationalisme breton*, pp. 23–26. These important memoirs of Olier Mordrel will hereafter be cited as OMM.

6. Morvan Lebesque, *Comment peut-on être breton?*, p. 26.

7. This was probably Danio's *Histoire de notre Bretagne*.

8. Pierre Laurent in his preface to Yann Poupinot, *La Bretagne contemporaine*, 1:7.

9. Eugen Weber and Hans Rogger, eds., *The European Right*, p. 24.

10. Maurice Marchal, "La question gallaise,"*Breiz Atao* 8 (August 1919): 2.

11. To this Charles Woodhouse adds: "So long as an ethnic minority could believe its interests in economic development and political power were not being blocked by cultural discrimination, the preservation and recognition of cultural identity by the larger society did not become a political or economic issue."See his introduction to Henry J. Tobias and Charles E. Woodhouse, *Minorities and Politics*, p. 4.

12. For example, see Marcel Guieysse, *La langue bretonne*, pp. 198–200 and the editorial of Jean La Bénelais [Olier Mordrel],"L'armée des mères," *Breiz Atao* 7 (July 1927): 815.

13. See Y.-B. Piriou, "Le Peuple Breton se penche sur son passé," *Le Peuple Breton* 33 (August 1966): 3.

14. Yves Hourmant, "Le symbôle: aliénation culturelle," *Le Peuple Breton* 32 (July 1966): 4.

15. Piriou, "Le Peuple Breton," p. 3.

16. The Catholic Breton organization called Bleun-Brug (Fleurs de Bruyère), founded in 1905 by the priest Jean-Marie Perrot, has long promoted this idea. For details see the biography by Henri Poisson, *L'abbé Jean-Marie Perrot*, especially the prefatory remarks by François Falc'hun, p. xi.

17. Guieysse, *La langue bretonne*, pp. 195–96.

18. Poisson, *L'abbé Jean-Marie Perrot*,pp. 2–3.

19. Reported at the XXIIIᵉ Congrès de Bleun-Brug and published in a pamphlet, *L'enseignement du breton et de l'histoire*, in 1933.

20. *An Oaled* 47 (1934): 60.

21. Edgar Morin, *The Red and the White*, p. 34.

22. Henri Poisson, *Yves Le Moal*, p. 199.

23. *Breiz Atao* 10 (October 1919): 3.

24. *Indépendance Bretonne* (St.-Brieuc), 31 October 1899. Reprinted in François Jaffrennou, *La genèse d'un mouvement, 1898–1911*, p. 56.

25. Norman Cohn, *The Pursuit of the Millennium*, pp. 59–60.

26. See chapter 6, "Industrialisation and the Crisis of the Intelligentsia," in Anthony D. Smith, *Theories of Nationalism*, pp. 109–50.

27. Karl Mannheim, *Ideology and Utopia*, p. 158.

28. At first most made their views known through the venerable Association Bretonne. Later they joined the Union Régionaliste Bretonne and the Fédération Régionaliste de Bretagne. The Comte de Lantivy-Trédion summarized the views of this group in two books, *La question bretonne* (1909) and *Vers une Bretagne organisée* (1911).

29. Olier Mordrel reported in 1938 that he became a nationalist only when he realized that Paris had no intention of ceding to the regionalists. He changed the

spelling of his name from Olivier Mordrelle to mark that change of attitude. See *Breiz Atao* 318 (December 1938): 1.

30. Henri Sée, "La population et la vie économique de Rennes vers le milieu du XVIIIe siècle d'après les rôles de la capitation," p. 96.

31. Yann Brekilien, *La vie quotidienne des paysans en Bretagne au XIXe siècle*, p. 347.

32. In the mid-nineteenth century rectors received twelve hundred to fifteen hundred francs per annum and vicars eight to eleven hundred francs. They also received many gifts, especially in kind, and a little land. According to Jean Meyer this "relative affluence afforded them a certain independence." See Jean Meyer, "Une mutation manquée: De la révolution politique aux débuts du monde industriel," p. 440.

33. André Siegfried in 1913 referred to Francophone eastern Brittany as "a land of submission." The description could have been applied with equal force to the rest of the peninsula. See his *Tableau politique de la France de l'ouest sous la troisième république*, p. 128.

34. According to a study by L. Girard cited by Meyer, "Mutation manquée," pp. 408, 424.

35. Siegfried, *Tableau politique*, p. 504.

36. Gilbert Le Guen, "D'une révolution manquée à une révolution possible," p. 464.

37. Meyer, "Mutation manquée," p. 403.

38. During the period 1876–1911 the urban population of Brittany increased by 260,000. At the same time the natural increase of the population amounted to 657,000 persons. See Le Guen, "Révolution manquée," pp. 464, 468. In 1901 Brittany's population of 3,221,169 amounted to 8.3 percent of the total for all of France.

39. Siegfried, *Tableau politique*, p. 222.

40. For the ten parliamentary elections during the period 1876–1910 the average rate of abstention across Brittany was almost 30 percent. Computed from figures in Siegfried, *Tableau politique*, pp. 94, 108, 127, 211.

41. Cited in Suzanne Berger, *Peasants against Politics*, p. 44.

42. The conservative vote dropped from 58 to 33 percent in Loire-Inférieure, from 49 to 33 percent in Ille-et-Vilaine, from 49 to 44 percent in Côtes-du-Nord and Morbihan, and from 38 to 28 percent in Finistère. The republican vote, on the other hand, rose respectively from 9 to 31 percent, from 25 to 39 percent, from 12 to 24 percent, and from 29 to 33 percent. See Siegfried, *Tableau politique*, pp. 94, 108, 127, 211.

43. Berger, *Peasants against Politics*, p. 41, makes the same point from a somewhat different perspective.

Chapter 3
1. *Bulletin* de l'Union Régionaliste Bretonne (hereafter cited as *Bulletin* de l'URB), 1901, p. 10.

2. The comparison is made by Jean La Bénelais [Olier Mordrel], *Galerie bretonne*, p. 1.

3. *Bulletin* de l'URB, 1902, p. 35.

4. In the following year Charles Le Goffic wrote that "the true Brittany is Breton-nant Brittany." See his *L'âme bretonne*, 1:4.

5. *Bulletin* de l'URB, 1908, p. 5.

6. Ibid., 1909, p. 9.

7. Ibid., 1904, p. 35.

8. Ibid., 1908, p. 6.

9. Comte René de Laigue, *Le congrès de 1907*, p. 3.

10. *Bulletin* de l'URB, 1907, p. 44.

11. *Le Pays Breton* 53 (26 January 1908): 1.

12. Yves Berthou once called this paper "le Faux-Breton de Sodome." See his *Les vessies pour des lanternes*, p. 193.

13. *Bulletin* de l'URB, 1908, pp. 39–40.

14. A ridiculously small statue was finally constructed after World War I on a site

near the battlefield of Ballon where Nominoë and his Breton army are supposed to have defeated the Franks in 848. It still stands today.

15. The charter of the FRB is found in *Bulletin* de la Fédération Régionaliste de Bretagne (hereafter cited as *Bulletin* de la FRB), 1911–12, pp. 4–7. In November 1911 Mellac and Herrieu declared *Le Pays Breton* the official organ of the new regionalist federation.

16. The FRB formally recognized the importance of the Breton language in its charter with a provision that three-fifths of its *conseil de direction* be Bretonnants. A second provision required that the FRB president, the second vice-president, and two of the three secretaries also had to be Bretonnants.

17. *Bulletin* de la FRB, 1911–12, p. 24.

18. Yann Poupinot, *La Bretagne contemporaine*, 1:88.

19. François Jaffrennou, "Le complot de l'U.R.B.," *Ouest-Eclair*, 24 September 1903. Cited in François Jaffrennou, *La genèse d'un mouvement, 1898–1911*, p. 110.

20. The statements in this paragraph are based on inspection of so-called *professions de foi* traditionally circulated by French parliamentary candidates in their constituencies during electoral campaigns. Beginning in 1881 those for winning candidates have been collected and published by the government according to the provisions of the Barodet law. Unfortunately, such documents for previous elections have been lost, while those of defeated candidates were seldom preserved in departmental archives.

21. France, Chambre des Députés, *Programmes, professions de foi et engagements électoraux* (Elections législatives des 26 avril et 10 mai 1914), in *Impressions, projets de loi, propositions, rapports, etc.*, Vol. 6, pp. 376–78, 728–29.

22. The hundredth and last number of *Le Pays Breton* announced that publication was temporarily suspended. *Le Réveil Breton* was renamed *Le Pays Breton* in 1947.

23. For the complete text see *Bulletin* de l'URB, 1919, pp. 8–10.

24. The text of this petition may be consulted in ibid., p. 12.

25. For the full text of this manifesto see ibid., pp. 52–55.

26. The details of this sordid little affair are found in Jean Choleau, "Par qui fut fondé le C.D.I.B.," *Le Pays Breton* 66 (1955): 788; *Le Réveil Breton* 3 (April–May–June 1921): 21; 6 (January–February–March 1922): 30–34; 17–18 (October 1924–May 1925): 28; and Jean Choleau, "Histoire de la F.R.B.," *Le Pays Breton* 43 (1948): 3.

27. [F. Simon], "Du sang inutile," *La Bretagne Intégrale* 7 (July 1922): 2.

28. *La Bretagne Intégrale* 9 (May 1923): 1.

29. *Bulletin* de l'URB, 1922, p. 2.

30. Ibid., p. 126.

31. By the end of the 1930s Jaffrennou was accusing the *Breiz Atao* group of being a Nazi fifth column in Brittany and was calling its leader Fanch Debauvais the *gauleiter* of Breton autonomism. See *An Oaled* 69 (July–September 1939): 250.

32. Pierre Mocaër, "Notre programme," *Buhez Breiz* 1 (January 1919): 4.

33. Le Moal to M. le chanoine Le Roy, 10 December 1923. Printed in Henri Poisson, *L'abbe Jean-Marie Perrot*, p. 77.

34. *Foi et Bretagne* 2 (February 1926): 12.

35. Although Madec resigned from Bleun-Brug soon after Duparc's disciplinary order, he continued as an active Breton militant. In 1928 he founded a popular democratic Breton movement called *Adsao* that was avowedly loyal to the French republic, libertarian, and vaguely socialist. Constantly harassed by Bishop Duparc, *Adsao* had a troubled, eight-year existence. In 1936 Abbé Madec died, a broken and discouraged man, and with him disappeared his movement.

36. Jean Choleau nicely captured the atmosphere of pettiness, ambition, and jealousy that did so much to discredit interwar Breton regionalism when he observed that "when three Bretons come together it is ordinarily against someone or something. It is first of all to try to demolish the society of which they are members, or at least to ruin its president. It is then to create a new society whose command posts they will divide among themselves . . . [and finally] to launch one journal against another journal, one review against another review." See Jean Choleau, "Tribune libre: considérations sur la Fédération," *Le Pays Breton* 58 (25 March 1953): 546.

Chapter 4

1. Regionalism, according to Yves Le Diberder, amounted to "death in small packets" because its "gutless" leaders possessed an "almost perfect incapacity for action." See *Brittia* 6(1913): 152, 167, and 9 (1913): 355.

2. Camille Le Mercier d'Erm, "Commémoratives: 1911–1961, cinquantenaire du P.N.B.," pp. 44–45.

3. The text of this manifesto is found in Louis-N. Le Roux, *Pour le séparatisme*, pp. ii–x.

4. Le Mercier d'Erm, "Commémoratives," p. 71.

5. Camille Le Mercier d'Erm, *Le nationalisme breton et l'Action Française*, p. 12.

6. "La Bretagne aux bretons," *Breiz Dishual* 1 (1912): 12.

7. *Breiz Dishual* 5 (1912): 2.

8. *Breiz Dishual* 8 (1913): 2.

9. Emile Masson, *Antée: Les bretons et le socialisme*, p. 15.

10. *Brittia* 1 (1912): 3. No more than sixteen persons can be identified as having belonged to the *Brittia* group, while fewer than two dozen were members of the Parti Nationaliste Breton. *Brug* seems to have been the one-man operation of Masson.

11. For Bretons like Abbé Perrot it was simply a question of honor and loyalty. A quarter century later he explained, "I can be reproached for nothing from the point of view of the loyalty I owe to the State. I know my duties as a French citizen; I have paid all my taxes and I have participated in the entire war beyond the measure of my duty." Letter dated 19 January 1939 cited in Henri Poisson, *L'abbé Jean-Marie Perrot*, p. 43. Mobilized at Lesneven in 1914, Perrot chose to go to war as a volunteer. On 22 July 1918 he was awarded the Croix de Guerre for exceptional bravery.

12. Cited in Henri Poisson, *Yves Le Moal*, p. 62.

13. Cited in Marcel Guieysse, *La langue bretonne*, p. 245.

14. Cited in Gilbert Le Guen, "D'une révolution manquée à une revolution possible," p. 490. Michel Huber's *La population de la France pendant la guerre* is flawed by its failure to include statistical data arranged according to department. It does confirm, however, that the war mortality rate for France was one in twenty-eight (p. 412). Huber's figures for the military districts of Rennes and Nantes—an area larger than Brittany since the latter included part of the Loire valley and the Vendée—show a total of 149,000 dead and missing (p. 426). But if naval losses (the French fleet is largely staffed by Breton sailors) and casualties among Bretons living in Paris and elsewhere outside Brittany are added to his figures, the nationalist claim of 240,000 Breton dead might conceivably be reached.

15. The nationalist historian Joseph Chardronnet writes that "one cannot exclude more unavowed motives on the part of a government always worried by and suspicious of the national loyalty of the Bretons." See his *Histoire de Bretagne*, p. 201.

16. Fanch Jaffrennou in *An Oaled* 68 (April–June 1939): 147. Several years ago Olier Mordrel wrote that it was the Dublin rising of Irish patriots on Easter Sunday 1916 that instantly transformed the fifteen-year-old François Debauvais into the Breton nationalist Fanch Debauvais. See [Olier Mordrel], "Fransez Debauvais, I," *Ar Vro* 1 (Pâques 1959): 14.

17. See Groupe Régionaliste Breton, *Notre doctrine et nos buts*, p. 2.

18. Reported by [Olier Mordrel], "Fransez Debauvais, II," *Ar Vro* 2 (June 1959): 2.

19. After he left the GRB de Roincé oddly began a new career as a propagandist for right-wing French nationalist movements. See [Maurice Marchal], *Le mouvement breton, Témoignage d'un ancien*, p. 2.

20. Maurice Marchal, "La question gallaise, II," *Breiz Atao* 9 (September 1919): 2.

21. Olier Mordrel, "La vie ou la mort," *Breiz Atao* 9 (September 1919): 3.

22. Figures taken from contribution lists published by *Breiz Atao* and its wartime successor *L'Heure Bretonne* show that more than four thousand cash donations totaling nearly one-half million francs had been received into the nationalist treasury by 1942.

23. Jean-Yves Keraudren [Théophile Jeusset], *A contre-courant*, p. 20.

24. [Marchal], *Mouvement breton*, p. 3.

25. Olier Mordrel, "Pour sauver la race, remplaçons l'immigré français par l'immigré de Grande-Bretagne," *Breiz Atao* 10–12 (October–December 1923): 378.

26. See Jean La Bénelais [Olier Mordrel], "Contre le service militaire obligatoire pour tous," *Breiz Atao* 7 (July 1923): 335, and Maurice Marchal, "La paix," *Breiz Atao* 6 (June 1925): 572.

27. The text of *Gwalarn's* founding manifesto may be consulted in *Breiz Atao* 2 (February 1925): 534.

28. Recalled in OMM, p. 106.

29. Maurice Marchal, "Equipe parlementaire," *Breiz Atao* 1 (January 1927): 744.

30. See Yann Poupinot, *La Bretagne contemporaine*, 2:91. At the beginning of 1927 Maurice Marchal noted that *Breiz Atao's* four hundred subscribers in 1920 had since increased tenfold. See his "Equipe parlementaire," p. 746.

Chapter 5
1. Camille Le Mercier d'Erm, "Paroles malheureuses," *Breiz Atao* 26 (7 October 1928): 1.

2. Kermorvan [Olier Mordrel], "La presse mondiale et le congrès de Kastellin," *Breiz Atao* 30 (2 December 1928): 2.

3. OMM, p. 135.

4. Cited in Yann Poupinot, *La Bretagne contemporaine*, 2:93.

5. Olier Mordrel, "Le rapport moral, congrès de Rennes," *Breiz Atao* 67 (22 September 1929): 2.

6. According to *Breiz Atao* 96 (12 April 1920): 1–2, many electors sold their votes for "a pack of cigarettes, a bottle of wine, or a 50-franc note." The article complained as well that the campaign period was too brief and that the political terrain had been insufficiently prepared. Debauvais added the following week that Mazéas's handbills had been too long and badly designed and that Breton voters didn't want to waste their ballots on an apparently hopeless candidacy. See Debauvais, "Impressions de campagne électorale," *Breiz Atao* 97 (19 April 1930): 1. See also OMM, p. 141.

7. See OMM, p. 142.

8. Olier Mordrel, "Je m'adresse aux forts," *Breiz Atao* 101 (18 May 1930): 4.

9. Duhamel's analysis of the PAB electoral failure is found in his letter of resignation from the nationalist movement, which may be read in *Breiz Atao* 139 (28 February 1931): 1.

10. "Réponse d'Olier Mordrel et Fanch Debauvais," *Breiz Atao* 139 (28 February · 1931): 1–2.

11. Reported in OMM, p. 145.

12. See "Au congrès de Rennes," *Breiz Atao* 142 (26 April 1931): 3.

13. In his memoirs Mordrel dismissed the five-member directorate that assumed control of *Breiz Atao* as "the cabal." See OMM, p. 146.

14. Ibid., p. 148.

15. See *La Nation Bretonne* 2 (21 June 1931): 6. Meavenn is one of the more curious of all Breton nationalists. A Bretonnant whom many of her associates ironically called "the red virgin," this reputed one-time mistress of Célestin Laîné nevertheless belonged to the left wing of the nationalist movement. Still active in the Breton movement, she briefly headed the Breton cultural and ideological review *Ar Vro* in the 1960s. For more details on the life of Meavenn see Jean La Bénelais [Olier Mordrel], *Galerie bretonne*, p. 20, and [Tony Le Montrer], *En Bretagne, rien de nouveau*, p. 24.

16. See *La Nation Bretonne* 4 (26 July 1931): 1.

17. "Programme du Parti Nationaliste Intégral Breton," *Breiz da Zont* 5 (Pâques 1931): 1.

18. Another group called the Nationalistes Bretons-Chrétiens splintered away from the Catholic extreme right of *Breiz Atao* in 1932. Its organ *Breiz Digabestr* (*La Bretagne sans entraves*) had an even more ephemeral existence than that of *Breiz da Zont*.

19. "Pourquoi War Zao?" *War Zao* 1 (5 July 1931): 1.

20. Ibid., p. 4.

21. The Ligue Fédéraliste de Bretagne was never more than its organ *La Bretagne*

Fédérale, which ceased publication in 1934. Never able to attract a following of any note in Brittany, most of the federalists eventually found homes in the peninsular sections of various left-oriented French political parties. As for Maurice Marchal, he completed his ideological metamorphosis from a youthful admirer of Charles Maurras by joining the Radical-Socialist party in 1936. See his *Le mouvement breton, Témoignage d'un ancien*, p. 4.

22. OMM, p. 154.

Chapter 6

1. Cited in [Tony Le Montrer], *En Bretagne, rien de nouveau*, p. 23.

2. Reported in *Ouest-Journal*, 8 August 1932, p. 1.

3. Taldir [François Jaffrennou], "Chronologie des attentats de Rennes et d'Ingrandes," *An Oaled* 43 (January–March 1933): 38.

4. Interview in *Ouest-Journal*, 9 August 1932, p. 1.

5. Reprinted in *Breiz Atao*, Numéro Spécial (13 August 1932): 2.

6. Maurice Marchal, "Et la république?" *La Bretagne Fédérale*, Numéro Spécial (3 September 1932): 1.

7. A nationalist pamphlet published some years later in fact claimed that during the six-month period following the bombing of the Boucher statue the police questioned more than two thousand persons and carried out four hundred searches in a vain attempt to find the authors of the deeds of 7 August and 20 November 1932. See Parti National Breton, *The Bretons' Struggle for Liberty*, p. 4. The nationalists also distributed this pamphlet in French, German, and Breton editions.

8. Lugan, "A propos de Gwenn-ha-Du," *Ar Vro* 13 (March 1962): 3–10.

9. On the Kuzul Meur see OMM, pp. 166–67.

10. [Olier Mordrel], "Fransez Debauvais," *Ar Vro* 6 (June 1960): 4.

11. The statutes of the reorganized PNB are found in *Breiz Atao*, Numéro Spécial (28 August 1932): 2.

12. Also in August 1932 was created Sparfelled Breiz (Les Faucons de Bretagne), the party youth organization. Its objective was the creation of a healthy, energetic, and disciplined Breton youth whose primary value system was based on obedience. It was hoped that this youth, through the study of the Breton language and history, would emerge as the vanguard of the PNB. The close resemblance between this organization and the Hitler Youth, the Italian Fascist Balilla, and the French Camelots du Roi is too obvious to miss. On the Sparfelled see *Breiz Atao*, Numéro Spécial (28 August 1932): 2.

13. See Parti National Breton, *Le nationalisme breton: aperçu doctrinal*, pp. 29–30, and Fanch Debauvais, "Le sens d'un mouvement," *Breiz Atao*, Numéro Spécial (28 August 1932): 2.

14. See "Un programme de revendications immédiates," *Breiz Atao*, Numéro Spécial (28 August 1932): 3.

15. The dedication in Trébeurden (Côtes-du-Nord) that same day of a bust of Aristide Briand—a Breton the nationalists usually excoriated as a French chauvinist—gave *Breiz Atao* another opportunity to attack Action Française. For the latter the left-leaning Briand was an archenemy and that was reason enough for *Breiz Atao* to eulogize the veteran French statesman. The nationalists accordingly distributed a leaflet at Trébeurden that sought to depict Briand as one of their own: "If French war-mongerers from the editors of *Action Française* and *L'Ami du Peuple* to the perfume manufacturer Coty want to treat Briand as a hooligan and a debauchee, we then have no reason to consider him an enemy." The text of this leaflet may be consulted in Ronan Caerléon, *Complots pour une république bretonne*, pp. 102–4.

16. A. C. [Olier Mordrel], "S.A.G.A.," *Breiz Atao* 170 (12 March 1933): 2.

17. See "Notre programme de Carhaix," *Breiz Atao* 183 (17 September 1933): 2.

18. OMM, p. 187.

19. On the beginnings of ABES see Yann Fouéré, "Nous devons obtenir l'ensignement du breton," *Bulletin* de l'URB, 1935, p. 6; Marcel Guieysse, *La langue bretonne*, pp. 246–51; and Yann Poupinot, *La Bretagne contemporaine*, 2:147.

20. OMM, pp. 201–2.

21. At *Peuples et Frontières* the Delaportes were succeeded by Yann Fouéré, who soon made of the publication a vehicle for progress reports on the ABES campaign and for the propagation of federalist ideas reminiscent of those earlier championed by Maurice Duhamel and Maurice Marchal. The federalists in fact were contemporaneously trying to make a comeback with the publication of their *Manifeste des bretons fédéralistes* but nobody paid them the slightest heed.

22. Debauvais was paid fifteen hundred francs per month, while the somewhat more prosperous Mordrel received only one thousand. See OMM, p. 203.

23. Ab Arzel, "Pas de guerre cette fois-ci," *Breiz Atao* 312 (2 October 1938): 1.

24. OMM, p. 208.

25. Ibid., p. 204.

26. *Breiz Atao* 302 (15 May 1938), cited in ibid., p. 221.

27. *Breiz Atao* 303 (29 May 1938): 4. The legal basis of the action was a Daladier decree-law dated 25 May 1938: "Quiconque aura entrepris, par quelque moyen que soit, de porter atteinte à l'intégrité du territoire national, ou de soustraire à l'autorité de la France une partie du territoire où cette autorité s'exerce, sera puni d'un emprisonment à cinq ans."

28. "Déclaration de Célestin Laîné," *Breiz Atao* 305 (26 June 1938): 1.

29. "Condamnation politique," *Breiz Atao* 306 (10 July 1938): 1.

30. The response of *Breiz Atao* readers was to send unprecedented sums to the PNB treasury. A fifty-thousand-franc subscription opened in December 1938 was nearly half covered by 15 January 1939. During the so-called Debauvais week of 27 March–3 April 1939 *Breiz Atao* asked all nationalists to forego alcoholic beverages, two principal meals, and all entertainment, contributing resultant savings to the PNB. The scheme netted fifty-two thousand francs. See OMM, pp. 226–27.

31. Both ibid., p. 229, and Hervé Le Boterf, *La Bretagne dans la guerre*, 1:74 indicate that Le Helloco and the *Gwalarn* were involved in such smuggling activities. The 1961 prizewinning novel by Michel Mohrt, *La prison maritime*, was based on these alleged PNB smuggling incidents. Le Boterf is a former member of the nationalist movement and Mohrt is clearly at home in such milieux.

32. Mordrel rather lamely explained years later that, outlawed by the French government and relentlessly pursued by its police, he and Debauvais were flung (*projeté*) into the enemy camp of France. See OMM, p. 233.

Chapter 7

1. Cited in Ronan Caerléon, *Complots pour une république bretonne*, p. 185.

2. OMM, p. 234.

3. These operations sometimes produced comic results. At Ker-Vreiz, for example, the police confiscated everything written in Breton and left alone all that in French. Thus the purely cultural review *Gwalarn* was seized, while a complete collection of *Breiz Atao* was left behind. See Yann Fouéré, *La Bretagne écartelée (1938–1948)*, p. 176, n. 15.

4. The complete text of *Diskleriadur*—distributed in Breton, French, English, German, and Dutch translations—may be read in Caerléon, *Complots*, pp. 194–95.

5. Ibid., p. 197.

6. Hervé Le Boterf, *La Bretagne dans la guerre*, 1:141. The incident is indirectly confirmed in OMM, p. 267.

7. The arriving nationalists were jeered by local Pontivy citizens as "dirty Boches." Caerléon reports that a group of PNB members were later saved from a severe hiding at the hands of the outraged inhabitants only by the timely intervention of German soldiers. See Caerléon, *Complots*, p. 224, and *L'Heure Bretonne* (14 July 1940): 1.

8. The complete text of the Pontivy declaration and its accompanying eighteen-point program may be read in *L'Heure Bretonne* 1 (14 July 1940): 2–3. It is reprinted in Caerléon, *Complots*, pp. 219–23.

9. Eberhard Jäckel, *La France dans l'Europe de Hitler*, p. 75.

10. Ibid., p. 76.

11. OMM, p. 303. The one-hundred-thousand-franc monthly subsidy was later halved by occupation authorities.

12. Raymond Delaporte, "Vers une politique constructuve," *L'Heure Bretonne* 24 (21 December 1940): 1.

13. By 1944 Radio-Rennes-Bretagne was being permitted hour-long daily broadcasts in the Breton language. Fouéré, Ecartelée, p. 74.

14. Le Boterf, *La Bretagne dans la guerre*, 2:104.

15. Ibid., p. 132.

16. During the eighteen months following July 1940 Bretons contributed nearly two hundred thousand francs to the PNB treasury. The name of each donor and the size of his or her gift were published in *L'Heure Bretonne*. Post-Vichy authorities later used such contribution lists as a basis for making their own lists of alleged Breton nationalist collaborators.

17. At first Vichy officials had refused such authorization on the ground that there was no generally recognized Breton language but a number of local dialects each requiring its own grammar, dictionary, and corps of instructors. This objection was rendered nugatory in July 1941 when Bretonnant scholars under the leadership of Roparz Hémon merged the 1908 KLT version of Breton with the orthographically dissimilar Vannetais dialect to form the so-called KLTG unified language. ("G" is for "Gwened," the Breton word for Vannes.) The major innovation of the new orthography involved the substitution of "zh" wherever KLT Breton had formerly used a "z" and Vannetais an "h." Hence "Breizh"—the new word for Brittany—to replace the KLT "Breiz" and the Vannetais "Breih."

18. Raymond Delaporte scorned this figure as ridiculous and instead demanded that such compensation be equal to 10 percent of a teacher's regular salary. He also called for state subsidies for the training of instructors qualified to teach Breton and the inclusion of Breton-language courses as part of the normal curriculum in Bretonnant western Brittany. See *L'Heure Bretonne* 102 (27 June 1942): 1.

19. Yann Fouéré, "Premier message," *La Bretagne* 1 (21 March 1941): 1.

20. *La Dépêche de Brest* had formerly been controlled by Dr. Victor Le Gorgeu, the longtime mayor of Brest. He lost it after successfully leading in December 1941 the opposition in Brest city council to the voting of an expression of confidence in Marshal Pétain's leadership. Angry Vichy officials retaliated on 31 December by dissolving the city council and removing Le Gorgeu as mayor. Four months later they helped oust him from financial and editorial control at *La Dépêche*, which they then allowed to pass to Fouéré. In 1944 named provisional commissaire for Finistère, Côtes-du-Nord, Morbihan, and Ille-et-Vilaine by liberation authorities, Le Gorgeu thus had a personal motive to proceed against alleged Breton nationalist collaborators like Yann Fouéré.

21. Article II of the prefectural decree of 7 December 1942 that created the CCB. Cited in Yvonnig Gicquel, *Le comité consultatif de Bretagne*, p. 44.

22. The editors of *Ar Falz* had voluntarily suspended its publication in 1939 before the war broke out and remained silent during the Vichy years. Postwar officials thus allowed them to resume its publication after the war.

23. Alan, "Réflexions pour 1943," *L'Heure Bretonne* 129 (8 January 1943): 1.

24. Cited in Fouéré, *Ecartelée*, p. 102.

25. See Caerléon, *Complots*, p. 321.

26. Most have been included in the terms of various French amnesty decrees in recent years and are now beginning to return to Brittany.

27. *L'Heure Bretonne* 184 (6 June 1944): 1.

28. Le Boterf, *La Bretagne dans la guerre*, 3:602.

29. This figure is based on data provided in OMM, p. 535–37.

30. Quoted in Paul Sérant, *Lâ Bretagne et la France*, p. 307.

31. This operation is generally referred to in nationalist works as the "rafle (comb-out) Allard" after the French general who had charge of its actual execution.

32. Since Delaporte had destroyed *L'Heure Bretonne* subscription lists and PNB membership rolls on the eve of the liberation, the police in part prepared their sus-

pect lists from prefectural registries of suspected Breton nationalists during the period 1932–40. This procedure led to some bizarre results, including the issuing of warrants for dead persons and the arrest of Bretons who had not been active in the nationalist movement for more than a decade. See Fouéré, *Ecartelée*, p. 119, and Le Boterf, *La Bretagne dans la guerre*, 3:610.

33. Reported by Fouéré, *Ecartelée*, p. 138. According to Olier Mordrel, banishment had the effect of concentrating Breton nationalists in the Paris area where they began to politicize the huge Breton population resident in the French capital. See OMM, p. 430.

34. See *Ouest-France*, 5 July 1945, p. 1.

35. Jasson's letter to his mother may be read in OMM, p. 426.

36. Typical renditions of this interpretation include Joseph Chardronnet, *Histoire de Bretagne*, pp. 224–34; Fouéré, *Ecartelée*, pp. 109–39; Caerléon, *Complots*, pp. 332–65; and Le Boterf, *La Bretagne dans la guerre*, 3:671–85.

37. Breton writers often invoke the findings of a delegation of eight Welshmen that visited Brittany in May 1947 in order to investigate charges that Breton militants were being unjustly persecuted by postwar French governments. Its report concluded that French authorities were in fact guilty of such conduct and went on to accuse Paris of following a policy of genocide in Brittany. This report cannot be taken seriously for three reasons: (1) its authors were all associated with the Welsh nationalist movement, which means that they can hardly be considered impartial observers of the alleged plight of their Celtic brothers in Brittany; (2) it was based on less than four days of observation, which was insufficient to get at the truth behind the charges of French persecution; and (3) its conclusions were in no way supported by reliable data. The text of this report may be consulted in *Bulletin* de l'Association Bretonne, 1947, pp. 71–90.

38. In an obvious attempt to curry favor with occupation officials *L'Heure Bretonne* regularly carried pieces that described in glowing terms life in STO labor camps in Germany. *La Bretagne* was far more circumspect and printed only those articles imposed on Fouéré by German authorities.

39. Jean Mabire, "Guerre secrète en Bretagne," p. 36.

40. Archives Départementales de Finistère, Folder M-107: *Elections législatives de 1936*.

41. G. Le Huedez, "Coup d'œil sur le mouvement breton," p. 64.

42. For a statement of this view see the influential study by Robert Aron, *The Vichy Regime, 1940–44*, pp. 72–73. The 1941 novel by Helen MacInnes, *Assignment in Brittany*, was perhaps the earliest expression of this argument.

43. Joseph Martray, "Le scandale de l'épuration en Bretagne," *Le Peuple Breton* 6 (15 March 1948): 8.

Chapter 8

1. But *Avel an Trec'h* (*Le Vent de la Victoire*), *An Avel* (*Le Vent*), and *Ar Vro* (*Le Pays*) each lasted for only a few issues and all had disappeared by 1948. Only *Al Liamm* (*Le Lien*), *Gwalarn*'s lineal successor, survived and is still being published today.

2. *Bulletin* de l'Association Bretonne, 1946, pp. 14, 27, 85–87.

3. See his "Le scandale de l'épuration en Bretagne," *Le Peuple Breton* 6 (15 March 1948): 5–8.

4. J. E. S. Hayward, "From Functional Regionalism to Functional Representation in France: The Battle of Brittany," p. 52.

5. Ibid., p. 54.

6. René Pleven, *L'Avenir de la Bretagne*, pp. 233–56.

7. The *force de frappe* phrase belongs to Hayward, "Functional Regionalism," p. 56.

8. CODER stands for Commission de Développement Economique Regional.

9. Phlipponneau then founded a tiny Breton-oriented publication of the left called *Le Fédéré* and became active in François Mitterand's FGDS socialist organization.

10. Ronan Caerléon, *La Révolution bretonne permanente*, p. 28.

11. *La Bretagne Réelle* 151 (1 November 1962): 1053, carried an advertisement for the Birmingham, Alabama *Thunderbolt*, the "official white racial organ of the National States Rights Party" dedicated to the fight against "communism and race-mixing."

12. *La Bretagne Réelle* 161 (1 March 1964): 20.

13. *La Bretagne Réelle* 5 (June 1954): 19.

14. These courses were summarized by Yann Poupinot in his two-volume work *La Bretagne contemporaine*.

15. Poupinot's principal collaborators—Henri Le Lan, Paul Morin, Yann Poilvet, Pierre Lemoine, Pierre Laurent, and Ned Urvoas—shared his background in the STO and the resistance.

16. Fouéré published the ideas presented during this tour in a pamphlet called *De la Bretagne à la France et à l'Europe*.

17. At the organizational meeting of the MOB in November 1957 Yann Fouéré had remarked that Brittany had long been living under an economically colonial regime. Cited in Caerléon, *Révolution bretonne*, p. 53. The so-called colonialist interpretation was subsequently given full treatment in Ned Urvoas, "Vers le front breton," *L'Avenir* 44 (September 1961): 3.

18. The language issue in fact never generated much enthusiasm among the MOB's membership and Poupinot was actively hostile to it. See his *Les bretons à l'heure de l'Europe*, pp. 110–15.

19. "L'heure de l'action," *L'Avenir* 42 (July 1961): 1.

20. Yann Poilvet, "Les temps des réalistes," *L'Avenir* 67 (5 January 1963): 1.

21. Ronan Le Prohon, "Tribune libre," *L'Avenir* 68 (19 January 1963): 4.

22. R. Dinan, "Raison d'un départ," *Le Peuple Breton* 1 (January 1964): 3.

23. The full text is in *Le Peuple Breton* 1 (January 1964): 1.

24. Jean-Marie Laigle, "Le Bretagne, colonie offerte à Citroën," *Le Peuple Breton* 16 (March 1965): 1, 4.

25. OMM, p. 499.

26. See *Ar Vro* 14 (June 1962): 10–16; 17 (February 1963): 23; and 18 (April 1963): 5–12.

27. SADED stands for Strollad Deskadurezh an Eil Derez (Institut de l'Enseignement du Sécond Degré). Dr. Etienne had already won a certain notoriety by refusing to give his children French names, which denied them legal existence in France and made them ineligible for French social welfare services. He was later prosecuted for withdrawing his children from French schools, insisting on his right to teach them at home in the Breton language. He eventually won both skirmishes with French authorities. For details see Paul Sérant, *La France des Minorités*, pp. 87–92.

28. *Breton News* 49 (Spring 1965): 1.

29. OMM, p. 455.

30. *Breton News* 49 (Spring 1965): 2.

Chapter 9

1. Its full text is reprinted in Ronan Caerléon, *La Révolution bretonne permanente*, p. 141.

2. An excerpt from the trial transcript may be found in ibid., pp. 137–38.

3. The explosive for the St.-Brieuc operation had been stolen on 13 January at Loudéac. See ibid., p. 170.

4. See *Douar Breiz* 3 (5 January 1969): 2–3.

5. Cited in Caerléon, *Révolution bretonne*, p. 248.

6. The text of the FLB manifesto is most easily consulted in Paul Sérant, *La Bretagne et la France*, pp. 414–21.

7. Caerléon, *Révolution bretonne*, pp. 174ff.

8. See OMM, p. 473.

9. Erwan Mescoat, "Le F.L.B. dans la trappe et le silence," *L'Avenir* 42 (8 May 1969): 6.

10. *New York Times*, 1 February 1969, p. 3.

11. *Breton News* 61 (Winter 1968–69): 2.

12. Yann Fouéré, "Le referendum et nous," *L'Avenir* 41 (10 April 1969): 4.

13. Mordrel announced his recommendation in "Manifeste pour une révision de la politique bretonne," *La Bretagne Réelle* 270 (1 April 1969): 1. Although he claimed that France had "changed" and that de Gaulle would eventually concede even more regional autonomy to Brittany than the referendum proposals anticipated, Mordrel admitted that one of his principal reasons for supporting de Gaulle was so as not to mix his ballot with the "Non" votes of the socialist and communist opposition.

14. Fouéré, "Le referendum et nous," p. 4.

15. Interestingly enough, in Bretonnant areas and in those cities where the largest number of alleged FLB members had been arrested—Rennes, Nantes, St.-Brieuc, St.-Nazaire, Châteaubriant, and Concarneau—the referendum was voted down.

16. See *Douar Breiz* 24 (20 November 1969): 10.

17. See "Le F.L.B. engage le combat légal," *L'Avenir* 46 (9 October 1969): 2.

18. *L'Avenir* 52 (9 April 1970): 1.

19. "Sav Breizh" means "Relèvement Bretagne."

20. According to *Douar Breiz* 42 (20 September 1970): 2, most of the former FLB prisoners joined an otherwise mysterious Front National Breton at Lorient.

21. Gwenc'hlan Le Scouézec and Serj Pineau, eds., *F.L.B. 72/procès de la Bretagne*, p. 10.

22. OMM, p. 483.

23. Six months of Durand's original one-year sentence had been suspended, as were five of Guénard's eight months. Since eight of the new fifteen-month sentences meted out to both men on 29 May were suspended as well, Durand actually had his sentence increased by one month and Guénard, by four.

24. The complete transcript of this trial fills most of the 340 pages of the Le Scouézec-Pineau volume cited in note 21 above.

25. Enthusiastic supporters of the defendants reacted to this announcement by hoisting black-and-white Breton nationalist flags over the Faculté des Sciences at Paris and atop the great spire of Notre Dame cathedral. It took an hour and a half for a company of Parisian firemen to remove, in full view of ORTF cameras, the offending flag from the spire of Notre Dame.

26. These new committees were actually renamed versions of the *comités de soutien* formed earlier to support the cause of the eleven FLB defendants.

27. The text of this communiqué may be read in "Etude," *Douar Breiz* 92 (5 April 1973): 2.

28. *Le Monde*, 16 February 1974, p. 9.

29. The reactions of *Humanité*, *L'Aurore*, and *Libération* are found in ibid.

30. *New York Times*, 24 April 1974, p. 8.

31. *Le Monde*, 16 February 1974, p. 9.

32. According to *Le Monde*'s Pierre Viansson-Ponté in ibid., p. 1.

33. *Le Figaro*, 16 February 1974, cited in ibid., p. 9.

34. Reported in *Le Monde*, 5 June 1974, p. 9.

Chapter 10

1. A poll by the *Glasgow Herald* in early 1976 reveals the reason for Wilson's abrupt approval for home rule in Scotland and Wales. It reported that if a new parliamentary election were held, Scottish nationalists would receive more votes than either the Labour or the Conservative party. Wilson thus had to act to undercut the Scottish nationalist movement, for it now threatens many of the forty-one formerly "safe" Labour seats in Scotland, and hence his majority in Commons. Important Conservative leaders, moreover, support his home-rule proposals in the hope that they will check the surging growth of Scottish nationalism, which they view as a grave threat to the continued functioning of British parliamentary government. In a

January 1976 speech in Commons in which he urged the fullest possible home rule for Scotland, former prime minister Edward Heath warned that he could "foresee a situation in Westminster where both major parties suffer great losses in Scotland and where there is a large Nationalist representation pledged to separation which would, in itself, damage Scotland, damage the Union, and make effective government in this House and Parliament impossible." Reported in *Daily Express*, 20 January 1976, p. 1.

2. Hechter's notion of ethnically based "internal colonies" is fully developed in his article "Towards a Theory of Ethnic Change."

3. The idea of an eventual European federation constructed out of small ethnic communities is the subject of a growing literature in France. Its most important titles to date include Guy Héraud, *L'Europe des ethnies* (1963); Yann Fouéré, *L'Europe aux cent drapeaux* (1968); and Paul Sérant, *La France des Minorités* (1965).

ᔰ Bibliography

I. Archival Material

Archives Départementales de Finistère. *Elections législatives de 1928, 1932, 1936*. Folders M-103, M-88, M-107, M-108.

Archives Départementales d'Ille-et-Vilaine. *Elections législatives de 1928*. Folder 3Md38.

Archives Départementales de Morbihan. *Elections législatives de 1910, 1914– 1932, 1936*. Folders M-243, M-244, M-3352, M-3547.

II. Government Documents

France. Assemblée Nationale. Annales. Vol. 21. *Enquête sur les actes du gouvernement de la défense nationale*. "Rapport de M. A. de La Borderie: Le camp de Conlie et l'armée de Bretagne." Paris: Imprimerie Nationale, 1874.

France. Chambre des Députés. *Programmes, professions de foi et engagements électoraux*. In *Impressions, projets de loi, propositions, rapports, etc.* Paris: Imprimerie Nationale, 1882–present. (Title varies.)

III. Periodicals

An Oaled (Carhaix). 1928–39.
Ar Falz (Rennes). 1933–.
Ar Vro (Rennes). 1959–67.
Avel an Trec'h (Rennes). 1946–48.
L'Avenir de la Bretagne (Rennes). 1958–.
Breiz (Rennes). 1956–.
Breiz Atao (Rennes). 1919–39, May 1944.
Breiz d'ar Vreiziz (Morlaix). 1928.
Breiz da Zont (Rennes). 1931–34.
Breiz Digabestr (St.-Servan). 1932.
Breiz Dishual (Rennes). 1912–14.
Bretagne Fédérale, La (Rennes). 1931–35.
Bretagne Intégrale, La (Rennes). 1921–32.
Bretagne Réelle, La (Merdrignac). 1954–.
Breton News (Dublin). 1960–.
Brittia (Lorient). 1912–14.
Brug (Pontivy and Vannes). 1913–14.
Buhez Breiz (Brest). 1919–24.

Bulletin de l'Association Bretonne (St.-Brieuc). 1843–58, 1875–. (Title varies.)
Bulletin de la Fédération Régionaliste de Bretagne (Rennes). 1911–13, 1919.
Bulletin de l'Union Régionaliste Bretonne (St.-Brieuc). 1898–1946.
Bulletin des Minorités Nationales en France (Rennes). 1936–37.
Consortium Breton, Le (Carhaix). 1927–28.
Douar Breiz (Mur-de-Bretagne). 1969–.
Foi et Bretagne (Rennes). 1926–28.
Glorieuse Bretagne des Armées et l'Idée Bretonne, La (Quimper). 1918–19.
Heure Bretonne, L' (Rennes). 1940–44.
Kaierou an Emsaver Yaouank. Les Cahiers du jeune militant (Rennes). 1959.
Labour: Etudes Travaillistes (St.-Malo). 1959.
Nation Bretonne, La (Rennes). 1931.
Pays Breton, Le (Lorient). 1908–14.
Pays Breton, Le (Fougères). 1947–64.
Peuple Breton, Le (La Baule). 1947–49.
Peuple Breton, Le (Rennes). 1964–.
Peuples et Frontières (Rennes). 1937–39.
Réveil Breton, Le (Lorient). 1907–8.
Réveil Breton, Le (Quimperlé). 1920–44.
Stur (Rennes). 1934–43.
Sturier-Yaouankiz. Périodique des Jeunes Bretons. 1960.
Tir na n-òg (Brest). 1946.
Triskell (Rennes). 1942–44.
War-Du ar Pal (Rennes). 1938–39.
War Zao (Pleudaniel). 1931.

IV. *Newspapers*

Bretagne, La (Rennes). 1941–44.
Daily Express (London). 1967.
Monde, Le (Paris). 1968, 1974–76.
New York Times. 1969, 1974.
Ouest-France (Rennes). 1945–48, 1967–68.
Ouest-Journal (Rennes). 1932.

V. *Printed Works Emanating from the Breton Movement*

Ar Brezoneg er Skol. *Enseigner le breton, exigence bretonne*. Rennes: Imprimerie Provinciale de l'Ouest, 1938.
Berthou, Yves. *Les vessies pour des lanternes*. Paris: Editeur Eugène Figuière et Cie, 1913.
Caerléon, Ronan. *Les bretons le dos au mur*. Paris: Editions de la Table Ronde, 1973.
———. *Complots pour une république bretonne*. Paris: Editions de la Table Ronde, 1967.
———. *La révolution bretonne permanente*. Paris: Editions de la Table Ronde, 1969.
Chardronnet, Joseph. *Histoire de Bretagne*. Paris: Nouvelles Editions Latines, 1965.
Charency, Cte. de; Gaidoz, H.; et de Gaulle, Charles. *Pétition pour les lan-*

gues provinciales au Corps Législatif de 1870. Paris: Picard et Fils, Editeur, 1903.

Comité Breton d'Organisation Fédéraliste. *Manifeste des fédéralistes bretons*. Rennes, 1938.

Danio, C. [Jeanne du Guerny]. *Histoire de Bretagne*. Rennes: Editions P.A.B., 1929.

_____. *Histoire de notre Bretagne*. Dinard: A l'Enseigne de l'Herminé, 1922.

Duhamel, Maurice. *Le fédéralisme international et le réveil des nationalités*. Rennes: Editions P.A.B., 1928.

_____. *La question bretonne dans son cadre européen*. Paris: Delpeuch, Editeur, 1929.

Estourbeillon, Régis de l'. *La nation bretonne*. Redon: Imprimerie Bouteloup, 1924.

_____. *Protestation de la Bretagne contre son morcellement en deux régions distinctes*. Redon: Imprimerie Bouteloup, 1926.

_____. *Du rôle et des devoirs des sociétés nationales bretonnes.* St.-Brieuc: Prud'homme, 1912.

_____. *La survivance des peuples*. n.p., n.d.

_____. *L'unité bretonne*. Redon: Imprimerie Bouteloup, 1927.

Fouéré, Yann. *De la Bretagne à la France et à l'Europe*. Lorient: Editions du C.O.B., 1957.

_____. *La Bretagne écartelée (1938–1948)*. Paris: Nouvelles Editions Latines, 1962.

_____. *L'Europe aux cents drapeaux*. Paris: Presses d'Europe, 1968.

_____. *Nous devons obtenir l'enseignement du breton*. Rennes: Imprimerie Provinciale de l'Ouest, 1937.

Gaulle, Charles de. *Les celtes au XIXe siècle. Appel aux représentants actuels de la race celtique*. Nantes: V. Forest et E. Grimaud, 1864.

_____. *Les celtes au XIXe siècle. Le réveil de la race*. New ed. Paris: Librairie Bretonne, 1903.

Groupe Feminin du P.A.B. *Merc'hed Breiz: Appel aux femmes et aux filles de la nation bretonne*. Rennes: Imprimerie Riou-Reuzé, 1929.

Groupe Régionaliste Breton. *Notre doctrine et nos buts*. Rennes: Aux Bureaux de Breiz Atao, 1926.

Guieysse, Marcel. *La langue bretonne*. Hennebont: Imprimerie J. Méhat, 1925.

_____. *La langue bretonne*. Quimper: Nouvelles Editions Bretonnes, 1936.

Jaffrennou, François. *La genèse d'un mouvement, 1898–1911*. Carhaix: Imprimerie-Librairie du Peuple, 1912.

Keraudren, Jean-Yves [Théophile Jeusset]. *A contre-courant*. Paris. Jean d'Halluin, 1965.

La Bénelais, Jean [Olier Mordrel]. *Galerie bretonne*. Merdrignac: Editions de la "Bretagne Réelle," 1953.

_____. *Pensées d'un nationaliste breton*. Rennes: Les Nouvelles Editions Bretonnes, 1933.

Laigue, Cte. René de. *Le congrès de 1907*. Vannes: Imprimerie Lafoyle Frères, 1907.

Lantivy, Cte. de. *L'idéal breton*. Vannes: Imprimerie ouvrière Vannétaise, 1922.

Lantivy-Trédion, Cte. de. *La question bretonne*. Paris: Nouvelle Librairie Nationale, 1909.

_____. *Vers une Bretagne organisée*. Paris: Nouvelle Librairie Nationale, 1911.

Le Barzic, Ernest. *Jean Choleau, son oeuvre*. Rennes: Imprimeries Simon, 1965?.

Le Baner, Alain. *Une nouvelle génération bretonne*. Rennes: Editions du P.N.B., 1942.

Lebesque, Morvan. *Comment peut-on être breton?* Paris: Editions du Seuil, 1970.

Le Boterf, Hervé. *La Bretagne dans la guerre*. 3 vols. Paris: Editions France-Empire, 1969–71.

Le Febvre, Yves. *La Bretagne et la 'Pensée Bretonne'*. Quimper: Editions "La Pensée Bretonne," 1914.

――――. *Considérations sur l'histoire bretonne*. Morlaix: Chevalier, 1916.

Le Goffic, Charles. *L'âme bretonne*. 4 vols. Paris: Honoré Champion, 1902–11.

Le Mercier d'Erm, Camille. *Bretagne et Germanie*. Dinard: A l'Enseigne de l'Herminé, 1935?.

――――. "Commémoratives: 1911–1961, cinquantenaire du P.N.B." *Ar Vro* 12 (1961): 38–50 and 13 (1962): 67–70.

――――. *Le nationalisme breton et l'Action Française*. Rennes: Editions du Parti Nationaliste Breton, 1913.

――――. *La question bretonne. Les origines du nationalisme breton: études critiques*. Quimper: Editions du Parti Nationaliste Breton, 1911.

[Le Montrer, Tony]. *En Bretagne, rien de nouveau*. Rennes: Imprimerie Provinciale, 1933.

L'enseignement du breton et de l'histoire. Quimper: Bleun-Brug, 1933.

Le Roux, Louis-N. *La Bretagne en marche, en avant*. Rennes: Editions de Breiz Atao, 1933.

――――. *Pour le séparatisme*. Quimper: Editions du Parti Nationaliste Breton, 1911.

Le Scouézec, Gwenc'hlan, and Pineau, Serj, eds. *F.L.B. 72/Procès de la Bretagne*. St.-Brieuc: Editions Kelenn, 1973.

L'instruction du peuple breton par le breton et l'oeuvre de 'Gwalarn'. Brest: Imprimerie Commerciale et Administrative, 1928.

[Marchal, Maurice]. *Le mouvement breton, Témoignage d'un ancient*. Rennes: Editions de la "Bretagne Réelle," 1954.

Masson, Emile. *Antée: Les bretons et le socialisme*. Guimgamp: Imprimerie Toullec et Geffroy, 1912.

Mordrel, Olier. *Breiz Atao, ou histoire et actualité du nationalisme breton*. Paris: Editions Alain Moreau, 1973.

Parti Autonomiste Breton. *Déclaration, statuts*. Rennes: Editions du P.A.B., 1929.

Parti National Breton. *The Bretons' Struggle for Liberty*. Rennes: Editions du P.N.B., 1935.

――――. *Le nationalisme breton: aperçu doctrinal*. Rennes: Editions du P.N.B., 1932.

Pennek, R. *Petite histoire de la Bretagne nationale*. Merdrignac: Editions de la "Bretagne Réelle," 1965.

Pleven, René. *L'avenir de la Bretagne*. Paris: Calmann-Lévy, 1961.

Poisson, Henri. *L'abbé Jean-Marie Perrot*. Rennes: Plihon, 1955.

――――. *Histoire de Bretagne pour les enfants*. Rennes: Imprimerie Commerciale de Bretagne, 1930.

――――. *Yves Le Moal*. St.-Brieuc: Les Presses Bretonnes, 1962.

Poupinot, Yann. *La Bretagne contemporaine*. 2 vols. Paris: Editions "Ker-Vreiz," 1954–55.

———. *Les bretons à l'heure de l'Europe*. Paris: Nouvelles Editions Latines, 1961.

Quilgars, Henri. *Ce qu'était l'Etat breton*. Rennes: Editions P.A.B., 1929.

VI. *Other Related Works*

Académie des Sciences Morales et Politiques. *Catalogue des actes de François Ier*. Vol. 2. Paris: Imprimerie Nationale, 1888.

Aron, Robert. *The Vichy Regime, 1940–44*. London: Putnam, 1958.

———. ed. *Histoire de notre temps*. Paris: Librairie Plon, 1967.

Balzac, Honoré de. *Les Chouans*. New York: Penguin Books, 1972.

Barbin, René. *L'autonomisme breton (1815–1930)*. Poitiers: l'Action Intellectuelle, 1934.

———. *Le mouvement breton, autonomisme et fédéralisme*. Carhaix: Editions "Armorica," 1937.

Barker, Ernest. *National Character and the Factors in Its Formation*. London: Methuen and Co., 1928.

Berger, Suzanne. "Bretons, Basques, Scots, and Other European Nations." *Journal of Interdisciplinary History* 3 (1972): 167–75.

———. *Peasants against Politics*. Cambridge, Mass.: Harvard University Press, 1972.

Brekilien, Yann. *La vie quotidienne des paysans en Bretagne au XIXe siècle*. Paris: Hachette, 1966.

Celtic League, The. *The Right of Brittany, Wales, and Scotland to Self-Determination and International Protection: A Memorandum Presented to the United Nations Organization*. Westport, Ireland: Foilseacháin Nái Siúnta Teorantei, 1960?.

Chassé, Charles. "L'infiltration autonomiste dans les Cercles celtiques." *Le Télégramme de Brest* 934 (15, 17, 19, and 21 October, 1947): 2.

Cohn, Norman. *The Pursuit of the Millennium*. Revised and expanded edition. New York: Oxford University Press, 1970.

Davis, Horace. *Nationalism and Socialism; Marxist Theories of Nationalism to 1917*. New York: Monthly Review Press, 1967.

Delumeau, Jean, ed. *Histoire de la Bretagne*. Toulouse: Privat, Editeur, 1969.

Egret, Jean. "Les origines de la Révolution en Bretagne (1788–1789)." *Revue Historique* 212 (1955): 189–215.

Enloe, Cynthia H. *Ethnic Conflict and Political Development*. Boston: Little, Brown and Co., 1973.

Figueras, André. "La Bretagne, dernière colonie française." *Le Charivari* 31 (November 1960): 21–24.

Gadhra, Nollaig O., ed. *Celtic Advance in the Atomic Age*. Annual volume of the Celtic League. Dublin: The Celtic League, 1967.

Gicquel, Yvonnig. *Le comité consultatif de Bretagne*. Rennes: Imprimerie Simon, 1960.

Gravier, J.–F. *L'aménagement du territoire et l'avenir des régions françaises*. Paris: Flammarian, 1964.

Hayward, J. E. S. "From Functional Regionalism to Functional Representation in France: The Battle of Brittany." *Political Studies* 17 (1969): 48–75.

Hechter, Michael. "The Political Economy of Ethnic Change." *American Journal of Sociology* 79 (1974): 1151–78.

_____. "Towards a Theory of Ethnic Change." *Politics and Society* 2 (1971): 21–45.

Heisler, Martin O., ed. *Politics in Europe*. New York: David McKay Co., Inc., 1974.

Héraud, Guy. *L'Europe des ethnies*. Paris: Presses d'Europe, 1963.

Huber, Michel. *La population de la France pendant la guerre*. New Haven: Yale University Press, 1931.

Jäckel, Eberhard. *La France dans l'Europe de Hitler*. Paris: Fayard, 1968.

Journal of Contemporary History 6. "Nationalism and Separatism." 1971.

Kohn, Hans. *The Idea of Nationalism*. New York: Collier Books, 1967.

La Borderie, Arthur de. *La Bretagne aux temps modernes, 1491–1789*. Rennes: Plihon, 1894.

_____. *Histoire de Bretagne*. 6 vols. Rennes: Plihon, 1896–1914.

Laroche, Fabrice. "Ni rouges ni blancs, bretons seulement." *Le Spectacle du Monde* (Summer 1973): 28–35.

Le Guen, Gilbert. "D'une révolution manquée à une révolution possible." In *Histoire de la Bretagne*, edited by Jean Delumeau, pp. 463–521. Toulouse: Privat, Editeur, 1969.

Le Huedez, G. "Coup d'œil sur le mouvement breton." *Cahiers du fédéralisme européen* 1 (1951): 63–66.

Lode, Claes. "The Process of Federalization in Belgium." *Delta* 4 (1963–64): 43–52.

Mabire, Jean. "Guerre secrète en Bretagne." *Miroir de l'Histoire* 223 (July 1968): 34–47.

MacInnes, Helen. *Assignment in Brittany*. New York: Dell, 1967.

Mannheim, Karl. *Ideology and Utopia*. New York: Harvest Books, 1962?.

Marcuse, Herbert. *One-Dimensional Man*. Boston: Beacon Press, 1964.

Meyer, Jean. "Une mutation manquée: De la révolution politique aux débuts du monde industriel." In *Histoire de la Bretagne*, edited by Jean Delumeau, pp. 381–461. Toulouse: Privat, Editeur, 1969.

Mohrt, Michel. *La prison maritime*. Paris: Editions Gallimard, 1961.

Morin, Edgar. *The Red and the White*. New York: Pantheon Books, 1970.

Pitré-Chevalier. *La Bretagne ancienne et moderne*. Paris: W. Coquebert, 1844.

Phlipponneau, Michel. *La gauche et les régions*. Paris: Calmann-Lévy, 1967.

Rader, Daniel L. "The Breton Association and the Press: Propaganda for a 'Legal Resistance' before the July Revolution." *French Historical Studies* 2 (1961): 64–82.

Rébillon, Armand. *Histoire de Bretagne*. Paris: Armand Colin, 1957.

Reece, Jack E. "Anti-France: The Search for the Breton Nation (1898–1948)." Ph.D. dissertation, Stanford University, 1971.

Riché, Pierre, and Devailly, Guy. "De l'Armorique à la Bretagne." In *Histoire de la Bretagne*, edited by Jean Delumeau, pp. 117–52. Toulouse: Privat, Editeur, 1969.

Sée, Henri. "La population et la vie économique de Rennes vers le milieu du XVIIIe siècle d'après les rôles de la capitation." *Mémoires* de la Société d'Histoire et d'Archéologie de Bretagne 4 (1923): 89–136.

Sérant, Paul. *La Bretagne et la France*. Paris: Fayard, 1971.

_____. "La Bretagne n'abdique pas." *Le Monde et la Vie* 171 (August–September 1967): 20–21.

_____. "Est-ce un crime d'être breton?" *Le Monde et la Vie* 172 (October–November 1967): 22–24.

_____. *La France des Minorités*. Paris: Robert Laffont, 1965.

Seton-Watson, Hugh. "Unsatisfied Nationalisms." *Journal of Contemporary History* 6 (1971): 3–14.

Shafer, Boyd C. *Faces of Nationalism*. New York: Harcourt, Brace, and Jovanovich, Inc., 1972.

Siegfried, André. *Tableau politique de la France de l'ouest sous la troisième république*. Paris: Armand Colin, 1913.

Simon, Walter B. "Occupational Structure, Multilingualism, and Social Change." In *Multilingual Political Systems*, edited by Jean-Guy Savard and Richard Vigneault, pp. 87–108. Quebec: Les Presses de l'Université Laval, 1975.

Smith, Anthony D. *Theories of Nationalism*. London: Duckworth, 1971.

Temps Modernes, Les. Nos 324–26: "Minorités nationales en France." August–September 1973.

Thompson, Frank G., ed. *Maintaining a National Identity*. Annual Book of the Celtic League. Dublin: The Celtic League, 1968.

Thompson, George, ed. *Recent Developments in the Celtic Countries*. Annual Book of the Celtic League. Dublin: The Celtic League, 1966.

Tobias, Henry J., and Woodhouse, Charles E. *Minorities and Politics*. Albuquerque: University of New Mexico Press, 1969.

Touchard, Henri. "Le moyen-âge breton." In *Histoire de la Bretagne*, edited by Jean Delumeau, pp. 153–215. Toulouse: Privat, Editeur, 1969.

Weber, Eugen, and Rogger, Hans, eds. *The European Right*. Berkeley: University of California Press, 1965.

Welsh Nationalist Party. *Breton Nationalism*. Cardiff: Welsh Nationalist Party, 1956?.

Index